EMPOWERING WOMEN

Grassroots Experience from Tamil Nadu

About the Authors

Prof. G. Palanithurai

Prof. Ganapathi Palanithurai, Chairperson, Rajiv Gandhi Chair, Chairperson, The Hunger Project of Tamil Nadu Council, Gandhigram Rural Institute is an academic activist working with the people in rural areas for building the capacity of the leaders and people to reinvent and strength grassroots democracy and to achieve sustainable Rural Development. He is heading the Department of Political Science and Development Administration, in Gandhigram Rural University, Tamil Nadu. His policy advocacy role at the governmental level is increasingly felt at present in all the three levels, namely, sub-regional, regional and national as he does more filed work than theorisation. He has been associating himself with Central Planning Commission, State Planning Commission of Tamil Nadu, State Finance Commission of Tamil Nadu and he carried out several research studies in decentralization for both governments. His activities are supported by Population Foundation of India, the Ford Foundation, UNICEF, Rajiv Gandhi Foundation, CAPART, Ministry of Rural Development and DANIDA (Danish-Indo Development Agency) in specific areas of activities in connection with empowerment of people. He is in the network of the Non-Governmental Organisations for Panchayat activities. He involves himself in capacity building exercise for local body leaders. He has evolved training module and manual for local body leaders. He has to his credit thirty nine books, seventy nine articles in reputed journals, twelve working papers, seven monographs and seven review articles on three major areas, namely, Legislative Behaviour, Ethnicity and Panchayati Raj System. He was a recipient of Fellowship from Sastri Indo-Canadian Institute, New Delhi and World Academy of Art and Science, USA. He has visited the US and Canada, on academic assignments. He was a visiting fellow in the MiGill University, Canada in 1989. He is a life member of Indian Institute of Public Administration, Indian Association of Public Administration, Indian Association of Political Science, Indian Association of American Studies and Indian Association of Canadian Studies. He is a member of the expert committee constituted by the Government of Tamil Nadu, to monitor the training programme for local body leaders.

Dr. T. Parthiban has obtained his Ph.D. from Gandhigram Rural Institute, Gandhigram, Tamil Nadu. He has had more than 10 years experience in different capacities starting from the Fellow in the UGC major Research Project in Gandhigram Rurai Institute, Gandhigram. He has served as an Investigator in National Commission for SCs/STs, Ministry of Social Justice and Empowerment, Government of India. He visited CODESRIA, Senegal through SEEPHIS Fellowship. He serves as a Research Consultant to the IDS, Sussex, UK Project entitled "Decentralization and poor: Political Penetration by caste based parties the PMK in Tamil Nadu."

Presently he is the Director of Centre for Sustainable Development, Madurai.

Vanishree Joseph is a Research Fellow, pursuing her research programme in "Gender and Governance". She has been involving in organizing Panchayat Women Leaders for social development activities. She has received awards for her contribution in the forms of articles and presentations in the areas of Gender and Governance based on her field activities. She has written a few monographs on the same area. She is in a network of scholars working in the field of Capability Approach.

EMPOWERING WOMEN

Grassroots Experience from Tamil Nadu

G. PALANITHURAI
T. PARTHIBAN
J. VANISHREE

CONCEPT PUBLISHING COMPANY, NEW DELHI

Cataloging in Publication Data—DK
Courtesy: D.K. Agencies (P) Ltd. <docinfo@dkagencies.com>

Palanithurai, G. (Ganapathy), 1953-
Empowering women : grassroots experience from Tamil Nadu / G. Palanithurai, T. Parthiban, J. Vanishree.
p. cm.
Study conducted in Thoothukudi District of Tamil Nadu, India.
Includes bibliographical references (p.)
Includes index.
ISBN 8180694542

1. Women in economic development—India—Thoothukudi (District). 2. Self-help groups—India—Thoothukudi (District). 3. Poor women—Government policy—India—Tamil Nadu. I. Parthiban, T., joint author. II. Vanishree, J. (Joseph), joint author. III. Title.

DDC 305.420 954 82 22

ISBN-13: 978-81-8069-454-7
ISBN-10: 81-8069-454-2

First Published 2007

Published and Printed by
Ashok Kumar Mittal
Concept Publishing Company
A/15-16, Commercial Block, Mohan Garden
NEW DELHI-110059 (India)

Phones: 25351460, 25351794
Fax: 091-11-25357103
E-mail: publishing@conceptpub.com

To

The Divine Mother

PREFACE

Poverty reduction and empowerment are uphill tasks that are being faced by governments, civil society organizations, investing agencies (to deliberately avoid the use of the concept of donor) and the affected collectivities themselves. Various approaches have been evolved over a period of time, a multitude of schemes and programmes have been carried out and yet the expected results have not been achieved. The reasons are being analysed elaborately globally and locally and one uniform answer emerging from all the analyses is that the affected or marginalized have not been prepared internally. Demands have not been generated by them and of aspirations have not been developed among the people who are vulnerable. Secondly, it has not been realized that however poor they are, they have got skills, capacity and capability. Moreover schemes and programmes are being carried out for poverty reduction with the perception that they are being done for charity.

Individuals, organizations and institutions which are involved in carrying out poverty reduction programmes, perceive themselves as donors and the people who receive benefits as beneficiaries. As a result, the self-respect and self-dignity of the people has been shattered. People reduce themselves to beneficiaries without self-dignity. Nowhere has it been proved that development is achieved at the cost of self-dignity. They become powerless, voiceless and helpless. In a society which is predominantly functioning in a highly hierarchical structure based on the caste system and a strong patriarchy one would find little opportunity to overcome barriers and obstacles. Unless the self is actualized and self-dignity is built up, it is very difficult to bring out the people who are in the extreme poverty bracket. That is why all over the world community-driven development and demand driven development are brought to the fore for discussion and adoption.

The new phenomenon of women's group, popularly called *Self-Help Group* is a silent revolution in Indian society. It is obvious from the literature that without bringing women into the economic domain, increasing economic growth is impossible. In the same way without mainstreaming women in governance and decision-making, poverty cannot be reduced and gender justice cannot be delivered. The new women force have started organizing themselves and coming out from their houses for the causes of collectives. There are many players in organizing such groups including government departments. NGOs who are strong in perspective building on women's advancement have started sensitizing women on the issues of women, children, governance and social development. The women who have been sensitized have come to the public space for discussing public issues. Further they have moved from credit to enterprise (production of marketable goods). They have got into a new zone of action which is totally new. A perspicacious researcher who is looking into the whole gamut of SHG activities can not be complacent as problems of SHGs are numerous and the support structure built up is very limited. A mushroom growth of groups formed by various agencies with varied perspectives with different levels of skills, aspirations and capability have started their credit activities. The institutions which have shown interest in forming groups have not shown the same interest in pursuing the groups from credit to enterprise. Moveover they do not have the wherewithal and the R & D. Without R & D these groups cannot move further. Likewise the government also does not have a strong R & D facilities. But there were stories coming out in the newspapers about the Thoothukudi SHG success in many fields which propelled me to look into it very deeply.

While visiting some of the areas and interacting with some of the members of SHG who are on the job, we came to know the powerful support structure emotionally created by the District Administration under the leadership of Mr. Rajaraman the then District Collector and the then Project Officer of DRDA Mr. Radha. Further it is noticed that the then District Collector Mr. Rajaraman and the then DRDA Project Officer Mr. Radha had extended unfathomable support to these SHGs for the success of their activities. But the support extended to them by the Collector and the Project Officer is not systemic but individualistic. It has been noticed now after that departure of the then Collector and Project Officer from the district the same support has not been extended to the SHGs.

We moved further our journey of probing the stories of the SHG members. We found stories of success and failures. But the District Administration has extended full co-operation to conduct the study. In this study we have concentrated on the groups which are supported by the government for their economic activities. Data have been generated from the government documents and the documents prepared by DRDA and case studies have been conducted on select individuals. In the case analysis process has been analysed to a limited extent. In this study we have not generalized anything but in fact we have brought to light the achievements and the actions to be taken. It is more of capturing the success and failures and they are to be further probed by others.

It is true that the women who got up early and went to bed last in the family as family chorus demanded their time. But after joining the group the women have not left any family chorus. They managed effectively and did everything in the family as usual and concentrated their attention on the new job. In the whole process women have been conscientised on credit and trained in enterprise but not on health. The major question is women health is more important than credit and enterprise. Even the NGOs have not done such exercises for women. If women that too SHG women are oriented in health, the status of women health would have been improved a lot. Despite all inherent weakness, the SHG women brought success stories and this propelled and motivated me to look in to the process of the women movement from home to enterprise.

To conduct this study I needed the support of a field researcher and my Ph.D. Scholar Dr. T. Parthiban after obtaining Ph.D. he was doing consultancy service to NGOs. He has come to my rescue. I requested him to carryout the field work and report the same to me. Another researcher, a JRF scholar who is working with me for her Ph.D. programme Ms.Vanishree helped me to finalize the draft. Hence, I express my sincere thanks to both of them.

Equally I express my thanks to the then District Collector of Thoothukudi District Mr. Rajaraman and DRDA Project Officer Mr. Radha for their support and cooperation. The SHG women who have spared their valuable time for us. Their frank and free comments have to be appreciated.

I express my sincere thanks to my colleagues in the Department and in my projects for their active support in completing this work in time. My family members especially my wife Ms. Mala a noble soul to me always bearing the burden of my family and taking care of my children. Many times I have not done justice to them. Yet they tolerate me with the thinking that I am doing a good work for the society. I register my thanks to my wife Ms. Mala.

G. PALANITHURAI
Gandhigram

CONTENTS

LIST OF TABLES

LIST OF DIAGRAMS

LIST OF ABBREVIATIONS

BLF	-	Block Level Federation
CSW	-	Central Social Welfare Department
DRD	-	Director of Rural Development
DRDA	-	District Rural Development Agency
EDP	-	Entrepreneurship Development Programme
GNP	-	Gross National Product
HDI	-	Human Development Index
IMF	-	International Monetary Fund
NABARD	-	National Bank for Agriculture and Rural Development
OBC	-	Other Backward Community
PLF	-	Panchayat Level Federation
PU	-	Panchayat Union
RASI	-	Rural Access to the Service through Internet
RSM	-	Rural Sanitary Mart
RTO	-	Road Transport Organization
SC	-	Scheduled Caste
SGSY	-	Swarnajayanti Gram Swarojkar Yojana
SHG	-	Self Help Group
ST	-	Scheduled Tribes
THADCO	-	Tamil Nadu Adi-Dravida Housing Development Corporation
TNCDW	-	Tamil Nadu Corporation for Development of Women

1 INTRODUCTION

"Women's Empowerment" is a concept and a construct which is used by everyone in the world in all fora and in all dimensions to indicate the increased activities for women's advancement. Thereby it has come to the centre stage of the political and administrative systems of the society. Movements from above and below have actively engaged women and others in pursuing the problems of women for decision-making and implementation. As a result, not only has the issue of women been brought to the forefront but the women themselves have come to that space for redressing their problems on their own with the help of the available support structure. As a result, the conditions of women are improving but the problems faced by them are also increasing as the empowerment process has to cross through a series of challenges and obstacles.

Over the past three decades, from the first United Nations International Conference on Women held in Mexico in 1975 to the present, activities have been initiated to promote the advancement and the rights of women. At the global level, all the three World Conferences are significant as they have brought proposals, issues, solutions and resolutions on the diverse problems of women. They have not only discussed the problems and passed resolutions but also moved further to exert pressure on governments to listen to their problems and to take steps to address their demands. Issues such as violence against women, poverty, illiteracy, women's health, reproductive rights, gender equity, women's under-representation in the decision-making bodies have been focused upon. In the1990s they have taken a further lead in mainstreaming their concern on human rights and the development agenda.

After the reform initiative for the globalization of the economy, the challenges of inequality and the feminization of poverty have been unequivocally exacerbated. So, the women's groups have started discussing the financing for development and they have started demanding specific allocation of resources for women's development.

Research Background

The late 1990s saw a significant refocusing of donor and government development efforts on the goal of poverty reduction. There were at least two reasons for this. First, after fifty years of international development effort, it was clear that the number of poor was continuing to grow. The total number living in poverty had grown from 1.2 billion to almost 1.5 billion. An increasing consensus among major donors on poverty reduction targets is to have focus on the coordination of development efforts to achieve synergy. Second, influential research by the World Bank and others has brought to light that billions of dollars of development funding was in many cases leaving little or significant impact on poverty reduction. This has prompted a major debate about the conditions under which aid will prove effective and a discussion of radical proposals for the reform of aid management and aid relationships.

This increased poverty focus is reflected in a range of new international development processes that, in intention at least, capture the pro-poor nature of contemporary international aid. They required developing country governments to develop a specific strategy for poverty reduction through the preparation of a Poverty Reduction Strategy Paper (PRSP) designed to ensure that policy is consistent with poverty reduction objectives. In principle, this should lead to an increased level of co-operation and joint action among a wide range of players—governments as well as multilateral and bilateral agencies. The specific interventions and activities which are identified to combat poverty will be different for different countries. There is emerging consensus that effective poverty reduction requires action on a range of broad, interlinked fronts.

To increase the income and the expenditure of the poor the old programmes for poverty alleviation did not work well. As a result steps were taken to integrate poverty alleviation programmes with over all development.

To improve access by the poor to assets, services and facilities required for functioning normally in society, including social and economic services, factor such as productive assets, including natural, financial and human capital is essential. There is a need for increased efficiency and improved effectiveness of public spending and for targeted assistance and safety nets and the recognition that these may well have to be funded by the public sector.

To empower the poor by facilitating their participation in political and social processes, in particular ensuring that they have the capacity to influence their immediate environment and to promote change in the aspects of exclusion include lack of political influence, abuse of fundamental human rights, discrimination on grounds of gender, ethnicity or language, and lack of dignity, and exclusion from normal social processes. In practical terms, this emphasis on empowerment, accountability and social inclusion may require an action on decentralization and local decision-making and a need to develop capacity at all levels of government and civil society. It may also suggest a need to address aspects of intra-household inequities.

To reduce vulnerability by addressing chronic insecurity, both at the individual level and at the meso level; concerns exist over the types of coping strategies which households typically adopt to manage risk, since these often result in increased vulnerability in the longer term; in practical terms, micro level risks can be addressed through insurance or risk-pooling schemes and through a complex range of diversification activities; also important in managing such risks is access to social networks for borrowing and other support.

The World Bank discusses a three-pronged strategy for poverty reduction. Specifically, the Bank advocates action in relation to:

a. Empowerment — to strengthen the focus of state institutions on poverty reduction.
b. Security — so that the poor can manage their risks more effectively.
c. Opportunity — such that economic options are strengthened.

Against this background the present study analyses the efforts of the Government of Tamil Nadu and their impact on the livelihoods of the poor. This study takes guidance from the conceptual framework developed by Amartya Sen.

Conceptual Framework—The Capability Approach (CA)

The main aim of this research study is to examine the role of the Government of Tamil Nadu in reducing poverty and inequality through increasing the capabilities of poor women. For sustainable poverty reduction, it is argued that issues of redistribution and social justice need to be addressed. Amartya Sen introduced the Capability Approach (CA) as a more appropriate theory of justice than existing theories in moral philosophy.

The CA is recognized as a valuable approach to the question of fundamental entitlements. Critical to this approach is the view of poverty as the failure to raise basic capabilities to achieve minimally acceptable levels of functioning. Against the dominant emphasis on economic growth and income as an indicator of a nation's quality of life, Sen insists on the importance of capabilities, i.e. what people are actually able to do and to be. In "Development as Freedom", Sen argues that capabilities provide the best basis for thinking about the goals of development. When nations are compared by international measures of welfare and when nations strive internally to achieve a higher level of development for their people, capabilities provide a holistic way of understanding the normative content of the idea of development. Limiting the goal of development to increasing GNP per capita ignores distributional inequalities, particularly central when thinking about gender equality. This also fails to disaggregate and separately consider important aspects of development such as health and education that do not necessarily demonstrably correlate with GNP, even when distribution is taken into account. For example, in comparing international data sets measuring the basic capabilities of longevity/survival and education, Sri Lanka and China stand out as being far ahead of other countries with a similar GNP per head such as India, and join or even overtake richer economies such as those of Mexico and Brazil.

Sen's functioning-capability-freedom framework moves the focus from income to capabilities, thereby allowing the poor to be seen as agents of change as opposed to victims requiring help. It also outlines the need for an integrated analysis of various institutions including the state, the market, the legal system, public interest groups and the media among others in terms of their contribution to enhancing the substantive freedom of individuals seen as active agents of change.

The Functioning-Capability-Freedom Framework

Amartya Sen's approach focuses chiefly on the freedom of individuals to pursue their own way of life, in which well-being is seen "in terms of a person's ability to do valuable acts or reach valuable states of being" (Amartya Sen 2002). This is the core of the Capability Approach (CA). According to the capability approach, the ends of well-being, justice and development should be conceptualized in terms of people's capabilities to function, that is, their effective opportunities to undertake the actions and activities that they want to engage in and be whom they want to be. These beings and doings, which Sen calls functionings, together constitute what makes a valuable life. The capability approach refuses to see people primarily as patients who can be helped by giving them a handout or a cure which they can take or leave, but rather as agents who can and should be given the power and the necessary conditions so that they can take their lives in their own hands. Sen's approach requires "a broader informational base, focusing particularly on people's capability to choose the life they have reason to value" (Amartya Sen 2002), to highlight the social and economic factors which give people the opportunity to do and to be what they consider valuable for their fulfillment. Thus the capability approach focuses directly on the substantive freedom of the individuals involved. Sen, as mentioned already, suggests that well-being be considered in terms of human functionings and capabilities. Functionings relate to what a person may value doing or being: they are the living conditions achieved by an individual and represent a set of interrelated activities and doings and beings that form his/her life. Capabilities concern the ability of an individual to achieve different combinations of functionings and define the freedom to choose the life that he/she prefers. These two categories are complementary but distinct: "A functioning is an achievement, whereas a capability is the ability to achieve. Functionings are, in a sense, more directly related to living conditions, since they are different aspects of living conditions. Capabilities, in contrast, are notions of freedom, in the positive sense: what real opportunities you have regarding the life you may lead" (Amartya Sen 2005).

The Capability Approach can be used in different ways depending on the context and it is not rigid because it is intentionally an open and flexible framework as Sen says: "the foundational affirmation of the importance of capabilities can go with various strategies of actual evaluation involving practical compromises. The pragmatic nature of practical reason demands this" (Amartya Sen 2005).

With these few propositions of Amartya Sen's Capability Approach, the present study makes an attempt, to evaluate the opportunities of Self-Help Groups (SHG) of women for carrying out various activities. The activities performed by these women are economic in nature, enhancing the economic conditions of their family. With this framework, the study analyses the well-being achieved by the women of Self-Help Groups. SHG women's capabilities to function, that is, their effective opportunities to undertake the action and activities that they want to engage in and be whom they want to be will be evaluated. A woman's earning and independent income through these self-help groups tend to have a clear impact on enhancing the social standing of women in the household and the society. Her contribution to the prosperity of the family is then more visible and she also has more voice because of being less dependent on others. This will be also analysed in the present study.

Objectives of the Study

- To study the role of the State Government in the process of development of poor women through SHGs.

- To evaluate the capability of women through their economic activities.
- To study the interface between DRDA and SHG.
- To find out the elements of sustainability of SHG entrepreneurship.

Methodology

The required secondary data were collected from books, articles and magazines. Data were also collected from the records of the Women's Development Corporation and the DRDA, Thoothukudi (also known as Tuticorin). Focus group discussions were conducted. An interview schedule was used for primary data collection. Primarily, this study relies on the case study method as groups have to be analysed individually. It is analytical in nature and descriptive in form. Group economic and social activities are analysed from the perspective of sustainability. Forty SHGs located in eight blocks in Thoothukudi District were selected for this study. The names of the selected SHGs are given Block-wise hereunder.

SELECTION OF THE SHGS' ENTERPRISES IN THOOTHUKUDI DISTRICT

Table 1.1 : Blocks of Selected SHGs in Thoothukudi District.

Sl. No.	*Name of the Block*	*No. of SHG*	*Total No. of Members*
1.	Thoothukudi	8	131
2.	Karukkulam	7	134
3.	Thiruvaikundam	4	73
4.	Alwarthirunagari	7	128
5.	Thiruchanthur	4	74
6.	Udankudi	6	97
7.	Kovilpatti	3	47
8.	Kayatharu	1	12
	Total	40	696

Source : Computed.

Table 1.2 : Selection of SHGs in Thoothukudi Block.

Sl. No.	*Name of the SHG*	*No.*	*Panchayat*	*Name of the Village/Town*	*Name of the Trade*
1.	Saranaaroja	20	Thoothukudi	Thoothukudi	Supermarket
2.	Kurinji	20	Thoothukudi	Thoothukudi	Ready made, canteen
3.	Oolovelukku	12	Thoothukudi	Thoothukudi	Honey sales
4.	Thirumakal	15	Thoothukudi	Thoothukudi	Ice cream
5.	Maniveenayagam	17	Thoothukudi	Thoothukudi	STD both
6.	Rasi Veediyal	12	Thoothukudi	Thoothukudi	Driving center
7.	Sathiya	19	Aathimarapatti	Aathimarapatti	Paper cup
8.	Jeyabharath	16	Sevariyapuram	Kaneshnagar	File pad. Envelop
	Total	131			

Source : Computed.

Table 1.3 : Selection of SHGs in Karukkulam Block.

Sl. No.	*Name of SHG*	*Total Members*	*Panchayat*	*Village/Town*	*Trade*
1.	Nehrugramayoga	19	Karukkgulam	Karukkgulam	Fisheries
2.	Nalmakalir	15	Periyathalai	Periyathalai	Crab flattening
3.	Thendral	20	Muthaloor	Muthaloor	Hallva
4.	Vasantham	20	Muthaloor	Muthaloor	Hallva
5.	M.G.R	20	Allwarkulam	Allwarkulam	Rental utensils
6.	Indira	20	Allwarkulam	Allwarkulam	Rental utensils
7.	Chandaragri	20	Allwarkulam	Allwarkulam	Rental utensils
	Total	134			

Source : Computed.

Table 1.4 : Selection of SHGs in Thiruvaikundam Block.

Sl. No.	*SHG Name*	*No.*	*Panchayat*	*Village/Town*	*Trade*
1.	Marutham	13	Korgai	Korgai Akkasalai	Goat farming
2.	Sugamsiddha Venayagam	20	Pathmanapa mangalam	Pathmanapa mangalam	Stone quarry
3.	Tholavelli-yamman	20	Amman Kovil	Sunganatha-puram	Stone tiller
4.	Kamarajar	20	Kottaikadu	Kottaikadu	Banana cultivation
	Total	73			

Source : Computed.

Table 1.5 : Selection of SHGs in Alwarthirunagari Block.

Sl. No.	*SHG Name*	*No.*	*Panchayat*	*Village/Town*	*Trade*
1.	Ponvela Dowcra	15	Kadaiyanodai	Kadaiyanodai	Pickles
2.	Annai Sivagami	20	Sugathanai	Therku marathanai	Jute
3.	Kamarajar	20	Sugathanai	Terku marathanai	Jute
4.	Karpagatharu	20	Karuvelampatti	Karuvelampatti	Palm candy Jaggery
5.	Muthumalai	18	Kurukattur	Thediyan Kudiyeruppu	Milch animals with Fish farming
6.	Sridevi	20	Karuvelampadu	Karuvelampadu	Milch animals forming
7.	Dowcra	15	Sethuguvaigathan	Sethuguvaigathan	Palm mats wearing

Source : Computed.

Table 1.6 : Selection of SHGs in Thiruchanthur Block.

Sl. No.	*SHG Name*	*No.*	*Panchayat*	*Village/Town*	*Trade*
1.	Sungamakalir kuttuaamaippu	18	Thiruchanthur	Thiruchanthur	Crosories
2.	Annai	20	Veerapandi pattanam	Adaikalpuram	Paper Cup
3.	Kirusthuraja	19	Veerapandi pattanam	Pelominagar	Provisional Store
4.	Parvathiyammal	17	Veerapandi pattanam	Chanmugapuram	Washing detergents
	Total	74			

Source : Computed.

Table 1.7 : Selection of SHGs in Udandkudi Block.

Sl. No.	*SHG Name*	*No.*	*Panchayat*	*Village*	*Trade*
1.	Karpagatharu	19	Chenmakkulam	Meiyanapuram	Crosories
2.	Indira	14	Chettiyapatti	Sevaloor	Palm leaf products
3.	Mariyammal	14	Chettiyapatti	Sevaloor	Palm leaf products
4.	Santhanamery	14	Chettiyapatti	Sevaloor	Palm leaf products
5.	Pathima	20	Kulasai	Kulasai	Palm leaf products
6.	Muththalamman	16	Puthukudiatchi	Manapad	Palm leaf products
	Total	97			

Source : Computed.

Table 1.8 : Selection of SHGs in Kovilpatti Block.

Sl. No.	*SHG Name*	*No.*	*Panchayat*	*Village/Town*	*Trade*
1.	Vinayagam	15	Kovilpatti	Kovilpatti	Stone quarry
2.	Suyachitta Everest	16	Sivanthipatti	Karisalkulam	Stone quarry
3.	Annaitherasa	16	Sivanthipatti	Karisalkulam	Stone quarry
	Total	47			

Source : Computed.

Table 1.9 : Selection of SHGs in Kayatharu Block.

Sl. No.	*SHG Name*	*No.*	*Panchayat*	*Village/Town*	*Trade*
1.	Annaivelankanni	12	Kayatharu	Chettikuruchi	Stone quarry
	Total	12			

Source : Computed.

The above groups are analysed both individually and collectively. The focus will be on building their capability, skill and capability, their access to credit and the support structure they have used to develop their group and the sustainability of their group activities. The Capability Approach will be a guideline and not a reference point for the analysis.

Chapterization

This report is organized in six chapters. The first chapter introduces the subject of the study, research questions, explains the conceptual framework spells out the objectives of the study, the methodology adopted and the sources of the data collected. Chapter two deals with the performance of the Tamil Nadu Government on SHGs. Chapter three analyses the performance of the Thoothukudi DRDA on SHGs. Chapter four provides some successful stories of SHG enterprises in Thoothukudi District. Chapter five presents an integrated analysis. Chapter six presents the major findings and recommendations.

2 GOVERNMENT OF TAMIL NADU AND SHGs : A State Profile

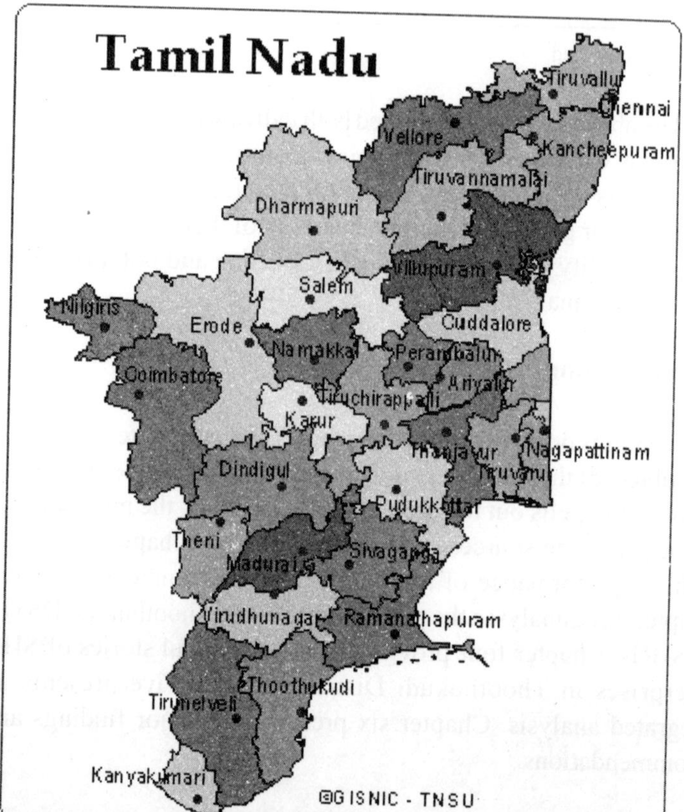

The population of Tamil Nadu State is 62 million as per the 2001 census as opposed to 55.9 million in 1991. The male-female ratio works out to 986 in 2001 as compared to 974 in 1991 and 977 in 1981. SC and ST population constitutes 11.3 million of whom 5.6 million are women. Tamil Nadu has emerged as the fifth largest economy in India. It has achieved solid development outcomes with a higher economic growth and a faster poverty reduction which is higher than the India average in the 1990s. It is one of India's most urbanized states with the third highest Human Development Index (HDI) among 29 states. Tamil Nadu has an educated hard working and disciplined workforce and a capable civil service. Tamil Nadu's HDI (2001) is 0.657 as compared to 0.571 for India as a whole. Tamil Nadu is generally regarded as a socially upheld state of the Indian Union. The Tamil Nadu Government has always been proud of its impressive performance in the social sector. Among the 15 major states of India Tamil Nadu holds impressive ranks in general literacy rates, sex ratio, birth rates, infant mortality rates etc. In terms of the quality of life Tamil Nadu was assessed to be the 4th among the 15 major states of India. But it is very striking that in terms of rural index, Tamil Nadu holds a lower 11th rank, below the low income states such as Madhya Pradesh, Rajasthan and Orissa. Tamil Nadu has an unfinished development agenda. The state has a relatively high poverty incidence of about 20 per cent. The following are the details of state profile.

The life of the poor in the rural areas is becoming more and more difficult as their livelihood opportunities are taken away as the globalization process is set in motion through the policies of the State and Central Governments since 1991 when the new Economic Policy was initiated. The worst affected are the agricultural labourers, fishermen, weavers, rural artisans and women. Basic services such as medical, water supply and sanitation services are becoming cost based and are provided on the basis of the charges paid by the users. Natural resources, which are the lifeline of the poor, are being exploited for producing marketable commodities by multi-national companies. Water is being sucked up, sand is being removed and blue metal is being quarried by companies. Communities at the local level are fighting against such kind of exploitation of natural resources at the expense of the poor. Panchayat leaders are fighting against this kind of exploitation with the support of the communities.

In the coastal areas shrimp cultivation is going on a large scale, eroding the natural resources, by which several thousands of fishermen and agricultural labourers have lost their livelihood. They are fighting against these new initiatives as they affect their life and livelihood security. When silicon soil was lifted from the Vanduvancheri Gram Panchayat area in Tanjore District, it was stopped by the Panchayat with the support of the community. The matter is now in court. When water was lifted from Sivaganga for bottling of mineral water, it was stopped by the local community which said that water was not a commodity but an entitlement of the people and the mineral water company should not be allowed to make it a commodity for the market to make profits. As the State Government stopped its subsidy for Khadhi and handloom products, the weavers lost employment opportunities and, as a result, they started migrating to different places in search of employment. Thus globalization has its own impact on the livelihood security of the people. The unskilled workers who were being used in the construction industry and road projects have been driven away as the activities have become totally mechanized and technology driven. As reform activities were initiated, the subsidy for electricity consumption by the small farmers has been cut and, as a result, the small farmers have had to give up their farm activities.

Being a frontline state in social development activities, Tamil Nadu has now reversed its policy options to cope with new economic pressures which globalization has set in motion. The problems arising out of the new policy options exert pressure on the Panchayats through the Gram Sabha. The Panchayat leaders are facing all these problems. Without having enough knowledge of this process every one is struggling. In Tamil Nadu, there are 12605 Gram Panchayats, 384 Block Panchayats and 29 District Panchayats. Of the 12605 Gram Panchayats, 3046 are headed by SC and ST men and women; of the 3046 Gram Panchayats, 1107 are headed by SC/ST women; 3150 Gram Panchayats are headed by other caste Hindu women leaders. The New Panchayat Act came into force in the year 1994. Basic services have been given to the Panchayat institutions despite several constraints and yet Panchayats are struggling to serve the people. By taking up the responsibilities, Panchayat leaders have assumed powers by which devolution is being evolved in Tamil Nadu.

While democracy is being deepened through decentralization

of powers, the economy is being globalised. It is a paradoxical situation at present that both work together to achieve development and prosperity. Decentralization of powers and globalization of the economy are institutionalized. There are opinions, views and observations about the process and the implications of the globalization of the economy and the decentralization of powers. Studies are pouring in on the implications of decentralization of powers—positive and negative—and they are location specific in nature and character. Likewise there are country-wide studies on globalization. Yet opposition to globalization and support for decentralization are emerging all over the world as if globalization is working against the interests of the people and decentralization is working towards the prosperity of the people. Despite the open support for decentralization, the process of decentralization is not smooth. Despite opposition to globalization the process of globalization proceeds apace through the policies of the government. It is a major question whether the government is working against the interests of the people in a democracy.

There is yet another issue to be seen in this context, namely, the position taken by individuals, organizations, associations and institutions on decentralization of powers and globalization of the economy. There are a large number of institutions totally opposed to the globalization process as if globalization of the economy causes only negative effects in the lives of the people. There are organizations that whole-heartedly support the globalization process as if it brings prosperity to everyone. On the other hand, for decentralization of powers, one can hear predominantly positive voices. It is true that both globalization and decentralization are worldwide phenomena and are historical processes. The delivery and the implications of globalization and decentralization depend on how best they are understood by the policy-makers and the stakeholders. Both have positive and negative aspects to them. So the focus should be on how best both can be utilized for the advancement of society and how best people can be saved from the ill-effects of the process of the globalization of the economy and the decentralization of powers. The reality can be understood by learning from one another.

Globalization works in the society through the policies and programmes of the government, both at the centre and in the states.

The impact of globalization will be felt at the grassroots and especially by the marginalized, weaker and poor segment of the society. It has to be mitigated through micro action in the field and macro action through policies and decisions. Grassroots leaders who manage local affairs have to be aware of the implications of globalization and, hence, they have to be sensitized. Globalization is a mix of challenges, threats and opportunities. People at the grassroots hardly have the capacity to understand its complex process, avoid its threats and harvest the opportunities. In this context Panchayats as people's institution of self-governance and instruments for ensuring their livelihood security have a critical role to play in arresting the ill-effects of globalization and exploiting the opportunities for which decentralization provides legitimate power to take decisions. Nothing prevents the grassroots leaders from making use of the opportunities, if any, in globalization to achieve development. The leaders at the grassroots have to have a clear picture about global issues also. So a link between the advocates and the adversaries of globalization and the grassroots leaders is imperative. This kind of synergisation should be a continuous process. It is necessary that Panchayats should be made to look at the reality from a scientific perspective for which they need to be oriented. The most important links between globalization and poverty reduction have to be analysed seriously at the micro level. There should be proper understanding by all concerned about the implications of globalization. To look at issues realistically and scientifically, to take the initiative to protect the people from the onslaught of the potential threats and to make use of the opportunities, a continuous dialogue and concerted action are imperative.

Globalization of the economy, localization of development, decentralization of powers, ensuring the livelihood security of the poor and the marginalized are ongoing activities. These activities are carried out in an isolated way without convergence and synergization. The activities are for different stakeholders and aim at different goals. But the human collectivity is always looking for prosperity, equity, equality and peace. Institutions which have evolved for governance over a period of time to manage development have to explore all the opportunities which are emerging in the world through the efforts of human beings. At present globalization is an endeavour to multiply prosperity in geometrical proportion. Decentralization is an endeavour to empower the powerless to determine their destiny. Human development is the major task which the government has to perform along with economic activity. Making development sustainable is the task of everyone at this juncture as the concept of development seems to be elusive.

In the whole process of development and democracy, learnings are very essential and, accordingly, individuals and collectivities can make use of the opportunities to achieve development and to protect themselves and others from the threats, if any, from the process. Globalization is on and human sufferings are also on the increase. Mechanization of economic activities through modern sophisticated technology has driven millions out of jobs. The growth of unemployment brings about acute social conflict. Aspirations for development and the desire to be in the democratic process are also on the increase in society.

Against this background research studies have to be undertaken on how the new dispensation provides opportunities for society to achieve prosperity, how it poses threats and how the threats are being managed. All these processes have to be studied scientifically. This will elicit valuable information for those who control the process of globalization and for those who control the localization of development. Both will have mutual understanding. Further the grassroots institutions have earmarked roles and responsibilities and the leaders have to administer economic development and social justice. The responsibility of ensuring the livelihood security of the poor is vested with the Panchayats. The Panchayat leaders have to be conscientised on the implications of globalization. Thus a linkage has to be established between the globals and the locals for mutual benefit and advantage. To establish such meaningful linkages, a series of activities are to be initiated.

STATE PROFILE: TAMILNADU

Table 2.1 : Basic Details.

Sl. No.	*Descriptions*	*Units*			*Units*	
1.	Total Area	129913.22	Sq. Kms.	Forest Area	21336.17	Sq. Kms.
2.	Net Sown Area	53032.94	.000	Net Irrigation Area	2885.85	.000
3.	Total Population	62110.84	.000	Total Literates	45652.11	.000
4.	Total Male	31268.65	.000	Total Female	30842.19	.000
5.	Urban Population	27241.55	.000	Rural Population	34869.29	.000
6.	Rural Population - Male	17508.99	.000	Rural Population - Female	17360.30	.000
7.	Urban population - Male	13759.67	.000	Urban Population - Female	13481.88	.000
8.	Total Male Literacy	25743.48	.000	Total Female Literates	19908.63	.000
9.	Rural Literates	23258.20	.000	Urban Literates	22361.24	.000
10.	Rural Literates - Male	13564.21	.000	Rural Literates - Female	9693.99	.000
11.	Urban Literates - Male	12163.55	.000	Urban Literates - Female	10197.70	.000
12.	Rural Male Literacy		77.47 %	Rural Female Literates		70.66 %
13.	Urban Male Literacy		88.40 %	Urban Female Literacy		82.58 %
14.	Proportion of Population Below Poverty Line	%	29.16	Urbanization	%	43.86
15.	Population Growth Per Annum	%	11.19	Literacy	%	73.47
16.	Population Density (Persons / Sq.Km.)	%	324	Male Literacy	%	82.33
17.	Workers as % of Total Population	%	44.78	Female Literacy	%	64.55
18.	Agriculture and Allied Activities	%	49.55	Urban Literacy	%	82.07
19.	Other Workers	%	45.21	Rural Literacy	%	66.66

Source : Director of Census Operations of Tamil Nadu, Chennai, Directorate of Economic and Statistics, Chennai - 6

Micro Finance Scenario: Project Details

The micro-finance initiatives of the nationalised banks have evolved as a sustainable social movement over a decade. At the national level, the formal banking system has reached the doorsteps of above 116 lakh poor households, providing micro-credit to them by organizing 7.17 lakh SHGs as of March 2003. The goal at the national level is to cover 100 million rural poor in the country with savings and credit by the year 2008 through SHGs. Tamil Nadu ranks second in the country in establishing SHGs. The states which have registered significant progress in the formation of SHGs are Andhra Pradesh and Tamil Nadu followed by Karnataka and Orissa. As on 31st December, 2003, about 1.51 lakh SHGs have been formed in Tamil Nadu State covering all the districts, blocks and Panchayats. The coverage details are shown in Table 2.2.

Table 2.2 : Overall Coverage of the Projects as on 31.12.2003.

1.	**Rural Areas**	
	Number of Districts covered	28
	Number of blocks covered	385
	Number of Panchayats covered	12619
	Total Number of SHGs formed	119014
	Total Number of Women enrolled	2023696
	Total Amount of Group Savings (Rs. Lakhs)	32539.29
2.	**Urban Areas**	
	Number of Town Panchayats covered	611
	Number of Municipalities covered	102
	Number of Corporations covered	6
	Total Number of SHGs formed	32529
	Total Number of Women enrolled	548938
	Total Amount of Group Savings (Rs. Lakhs)	6825.06
	Grand Total of Rural and Urban	
	Number of SHGs	151543
	Number of Women enrolled	2572634
	Amount of Group Savings (Rs. in Lakhs)	39364.35

Source : TNCDW, Chennai.

Table 2.3 : District-wise Coverage of the Project (as on 31.12.2003).

Sl. No.	Name of District	Blocks Covered	Number of Panchayats Covered	Rural Panchayats			Urban Local Bodies			Grand Total		
				Groups Formated	Women Enrolled	Group Savings Rs. in Lakhs	Formed	No. of Women Enrolled	Group Saving Rs. in Lakhs	Group Formed	Women's Enrolled	Total Savings Rs. in Lakhs
1	2	3	4	5	6	7	8	9	10	11	12	13
1.	Virudhunagar	11	450	3413	911.3	934	934	17041	245.34	4347	77878	1156.64
2.	Villupuram	22	1104	6672	2269.05	752	752	14629	189.92	7424	143672	2459.42
3.	Vellor	20	753	3938	1178.19	522	522	8489	50.46	4460	74231	1228.65
4.	Trichy	14	408	4587	1023.46	1335	1335	21905	286.87	5922	96795	1310.33
5.	Thoothukudi	12	408	3465	905.35	940	940	17121	220.35	4405	78024	1125.7
6.	Thiruvarur	10	430	4902	1288.35	513	513	8963	126.78	5415	95755	1415.13
7.	Thiruvallur	14	539	4418	1130.69	778	778	12231	113.48	5196	81951	1244.17
8.	Theni	8	130	2591	459.18	1313	1313	20714	223.94	3904	62493	683.12
9.	Thanjavur	14	589	6058	1321.75	747	747	12758	159.85	6805	115364	1481.6
10.	Tirunelveli	19	425	4773	1170.93	2151	2151	40152	448.8	6924	125163	1619.73
11.	T.V. Malai	18	860	4941	683.9	413	413	7573	58.58	5354	92865	742.48
12.	Sivagangai	12	445	3424	889.43	472	472	8628	105.81	3896	66251	995.24
13.	Salem	20	385	4785	1446.89	1302	1302	21397	283.4	6087	101951	1730.29

(Table Contd. ...)

(Contd. ...)

1	2	3	4	5	6	7	8	9	10	11	12	13
14.	Ramnad	11	429	3640	1649.35	735	735	13971	151.9	4375	80723	1901.25
15.	Pudukottai	13	498	4498	977.18	352	352	5996	76.42	4850	80310	1053.6
16.	Perambalur	10	322	3673	673	256	256	4372	41.8	3929	65234	714.8
17.	Niligiris	4	35	2103	375.95	1414	1414	21995	304.22	3517	55430	680.17
18.	Namakkal	15	331	3438	1273.8	982	982	16751	302.5	4420	76876	1576.3
19.	Nagapattinam	11	434	5460	1257.37	666	666	10802	188.12	6126	101756	1445.49
20.	Madurai	13	431	3688	1137.62	781	781	14886	221.12	4469	87538	1358.74
21.	Karur	8	158	3025	644.31	468	468	6304	73.57	3493	48475	717.88
22.	Kanyakumari	9	99	2954	879.12	3075	3075	58275	798.71	6029	113451	1677.83
23.	Kancheepuram	13	648	4997	1093.14	2339	2335	33705	223.15	7336	113849	1316.29
24.	Erode	20	343	5232	856.34	1847	1847	27326	334.9	7079	102200	1191.24
25.	Dindigul	14	306	3375	545.76	745	745	11352	135.12	4120	62117	680.88
26.	Dharmapuri	18	588	5460	3771.7	439	439	8307	380.85	5899	109359	4152.55
27.	Cuddalore	13	682	5157	1903.7	1002	1002	19463	387.07	6159	118477	2290.77
28.	Coimbatore	19	389	4347	822.03	2807	2807	41608	417.4	7154	102222	1239.43
29.	Chennai	0	0	0	0	2449	2449	42224	174.63	2449	42224	174.63
30.	Total	385	12619	119014	32539.3	32529	32529	548938	6825.1	151543	2572634	39364.35

Source : TNCDW, Chennai.

As far as rural areas are concerned, 12,619 Panchayats of 385 blocks in 28 districts have been covered by the project. 20,23,696 women are enrolled with 1,19,014 Self-Help Groups in 29 districts. They have saved Rs. 32539.29 lakhs; 6 Corporations, 102 Municipalities and 611 Town Panchayats are covered in urban areas; here, 5,48,939 women are enrolled with 32,529 Self-Help Groups and they have saved Rs. 6825.06 lakhs; totally, 25,72,634 women are enrolled with 1,51,543 Self-Help Groups both in rural and urban areas and their savings is Rs. 39364.35 lakhs.

Table 2.3 presents describes the details of women's Self-Help Groups in 29 districts including urban areas. It is observed that the number of women enrolled in all the districts is 25,72,634 who have to saved a sum of Rs.39364.35 lakhs through 1,51,543 SHGs formed; 1,19,014 groups are found in rural Panchayats of 29 districts and 32,529 groups are found in urban areas including Chennai. The total blocks where the SHGs are formed are 385 of the all the districts covered by the Project. The total numbers of Panchayats under these blocks are 12,619.

Table 2.4 : Coverage of Habitations.

Sl. No.	*Details of Coverage*	*Total Number*	*Number Covered*	*Percentage*
1.	Coverage of Habitations	67716	58388	86.2
2.	Coverage of SC/ST Habitations	22866	20613	90.2
3.	Coverage of BPL Families			
	i. Rural	2686613	1724234	64.2
	ii. Urban	1756949	639709	36.4
	iii. Total	443562	2363943	53.2

Source : TNCDW, Chennai.

District-wise coverage of habitations and BPL families are shown in the following tables:

Table 2.5 : Coverage of Habitations — All and SC/ST Habitations — Physical Achievement.

Sl. No.	*Name of the District*	*Total Habitations*	*Habitations Covered as on Dec. 2003*		*%age of Coverage*	
			All	*SC/ST*	*All*	*SC/ST*
1.	Virudhunagar	1454	1454	798	100.00	100.00
2.	Villupuram	2892	2304	865	79.67	81.22
3.	Vellore	3563	2580	811	72.41	83.18
4.	Trichy	2541	2084	1271	82.01	97.47
5.	Thoothukudi	2113	2113	444	100.00	100.00
6.	Thiruvarur	2131	2060	114	96.67	98.16
7.	Thiruvallur	2579	1793	654	69.52	74.39
8.	Theni	476	456	59	95.80	95.16
9.	Thanjavur	1980	1976	1314	99.80	98.35
10.	Tirunelveli	2032	1149	136	56.55	66.34
11.	Thiruvannamalai	3148	2254	901	71.60	80.16
12.	Sivagangai	2787	2265	806	81.27	86.39
13.	Salem	3483	3280	551	94.17	74.56
14.	Ramnad	1915	1846	390	96.40	96.53
15.	Pudukottai	3938	3680	1451	93.45	99.59
16.	Perambalur	1096	1022	625	93.25	92.73
17.	Nilgiris	1389	1256	396	90.42	100.00
18.	Namakkal	1883	1640	982	87.10	87.91
19.	Nagapattinam	1989	1960	415	98.54	100.00
20.	Madurai	1855	1731	233	93.32	89.96
21.	Karur	1661	1467	901	88.32	82.36
22.	Kanniyakumari	1885	1885	218	100.00	77.86
23.	Kancheepuram	2145	2000	1200	93.24	92.31
24.	Erode	3997	3084	1341	77.16	90.00
25.	Dindigul	2963	179	190	60.72	86.36
26.	Dharmapuri	5542	5117	230	92.33	61.50
27.	Cuddalore	2290	2212	979	96.59	98.69
28.	Coimbatore	1989	1921	1447	96.58	95.89
29.	Chennai	-	-	-	-	-
	Total	67716	58388	20613	86.22	90.15

Source : TNCDW, Chennai.

The total habitations covered under the project are 67,716 where in SC/ST habitations are 90.15 per cent and overall habitations are 86.22 per cent. The highest overall habitations were 5117 in Dharmapuri District and the lowest overall habitations were 476 in

Theni District. As far as SC/ST habitations are concerned, 59 was the lowest in Theni District whereas as the highest 1451 SC/ST habitations were in Pudukottai District.

Table 2.6 : Coverage of BPL Families.

Sl. No.	*Name of the District*	*Rural*			*Urban*		
		Total No. of BPL Families	*Number Covered*	*%*	*Total No. of BPL Families*	*No. Covered*	*%*
1.	Virudhunagar	78053	62364	79.90	30750	17929	58.32
2.	Villupuram	242282	116599	48.13	28086	13476	47.98
3.	Vellore	202072	58201	28.80	280284	62200	22.19
4.	The amount of loan was ranging from Rs.Trichy	83868	74890	89.30	60630	21905	36.13
5.	Thoothukudi	91274	60833	66.65	36910	16915	45.83
6.	Thiruvarur	77543	75217	97.00	15625	14688	94.00
7.	Thiruvallur	104141	104141	100.00	58080	58080	100.00
8.	Theni	51391	39069	76.02	33521	18886	56.34
9.	Thanjavur	112171	61995	55.27	77221	60226	77.99
10.	Tirunelveli	121015	84374	69.72	63744	39226	61.54
11.	Thiruvannamalai	121149	85304	70.41	15951	9591	60.13
12.	Sivagangai	22379	19479	87.04	3438	2241	65.18
13.	Salem	128818	78269	60.76	158866	20697	13.20
14.	Ramnad	64457	63492	98.50	24373	24373	100.00
15.	Pudukottai	70575	28145	39.88	4030	2015	50.00
16.	Perambalur	14	60862	82.70	7739	4372	56.49
17.	Nilgiris	32606	30639	93.97	16526	2441	14.77
18.	Namakkal	74337	15031	20.22	36330	3682	10.63
19.	Nagapattinam	74192	72036	97.09	36602	10757	29.39
20.	Madurai	120514	71899	59.66	104937	14800	14.10
21.	Karur	53346	41058	76.97	17840	6142	34.43
22.	Kanniyakumari	60291	54742	90.80	240026	57779	24.07
23.	Kancheepuram	125893	78898	62.67	97602	32367	33.16
24.	Erode	99402	74874	75.32	28486	27326	95.93
25.	Dindigul	86321	12691	14.70	39052	2838	7.27
26.	Dharmapuri	148736	100414	67.51	27662	8033	29.04
27.	Cuddalore	11413	44187	38.71	12332	4000	32.44
28.	Coimbatore	125632	54531	43.41	158082	40050	25.33
29.	Chennai	-	-	-	42224	42224	100.00
	Total	2686613	1724234	64.18	1756949	639709	36.41

Source : TNCDW, Chennai.

The total number of BPL families in rural areas of all the districts covered by the project were 26,86,613 of which 17,24,234 were benefited as against 6,39,709 BPL families which were benefited among 17,56,49 BPL families in urban areas. As low as 12,691 BPL families were covered in Dindigul District and as high as 1,16,599 BPL families were covered in Villupuram District rural areas. The lowest and highest coverage of BPL families in urban areas were 2015 in Puthukottai District and 62,200 in Vellure District respectively.

PLFs and BLFs

Under the project, within a period of six months to one year of group formation, Panchayat Level Federation (PLF) was formed in each Village Panchayat by grouping all the SHGs functioning in the Panchayat for the betterment of the members. The PLFs are expected to act as a facilitator to the SHGs for achieving sustainability of the groups in the long run. Hence, the project authorities are insisting on the formation of PLFs and Block Level Federations (BLFs). At the State level, as of December 2003, out of the 12619 Panchayats, in about 80 per cent of the Panchayats, PLFs have been formed and in respect of BLFs, the proportion is found to be low at 15 per cent of the blocks. The details are presented hereunder.

District-wise details reveal that in the districts of Salem, Erode, Perambalur, Kanniyakumari, Nilgiris and Virudhunagar, cent per cent has been achieved in the formation of PLFs. Among the districts, Dharmapuri has got the lowest percentage in the formation of PLFs (31%). In the case of BLFs, action has been initiated only in 6 districts, of which 4 districts have formed cent per cent BLFs.

On a policy issue, the question arises as to how effective are the Federations in discharging their allotted functions and what are the constraints that have stood in the way of the Federations playing a more pro-active and effective role in the SHG movement. Looking at the three-tier structure of the SHGs, it is seen that the district level entities are still to take root. Turning to the Panchayat Level Federations, it is heartening to note that the establishment of PLFs has gained momentum and the coverage has been impressive at nearly 80 per cent. At the block level, however, the momentum has just started picking up and the present level of coverage, which stands at 15 per cent, requires to be significantly increased for purposes of optimal realization of benefits from this new institutional mechanism for the SHGs.

Table 2.7 : District-wise Formation of PLFs and BLFs.

Sl. No.	*Name of the District*	*Total No. of Panchayats*	*No. of PLFs formed*	*% Covered*	*Total No. of Blocks*	*No. of BLFs formed*	*% Covered*
1.	Virudhunagar	450	448	100	11	0	0
2.	Villupuram	1104	797	72	22	0	0
3.	Vellore	753	347	46	20	0	0
4.	Trichy	408	390	966	14	7	50
5.	Thoothukudi	408	397	97	12	0	0
6.	Thiruvarur	430	387	90	10	0	0
7.	Thiruvallur	539	335	62	14	0	0
8.	Theni	130	100	77	8	0	0
9.	Thanjavur	589	297	50	14	0	0
10.	Tirunelveli	425	331	78	19	0	0
11.	Thiruvannamalai	860	761	88	18	0	0
12.	Sivagangai	445	350	79	12	12	100
13.	Salem	385	385	100	20	0	0
14.	Ramnad	429	402	94	11	0	0
15.	Pudukottai	498	309	62	13	0	0
16.	Perambalur	322	322	100	10	10	100
17.	Nilgiris	35	35	100	4	0	0
18.	Namakkal	331	327	99	15	4	27
19.	Nagapattinam	434	415	96	11	0	0
20.	Madurai	431	288	67	13	0	0
21.	Karur	158	117	74	8	3	38
22.	Kanniyakumari	99	99	100	9	0	0
23.	Kancheepuram	648	626	97	13	0	0
24.	Erode	343	343	100	20	20	100
25.	Dindigul	306	249	81	14	0	0
26.	Dharmapuri	588	183	31	18	0	0
27.	Cuddalore	682	662	97	13	0	0
28.	Coimbatore	389	355	91	19	0	0
29.	Chennai	0	0	0	0	0	0
	Total	12619	10057	79.7	385	56	14.5

Source : TNCDW, Chennai.

The Federations are beginning to function and, given the relative state of infancy, an element of support in the form of capacity building for the members and the organizations and provision of hand holding facilities and escort services to the Federations involved particularly in economic activities has been receiving attention and fully empowering the Federations in all the three-tiers is a challenge for all the stakeholders.

Revolving Fund Assistance

Before the linkage of SHGs with any financial institution, credit discipline is imbibed among the members through loans from own savings within the group members. After six months from the time of group formation, the SHGs have to pass a credit rating to become eligible for receiving bank assistance. As on 31st December, 2003, out of the 105733 eligible SHGs which have passed the credit rating, about one-third have been sanctioned with Revolving Fund Assistance to the tune of about Rs. 8070 lakhs.

Table 2.8 : Revolving Fund Assistance Provided as on 31.12.2003.

Sl. No.	*Name of the District*	*Total No. of Sanctioned RF*	*Amount Sanctioned*	*No. of SHGs Disbursed RF*	*Amount Disbursed*
1	2	3	4	5	6
1.	Virudhunagar	633	158.25	626	154.00
2.	Villupuram	2748	410.55	2748	410.55
3.	Vellore	1360	312.38	1073	268.25
4.	Trichy	1474	368.50	1287	321.75
5.	Thoothukudi	765	191.25	765	191.25
6.	Thiruvarur	1321	316.95	1250	299.05
7.	Thiruvallur	1214	303.50	1205	301.25
8.	Theni	352	88.00	335	84.00
9.	Thanjavur	1260	316.00	1042	272.25
10.	Tirunelveli	1595	267.34	939	234.10
11.	Thiruvannamalai	1231	307.75	1198	299.50
12.	Sivagangai	629	154.35	626	154.35
13.	Salem	2641	660.25	2483	620.75
14.	Ramnad	829	243.47	827	238.47
15.	Pudukottai	1237	254.50	1114	227.15
16.	Perambalur	1180	294.50	1052	263.00
17.	Nilgiris	489	122.25	344	86.00
18.	Namakkal	1056	264.00	969	242.25

(Table Contd. ...)

(Contd. ...)

1	2	3	4	5	6
19.	Nagapattinam	1761	440.18	1780	440.16
20.	Madurai	713	178.25	713	178.25
21.	Karur	459	114.75	442	110.50
22.	Kanniyakumari	543	115.10	546	115.10
23.	Kancheepuram	805	185.75	805	185.75
24.	Erode	2379	594.75	2340	585.00
25.	Dindigul	583	198.75	576	142.30
26.	Dharmapuri	1073	268.25	1024	256.0
27.	Cuddalore	987	246.75	987	246.75
28.	Coimbatore	2774	693.50	2745	686.25
29.	Chennai	0	0.00	0	0
	Total	34094	8069.82	31841	7615.98

Source : TNCDW, Chennai.

Loan for Economic Activity

Micro-finance has emerged as one of the most successful and powerful facilitating medium for enabling the poor and disadvantaged sections of the society to access institutional credit. Micro-finance provides opportunity to the poor for receiving adequate amount of credit easily to start the chosen income generating activity. Under the project, the eligible SHGs which have been credit rated as per the prescribed guidelines are eligible to receive economic activity loan either with subsidy or without subsidy. The banks sanction economic activity loan on the basis of project proposals submitted by the SHGs. The SHGs receive loan from various sources, viz., SGSY, NABARD, THADCO and NGO. As on 31st December, 2003, 109046 SHGs have been disbursed loans for economic activity to the tune of Rs. 56415 lakhs. The details are presented hereunder:

Table 2.9 : Loan for Economic Activities.

Total No. of SHGs functioning for more than 6 months	131044
Number of SHGs Rated	117042
Number of SHGs eligible from the Rated List	105733
Number of SHGs Sanctioned Loan	112712
Amount of Loan Sanctioned (in Rs. in Lakhs)	61727.37
Number of SHGs Disbursed Loans	109046
Amount of Loan Disbursed (Rs. in Lakhs)	56415.23

Source : TNCDW, Chennai.

District-wise details are furnished in the following table:

Table 2.10 : District-wise Disbursement of EA Loan.

Sl. No.	*Name of the District*	*Groups Formed*	*No. of SHGs more than 6 months*	*Total No. of SHGs related as per the Credit Guidelines*	*No. of SHGs eligible from the rated list*	*Total No. of SHGs Sanctioned Loan*	*Amt. of Loan Sanctioned Rs. in Lakhs*	*Total Amt. of Loan Disbursed Rs. in Lakhs*
1	**2**	**3**	**4**	**5**	**6**	**7**	**8**	**9**
1.	Villupuram	6672	6603	5523	3891	5306	2826.05	5173
2.	Dharmapuri	5720	5457	5420	5288	8751	8255.78	8704
3.	Namakkal	3438	3717	3262	3262	4246	3893.36	3998
4.	Cuddalore	5157	5629	5133	4461	4132	1495.47	4132
5.	Ramnad	3640	4119	4549	4552	4037	3315.56	4015
6.	Thiruvarur	4902	5027	4397	4260	4875	1420.60	4717
7.	Vellore	3938	3342	2843	2459	3330	1550.13	2468
8.	Madurai	3688	3972	3705	3297	3856	3204.34	3856
9.	Thiruvallur	4418	4228	3482	3342	2818	859.47	2709
10.	Salem	4785	5246	4925	471	5389	3437.68	4954
11.	Karur	3025	3138	2781	2507	2692	1799.79	2657
12.	Thoothukudi	3465	3921	3796	3796	4912	2444.94	4912
13.	Theni	2591	3156	2731	2542	1543	841.51	1511

(Table Contd. ...)

(Contd. ...)

1	2	3	4	5	6	7	8	9
14.	Virudhunagar	3413	3874	3874	3872	4177	2319.23	4154
15.	Sivagangai	3424	3599	3147	2864	2966	2333.21	2963
16.	Tirunelveli	4773	6399	5291	4783	4324	2238.14	3573
17.	Trichy	4587	5586	408	4209	3917	1262.76	3716
18.	T.V. Malai	4941	4612	4908	3783	3080	1943.89	2953
19	Pudukottai	4498	4659	4164	3770	2041	1359.87	3203
20.	Nilgiris	2103	2997	4080	2320	1762	958.44	1494
21.	Erode	5232	6214	2942	5727	5224	1564.94	5127
22.	Coimbatore	4347	5594	5894	4357	5117	2188.61	4939
23.	Kancheepuram	4997	5493	2905	2017	2284	639.05	2144
24.	Kanniyakumari	2954	5754	5486	5028	6256	3911.91	6235
25.	Perambalur	3673	3285	2862	2501	2340	1215.31	2156
26.	Thanjavur	6058	5069	4985	4916	4968	1455.92	4630
27.	Nagapattinam	5460	5639	5517	5074	6351	2079.42	6269
28.	Dindigul	3375	3783	2919	2438	2005	909.82	1671
29.	Chennai	0	932	69		13	2.17	13
	Total	119014	131044	117042	105733	112712	61727.37	109046

Source : TNCDW, Chennai.

Table 2.11 : Economic and Special Activities by SHGs at State Level.

S. No.	*District*	*Economic activities taken up by SHGs*	*Special activities taken up by SHGs*
1	**2**	**3**	**4**
1.	Coimbatore	Area sheath plate, Paper cups, Coir and Jute bag	Mineral water supply, Tamarind Paste and powder, Chappal Toll at Temples
2.	Cuddalore	Cashew processing, Coir making, bakery Unit	Curry Leaves Powder, Drum Stick Leaves Power, Being supplied to Anganwadi Centres
3.	Erode	Quarry, Door Mats, Kora Silk	Textile Weaving
4.	Kancheepuram	Canteen, Readymade Garments	
5.	Kanniyakumari	Coir Products, Coastal Area Products, Lace and Embroidery Works.	Physically Handicapped Groups (SGSY Funds)
6.	Karur	Textile, Cotton Sarees, Bed Spreads	Chappal by Subamathi Groups
7.	Madurai	Readymade Garments, Aavin Booth, Cell Phone Repair	Already visited by DRD
8.	·Nagapattinam	Canteen, Paper cup, Area sheath plate	Wasteland Development (Orehid) Tourism
9.	The Nilgiris	Construction of Foot-path. Paper Cups, Motor Pump Repairs, Floriculture	Masonry Training to SHG
10.	Perambalur	Greetings Cards, Wood Carving	Eunuchs, Youth groups and CSW groups have been formed
11.	Pudukottai	Waste paper products, ration shop, terracotta	Male SHG Formation (SGSY), Hliet Brewers Rehabitation, Waste Land Development, Mathi Literacy, Child Labourer's Mothers SHG, Adolescent Girl Groups

(Table Contd. ...)

(Contd. ...)

1	2	3	4
12.	Ramnad	Charcoal Production, Home Appliances Repair, Cell Phone Repair, Palm Leaf Products, Dry Fish Processing	Tie up with National Minorities Finance Development Corporation for giving Loans through Co-op Banks at minimum rate of Interest.
13.	Salem	Silver Anklet Making, Tractor, Departmental Store	
14.	Thiruvallur	Ration Shop, Jute bag, Readymade Garments	
15.	Trichy	Jute bags, Greeting cards	Conducted Eye camp (Mission for Women Vision), AIDS Awareness Camps, Special Skill Training for Women Prisoners
16.	Thanjavur	Terracotta, Medicinal Plants, Turkey Farm	Nachiyar Koil Kuthu Vilakku by artisans groups, Folk Arts Groups
17.	Vellore	Natural Colour, Bathik Printings, Organic Farm, Palm Leaf Products	CSW groups are given employment opportunities at Match Industry
18.	Virudhunagar	Readymade Garments, Candle Making	Selling forms at RTO Office, Beauty Parlour, Lease Land for Vegetable Cultivation

Source : TNCDW, Chennai.

Sum Up

The State profile shows that Villupuram District has formed more number of Self-Help Groups compared to other districts by forming 6672 SHGs as on 31.12.2003. But Erode District stands first in the rated list of SHGs by having 5727 SHGs. Dharmapuri District ranks first in the amount of loan sanctioned and loan disbursed at Rs. 8255.78 lakhs and Rs. 8704 lakhs respectively. With these loans SHGs in various districts have taken up different economic activities. Their activities not only generate income to them but also their products are environment friendly. Opportunity has been provided to eunuchs also in Perambalur District and this will lead to a decent standard of living and earns respect for them from society. Apart from the economic activities these women have engaged in social activities like conducting medical camp. An SHG of Trichy District frequently conducts eye camp under the caption "Mission for Women Vision". These activities show women's unified empowering role. This role has to be related to women's power in terms of economic independence and social emancipation.

3 THOOTHUKUDI DRDA AND SHG

A Profile of Thoothukudi

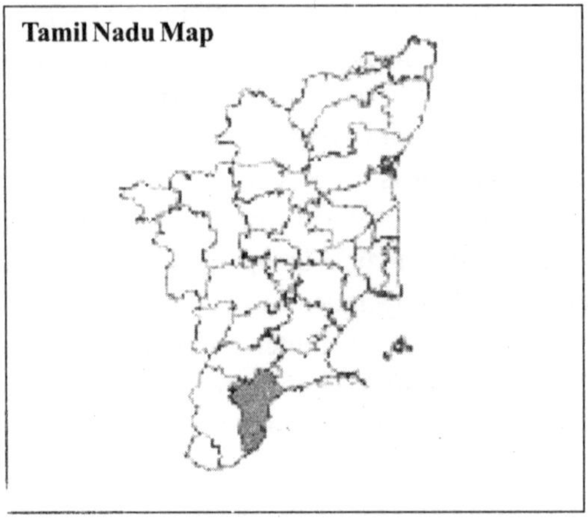

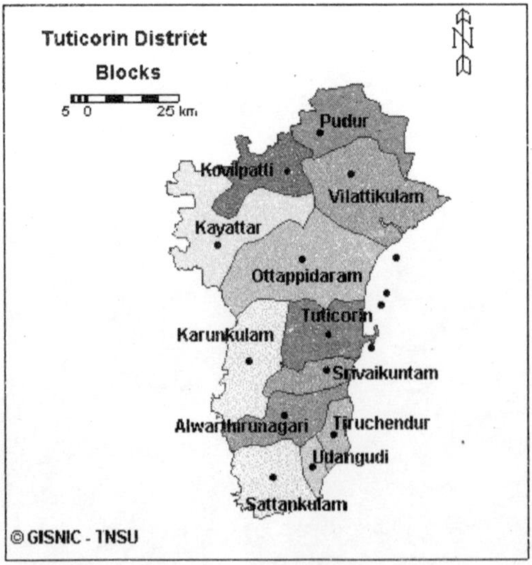

The district of Thoothukudi is situated in the extreme south-eastern corner of Tamil Nadu State. It is bounded on the north by the districts of Tirunelveli, Virudhunagar and Ramanathapuram, on the east and south-east by the Gulf of Mannar and on the west and south-west by the district of Tirunelveli. The total area of this district is 4621 sq. kms. and the administrative headquarters Thoothukudi, is an urban agglomeration and also one of the taluk headquarters within the district.

Its socio-economic condition is better than other that of districts of Tamil Nadu. It ranks fifth in the per capita income among the districts of Tamil Nadu, third in the literacy rate and second in the combined gross enrolment ratio. It also fares well in the Gender Development Index in Tamil Nadu, coming next to Chennai, Kanchipuram, Kanniyakumari respectively.

Sl.No.	*Revenue Divisions*	*Taluks comprising Revenue Division*	
1.	Thoothukudi	a.	Thoothukudi
		b.	Srivaikundam
2.	Tiruchendur	a.	Tiruchendur
		b.	Sattankulam
3.	Kovilpatti	a.	Kovilpatti
		b.	Ettayapuram
		c.	Vilathikulam
		d.	Ottapidaram

Revenue Firkas : 40
Revenue Villages : 468

For the purpose of elections, this district is divided into 7 Assembly constituencies and covers 3 Parliamentary Constituencies, as given bellow:

1. Parliamentary Constituencies

1. Tirunelveli,
2. Tiruchendur, and
3. Sivakasi.

2. *Assembly Constituencies*

1. Vilathikulam,
2. Ottapidaram,
3. Kovilpatti,
4. Sattankulam,
5. Tiruchendur,
6. Srivaikuntam, and
7. Thoothukudi.

Local Bodies

- Corporation : Nil
- Municipalities : 2
- Panchayat Unions : 12
- Town Panchayats : 20
- Village Panchayats : 408
- Revenue Firkas : 40
- Revenue Villages : 468

Area and Population

Thoothukudi District has a geographical area of 4,621 sq.km.

Sl. No.	*Name of the Taluk*	*Area in Hectares*	*Male*	*Female*	*Total*
1.	Thoothukudi	21706.22	162671	160009	322680
2.	Tiruchendur	33330.83	131196	146046	277242
3.	Kovilpatti	88851.99	142094	146379	288473
4.	Sathankulam	34379.26	46420	54991	101411
5.	Srivaikuntam	55620.84	94289	100851	195140
6.	Vilattikulam	109788.55	79057	82290	161347
7.	Ottapidaram (SC)	72972.97	54033	55594	109627
	District Total	416650.66	709760	746160	1455920

Source : Provisional Population as per Census 2001 : 15,65,743.

District Profile : Thoothukudi

	Units			Units	
Total Area	***4590.54***	***Sq.Kms.***	***Forest Area***	***110.12***	***Sq.Kms.***
Net Sown Area	1594.53	.000	Net Irrigation Area	372.46	.000
Total Population	1565.53	.000	Total Literates	1283.81	.000
Total Male	764.09	.000	Total Female	801.66	.000
Urban Population	661.93	.000	Rural Population	903.81	.000
Rural Population Male	437.60	.000	Rural Population Female	466.21	.000
Urban Population Male	326.49	.000	Urban Population Female	335.49	.000
Total Male Literacy	677.44	.000	Total Female Literates	606.37	.000
Rural Literates	706.72	.000	Urban Literates	577.12	.000
Rural Literates Male	377.30	.000	Rural Literates Female	329.43	.000
Urban Literates Male	300.08	.000	Urban Literates Female	277.05	.000
Rural Male Literacy	86.22%		Rural Female Literates	70.66%	
Urban Male Literacy	91.91%		Urban Female Literacy	82.58%	

Description	*Units*	*District*	*State*	*Description*	*Units*	*District*	*State*
Proportion of Population Below Poverty Line	%	37.81	29.16	Urbanization	%	42.28	43.86
Population Growth per Annum	%	7.54	11.19	Literacy	%	81.96	73.47
Population Density (Perons/ Sq.Km.)	Nos.	315	324	Male Literacy	%	88.66	82.33
Workers As % of Total Population	%	43.03	44.78	Female Literacy	%	75.64	64.55
Agriculture and Allied Activities	%	35.44	49.55	Urban Literacy	%	87.17	82.07
Other Workers	%	57.77	45.21	Rural Literacy	%	78.13	66.66

Source : Director of Census Operations of Tamil Nadu, Chennai
Directorate of Economic and Statistics, Chennai - 6

Only 2 SHGs received SGSY loans with subsidy in Thoothukudi PU during 2002-2003. The amount of loan ranged from Rs. 3,00,000 to Rs. 2,04,000 for the trades of soda manufacturing and cloth merchandise. The total amount of loan was Rs. 5,04,000. Out of this,

Table 3.1 : SGSY 2002 -2003 Thoothukudi Panchayat Union.

Sl. No.	*SHG Name*	*Total Members*	*Enterprise*	*Total Amount*	*Subsidy*	*Loan*	*Bank Name*
1.	Tenseela Mahalir Mandram	20	Soda manu-facturing	300000	125000	175000	Indian Overseas Bank, Mappi-llaiyurani
2.	Indira Mahalir Mandram	17	Cloth merchan-dise	204000	102000	102000	Indian Overseas Bank, Mappi-llaiyurani

Source : DRDA, Thoothukudi.

Rs. 2,27,000 was subsidy and Rs. 2,77,000 the repayable loan.The average amount of subsidy for an SHG was Rs.1,38,500.

Ten SHGs were benefited from SGSY loan with subsidy in Karungulam PU during 2002-2003. The amount of loan was ranged from Rs.1,60,000 to Rs. 2,73,000 for the trades of goats rearing, milch animal rearing and dairy units. The total amount of loan was Rs. 26,62,102, of which Rs.1,45,433 was subsidy and Rs.15,16,673 was repayable loan. The average amount of subsidy for an SHG was Rs.1,51,667.

Only 2 SHGs received loans with subsidy under SGSY in Thiruvaikundam PU during 2002-2003. The amount of loan ranged from Rs. 2,08,000 to Rs. 1,25,000 for the trades of goat rearing and power tiller. The total amount of loan was Rs.3,33,000. Out of this, Rs.1,66,500 was subsidy and Rs.1,66,500 was repayable loan. The average amount of subsidy for an SHG was Rs.83,250.

A total of 16 SHGs received SGSY loans with subsidy in Alvarthirunagari PU during 2002-2003. The amount of loan ranged from Rs. 1,52,000 to Rs. 3,00,000 for the trades of groundnut merchandise, readymade garments, dairy units, coconut frond products, jaggery, palm frond mat weaving, goat rearing and wax candle making. The total amount of loan was Rs. 34,21,000. Out of this, Rs.16,73,000 was subsidy and Rs. 17,48,000 was repayable loan. The average amount of subsidy for an SHG was Rs.1,09,250.

Table 3.2 : Karungulam Panchayat Union.

Sl. No.	*SHG Name*	*Total Members*	*Enterprise*	*Total Amount*	*Subsidy*	*Loan*	*Bank Name*
1.	Ulaikkum Mahalir Munnetra Sangam	15	Goat rearing	237217	118608	118609	Indian Overseas Bank, Vallanadu
2.	Ulaikkum Mahalir Munnetra Sangam	16	Goat rearing	253758	125000	128758	Indian Overseas Bank, Vallanadu
3.	Thamarai Gramodaya Mahalir	10	Goat rearing	160044	80022	80022	UCO Bank, Karungulam
4.	Ambedkar Gramodaya Mahalir	12	Goat rearing	189774	94887	94887	UCO Bank,Karungulam
5.	Ulaikkum Pengal Munnetra Sangam	14	Dairy unit	252000	125000	127000	Indian Overeas Bank, Vallanadu
6.	Malligai Giramodaya Mahalir	14	Goat rearing	219096	109548	109548	UCO Bank, Karungulam
7.	Roja Kiramothaya Mahalir	20	Milch animals	210000	105000	105000	Pandian Grama Bank, Seythunganallur
8.	Pitchipoo Gramodaya Mahalir	15	Milch animals	273000	125000	148000	Pandian Grama Bank, Seythunganallur
9.	Roja Gramodaya Mahalir	15	Goat rearing	233217	116608	116609	UCO Bank, Karungulam
10.	Ulaikkum Pengal Munnetra Sangam	14	Milch animals	234000	117000	117000	Indian Overseas Bank, Vallanadu

Source : DRDA, Thoothukudi.

Table 3.3 : Thiruvaikundam Panchayat Union.

Sl. No.	SHG Name	Total Members	Enterprise	Total Amount	Subsidy	Loan	Bank Name
1.	Marutham Mahalir Mandram	13	Goat rearing	208000	104000	104000	Central Bank of Mukkani
2.	Tholavilli Amman	19	Power tiller	125000	62500	62500	Pandian Grama Bank Sivakalai

Source : DRDA, Thoothukudi.

Table 3.4 : Alvarthirunagari Panchayat Union.

Sl. No.	*SHG Name*	*Total Members*	*Enterprise*	*Total Amount*	*Subsidy*	*Loan*	*Bank Name*
1	**2**	**3**	**4**	**5**	**6**	**7**	**8**
1.	Bharathi Pengal	11	Groundnut merchandise	210000	105000	105000	Pandian Grama Bank, Srivenkatesapuram
2.	Gandhi Pengal	10	Readymade garments	200000	100000	100000	Pandian Grama Bank, Srivenkatesapuram
3.	Roja Pengal	11	Dairy unit	230000	115000	115000	Pandian Grama Bank, Srivenkatesapuram
4.	Thamarai Pengal	10	Coconut frond products	152000	76000	76000	Canara Bank,Athur
5.	Agnithai Mahalir	10	Dairy unit	210000	105000	105000	Indian Overseas Bank, Thenthirupparai
6.	Parani Pengal	10	Dairy unit	210000	105000	105000	Indian Overseas Bank, Thenthirupparai
7.	Mahilchi Pengal	15	Jaggery. palm frond mat weaving	200000	100000	100000	Pandian Grama Bank, Srivenkatesapuram
8.	Thorkal Mahalir	10	Jaggery, palm frond mat weaving	220000	110000	110000	Pandian Grama Bank, Srivenkatesapuram
9.	Muthamil Mahalir Mandram	13	Dairy unit	275000	125000	125000	Indian Overseas Bank, Thenthirupparai
10.	Sakthi Pengal	12	Wax candle making	120000	60000	60000	Pandian Grama Bank, Srivenkatesapuram

(Table Contd. ...)

(Contd. ...)

1	2	3	4	5	6	7	8
11.	Karpagatharu Pengal	14	Dairy unit	300000	125000	175000	Pandian Grama Bank, Srivenkatesapuram
12.	Parvathi Mahalir	10	Dairy unit	210000	105000	105000	Pandian Grama Bank, Srivenkatesapuram
13.	Rose Mahalir	12	Dairy unit	250000	125000	125000	Pandian Grama Bank, Srivenkatesapuram
14.	Anbu Pengal	12	Goat rearing	200000	100000	100000	Pandian Grama Bank, Srivenkatesapuram
15.	Isreal Mahalir	11	Dairy unit	230000	115000	115000	Indian Overseas Bank, Thenthirupperai
16.	Mahanathi	11	Goat rearing	204000	102000	102000	Indian Overseas Bank, Thenthirupperai

Source : DRDA, Thoothukudi.

Table 3.5 : Thiruchendur Panchayat Union.

Sl. No.	*SHG Name*	*Total Members*	*Enterprise*	*Total Amount*	*Subsidy*	*Loan*	*Bank Name*
1.	Ambedkar	10	Chair and vessels hiring	240000	120000	120000	Indian Over-seas Bank Thiru-chenthur

Source : DRDA, Thoothukudi.

Only one SHG was provided with subsidized loan in Thiruchendur PU during 2002-2003. The amount of loan was Rs. 2,40,000 of which Rs. 1,20,000 was repayable loan and Rs.1,20,000 was subsidy for the trade of chair and vessels hiring.

Table 3.6 : Udangudi Panchayat Union.

Sl. No.	*SHG Name*	*Total Members*	*Enterprise*	*Total Amount*	*Subsidy*	*Loan*	*Bank Name*
1.	Karpagatharu	16	Palm frond mat weaving	112800	56400	56400	State Bank of India Udan-kudi
2.	Yamunai Mahalir	13	Groceries shop	200000	100000	100000	Indian Bank, Kula-sekaran Pattinam
3.	Suriyakanthi Amman	16	Palm frond mat weaving	210000	105000	105000	State Bank of India Udan-gudi
4.	Karpagatharu	!5	Palm frond	105960	52980	52980	State Bank of India Udan-gudi

Source : DRDA, Thoothukudi.

SGSY loans with subsidy were provided to 4 SHGs in Udangudi PU during 2002-2003. The amount of loan was ranged from Rs. 1,05,960 to Rs. 2,10,000 for the enterprise such as palm frond mat weaving, groceries shop and jaggery making. The total amount of loan was Rs. 6,28,760, of which Rs. 3,14,380 was subsidy and Rs. 3,14,380 was repayable loan. The average amount of subsidy for an SHG was Rs.78,595.

A total of 13 SHGs, were benefited from SGSY loans with subsidy in Sathankulam PU during 2002-2003. The amount of loan ranged from Rs.1,00,000 to Rs. 3,00,000 for trades such as goat rearing, dairy units and palm frond products. The total amount of loan was Rs. 20,42,000. Out of this, Rs. 9,96,000 was subsidy and Rs.10,46,000 was repayable loan. The average amount of subsidy for an SHG was Rs. 80,460.

Three SHGs in Kovilpatti PU received SGSY loans with subsidy during 2002-2003. The amount of loan was Rs. 2,93,000 for two SHGs and Rs. 3,20,000 for one SHG to establish dairy units. The total amount of loan was Rs. 9,10,000, of which Rs. 3,57,000 was subsidy and the remaining Rs. 4,47,000 was repayable loan. The average amount of subsidy for an SHG was Rs.1,90,000.

Three SHGs in Kayatharu PU received SGSY loans with subsidy during 2002-2003. The amount of loan was Rs. 3,20,000, Rs. 2,20,000 and Rs. 2,80,000 dairy units. The total amount of loan was Rs. 8,20,000, of which Rs. 3,60,000 was the subsidy and the remaining Rs. 4,60,000 was repayable loan. The average amount of subsidy for an SHG was Rs. 1,20,000.

Only two SHGs received SGSY loans with subsidy in Ottapidaram PU during 2002-2003. The amount of loan was Rs. 2,60,000 and Rs. 2,67,325 for the trades of charcoal making and goat rearing. The total amount of loan was Rs. 5,20,325 was subsidy of which Rs. 2,50,000 and the remaining amount of Rs. 2,77,325 was repayable loan. The average amount of subsidy for an SHG was Rs.1,25,000.

Table 3.7 : Sathankulam Panchayat Union.

Sl. No.	SHG Name	Total Members	Enterprise	Total Amount	Subsidy	Loan	Bank Name
1.	Rose Mahalir Mandram	20	Goat rearing	300000	125000	175000	Tamil Nadu Mercantile Bank, Prakasapuram
2.	Punitha Anthoniyar Sakuma Sevai Sangam	10	Palm frond products	100000	50000	50000	Tamil Nadu Mercantile Bank, Tattarmadam
3.	Kalaiselvi Mahalir Mandram	10	Palm frond products	100000	50000	50000	Tamil Nadu Mercantile Bank, Kommadikottai
4.	Mariyaal Mahalir Mandram	10	Palm frond products	100000	50000	50000	Tamil Nadu Mercantile Bank, Kommadikottai
5.	Vadamalli Pengal Koovaikinaru	10	Palm frond products	100000	50000	50000	Pandian Grama Bank, Venkatesapuram
6.	Roja Pengal	12	Palm frond products	100000	50000	50000	Pandian Grama Bank, Venkatesapuram
7.	Samathanam Pengal	10	Dairy unit	214000	107000	107000	Pandian Grama Bank, Peykulam
8.	Santhosam Pengal	10	Dairy unit	214000	107000	107000	Pandian Grama Bank, Srivenkatesapuram, Branch Peykulam
9.	Gangai	12	Goat rearing	110000	55000	55000	Indian Bank, Padukkapathu
10.	Marikolunthu Mahalir	10	Goat rearing	200000	100000	100000	Pandian Grama Bank, Srivenkatesapuram Branch Peykulam
11.	Selvam Mahalir	10	Goat rearing	110000	55000	55000	Indian Bank, Padukkapathu
12.	Weeds Mahalir	12	Goat rearing	180000	90000	90000	Pandian Grama Bank, Thattarmadam
13.	Weeds Mahalir	10	Dairy unit	214000	107000	107000	Pandian Grama Bank, Thattarmadam

Source : DRDA, Thoothukudi.

Table 3.8 : Kovilpatti Panchayat Union.

Sl. No.	SHG Name	Total Members	Enterprise	Total Amount	Subsidy	Loan	Bank Name
1.	Malligai Mahalir	11	Dairy unit	295000	125000	170000	Thodakka Velanmai Bank, Sethukkuvaithan
2.	Jeevaroja Mahalir	12	Dairy unit	295000	125000	170000	Thodakka Velanmai Bank, Sethukkuvaithan
3.	Kaleeswari Mahalir	16	Dairy unit	320000	125000	195000	State Bank of Trivancore, Kovilpatti

Source : DRDA, Thoothukudi.

Table 3.9 : Kayatharu Panchayat Union.

Sl. No.	SHG Name	Total Members	Enterprise	Total Amount	Subsidy	Loan	Bank Name
1.	Vinayagar Mahalir Suya Utha-vikulu, South Pommaiyapuram	16	Dairy unit	320000	125000	195000	Bank of India, Kamanaickenpatti
2.	Kurinchi Arivoli Mahalir Suya Uthavikulu, Va.Ramalingapuram	11	Dairy unit	220000	110000	110000	Pandian Grama Bank, Nalattinputhur
3.	Selvi Amman Mahalir Suya Uthavikulu, South Pommaiyapuram	11	Dairy unit	280000	125000	155000	Bank of India, Kamanaickenpatti

Source : DRDA, Thoothukudi.

Table 3.10 : Ottapidaram Panchayat Union

Sl. No.	SHG Name	Total Members	Enterprise	Total Amount	Subsidy	Loan	Bank Name
1.	Mathulampoo Suya Uthavikulu, Kodiankulam	14	charcoal making	260000	125000	135000	Pandian Grama Bank, Akkanaickenpatti
2.	Kurinchimalar Mahalir Mandram, Kuppanapuram	17	goat rearing	267325	125000	142325	Pandian Grama Bank, Paduvanthanai

Source : DRDA, Thoothukudi.

Table 3.11 : Vilathikulam Panchayat Union.

Sl. No.	SHG Name	Total Members	Enterprise	Total Amount	Subsidy	Loan	Bank Name
1.	Kaliamman Mahalir Mandram	13	Dairy unit	295000	125000	170000	Thodakka Velanmai Bank, Setnukkuvaithan
2.	Vellai Roja	12	Goat rearing	270000	125000	145000	Bharatha State Bank, Vilathikulam
3.	Scodu Malligai	15	Goat rearing	250942	1250000	125942	Bharatha State Bank, Vilathikulam
4.	Malligai Mahalir Mandram	12	Charcoal making	250000	125000	125000	Bharatha State Bank, Vilathikulam
5.	Scott Thendral Mahalir Mandram	12	Charcoal making	250000	125000	125000	Bharatha State Bank, Vilathikulam
6.	Roja Mahalir Kulu	12	Charcoal making	250000	125000	125000	Thodakka Velanmai Bank, Veilaiammalpuram
7.	Ovvaiyar Mahali Kulu	12	Charcoal making	250000	125000	125000	Thodakka Velanmai Bank, Vellaiammalpuram
8.	Kalaimakal	10	Herbal plants raising and goat rearing	275000	125000	150000	Canara Bank, Ettaiyapuram
9.	Jansirani Mahalir	10	Herbal plants raising and goat rearing	275000	125000	150000	Canara Bank, Ettaiyapuram
10.	Vinayaga Adu Valarpavar Kulu, M. Kumarattaiyapuram	10	Goat rearing	250000	125000	125000	Canara Bank, Ettaiyapuram
11.	Vasuki Mahalir Suya Uthavikulu, Pommaiyapuram	10	Herbal plants raising and goat rearing	275000	125000	150000	Canara Bank, Ettaiyapuram
12.	Roja Mahalir Suya Uthavikulu, Lekkampatti	11	Goat rearing	251600	125000	126600	Tamil Nadu Mercantile Bank, Vilathikulam
13.	Kurinchi Mahalir Suya Uthavikulu, Virusampatti	12	Goat rearing	270000	125000	145000	Pandian Grama Bank, Vilathikulam

Source : DRDA, Thoothukudi.

Table 3.12 : Pudur Panchayat Union.

Sl. No.	*SHG Name*	*Total Members*	*Enterprise*	*Total Amount*	*Subsidy*	*Loan*	*Bank Name*
1.	Kamaraj	Not available	Milch animals rearing	250000	125000	125000	Indian Overseas Bank, Nagalapuram
2.	Rajivgandhi	Not available	Milch animals rearing	250000	125000	125000	Indian Overseas Bank, Nagalapuram
3.	Suriya Tokka Mahalir Mandram	14	Goats rearing	203000	101500	101500	Thodakka Velanmai Koottu-ravu Bank, Muthalapuram
4.	Arringar Anna	10	Coal making	250000	125000	125000	Indian Overseas Bank, Nagalapuram
5.	Nila	12	Goats rearing	260000	125000	135000	Indian Overseas Bank, Nagalapuram
6.	Jeeva	12	Goats rearing	260000	125000	135000	Indian Overseas Bank, Nagalapuram
7.	Sinthu	10	Coal making	250000	125000	125000	Indian Overseas Bank, Nagalapuram

Source : DRDA, Thoothukudi.

Table 3.13 : 2001-2002 (1. Thoothukudi Panchayat Union).

Sl. No.	SHG Name	Total Members	Enterprise	Total Amount	Subsidy	Loan	Bank Name
1.	Kasthuribai	11	Milch animal rearing	259600	125000	134600	Bharatha State Bank, Harbor
2.	Jawaharlal	12	Milch animal rearing	283200	125000	158200	Bharatha State Bank, Harbor
3.	Alwin Mahalir Mandram	13	Frond basket making	130000	65000	65000	Tamil Nadu Mercantile Bank, Pudukottai
4.	Alagu Mutharamman Mahalir Mandram	20	Frond basket making	180000	90000	90000	Indian Overseas Bank, Mappillaiyurani
5.	Alli Mahalir Mandram	12	Cloth merchant	150000	75000	75000	Indian Overseas Bank, Mappillaiyurani

Source : DRDA, Thoothukudi.

Table 3.14 : Karungulam Panchayat Union.

Sl. No.	SHG Name	Total Members	Enterprise	Total Amount	Subsidy	Loan	Bank Name
1.	Ulaikkum Pengal Munnetra Sangam	14	Milch animals rearing	294000	125000	169000	Pandian Grama Bank, Thiruvaikundam
2.	Sendu Kiromatha Mahalir	13	Milch animals rearing	294000	125000	148000	Indian Overseas Bank, Ramanujampudur
3.	Lilly	12	Goat rearing	237597	118798	118799	Indian Overseas Bank, Ramanujampudur
4.	Ulaikkum Pengal Munnetra Sangam	20	Goat rearing	252721	125000	127721	Indian Overseas Bank, Vallanadu
5.	Pitchipoo Gramodaya Mahalir	16	Goat rearing	253758	125000	128758	UCO Bank, Karungulam

Source : DRDA, Thoothukudi.

A total of 13 SHGs in Vilathikulam PU were benefited from SGSY loans with subsidy during 2002-2003. The amount of loan ranged from Rs. 2,50,000 to Rs. 2,95,000 for enterprises such as goat rearing, milch animal rearing, charcoal making, herbal plants arising and dairy unit. The total amount of loan was Rs. 34,12,542. Out of this, Rs.16,25,000 was subsidy and Rs.17,875,42 was repayable loan. The average amount of subsidy for an SHG was Rs.1,37,503.

SGSY loans with subsidy were provided to 7 SHGs in Pudur PU during 2002-2003. The amount of loan ranged from Rs. 2,03,000 to Rs. 2,60,000 for the trades of goat rearing, milch animals rearing and charcoal making by the members of SHGs. The total amount of loan was Rs. 17,23,000, of which Rs. 8,56,500 was subsidy and Rs. 8,66,500 was repayable loan. The average amount of subsidy for an SHG was Rs. 1,23,785.

A total of 5 SHGs were benefited from SGSY loans with subsidy in Thoothukudi PU during 2001-2002. The amount of loan ranged from Rs.1,30,000 to Rs. 2,59,600 for enterprises such as frond basket making, milch animal rearing and cloth merchandise. The total amount of loan was Rs. 10,02,800, of which subsidy was Rs. 4,80,000 and loan Rs. 5,22,800. The average amount of subsidy for an SHG was Rs. 1,04,560.

SGSY loans with subsidy were provided to 5 SHGs in Karungulam PU during 2001-2002. The amount of loan ranged from Rs. 2,37,597 to Rs. 2,94,000 for the trades of goat rearing and milch animals rearing by the members of SHGs. The total amount of loan was Rs. 13,32,076. The subsidy provided to all the SHGs was Rs. 6,18,798 and the repayable loan amount was Rs. 7,13,278. The average amount of subsidy for an SHG was Rs. 1,42,655.

Five SHGs were benefited from SGSY loans with subsidy in Thiruvaigundam PU during 2001-2002. The amount of loan ranged from Rs. 2,51,000 to Rs. 2,94,000 for enterprises such as goat rearing, milch animals rearing, cooking vessels merchandise, coconut frond roof making and tamarind making. The total amount of loan was Rs. 13,95,000. Out of this Rs. 6,25,000 was subsidy and Rs.7,70,000 was repayable loan. The average amount of subsidy for an SHG was Rs. 1,54,000.

Table 3.15 : Thiruvaigundam Panchayat Union.

Sl. No.	*SHG Name*	*Total Members*	*Enterprise*	*Total Amount*	*Subsidy*	*Loan*	*Bank Name*
1.	Kamarajar	20	Goat rearing. milch animals rearing	294000	125000	169000	Canara Bank, Eral
2.	Nattathi Mahalir Mandram	15	Goat rearing, milch animals rearing, cooking vessels merchantise	280000	125000	155000	Pandian Grama Bank, Sebathaiapuram
3.	Mahatma Gandhi Pengal	15	Coconut frond roof making and tamarind making	282000	125000	157000	Canara Bank, Thiruvaikundam
4.	Thamira Mahalir Mandram	18	Goat rearing	288000	125000	163000	Canara Bank, Eral
5.	Mahatma Gandhi	15	Readymade cloth merchandise	251000	125000	126000	Tamil Nadu Mercantile Bank, Siruthondanallur

Source : DRDA, Thoothukudi.

Table 3.16 : Alvarthirunagari Panchayat Union.

Sl. No.	SHG Name	Total Members	Enterprise	Total Amount	Subsidy	Loan	Bank Name
1.	Pothigai Mahalir Mandram	11	Goat rearing	204000	102000	102000	Indian Overseas Bank, Thenthirupperai
2.	Roja Mahalir Suya Uthavikulu	13	Dairy unit	275000	125000	150000	Indian Overseas Bank, Thenthirupperai
3.	Annai Therasa Mahalir	10	Goat rearing	212000	106000	106000	Pandian Grama Bank, Srivenkatesapuram
4.	Kalaivani Pengal	14	Dairy unit	300000	125000	175000	Pandian Grama Bank, Srivenkatesapuram
5.	Kathambam Pengal	14	Dairy unit	295000	125000	170000	Thodakka Velanmai Bank, Sethukkuvaithan
6.	Vadamalar Pengal	10	Dairy unit	236000	118000	118000	Thodakka Velanmai Bank, Sethukkuvaithan
7.	Annai Therasa Mahalir Membattu Sangam	12	Dairy unit	276000	125000	151000	Thodakka Velanmai Bank, Sethukkuvaithan
8.	Ambedkar Mahalir	13	Dairy unit	275000	125000	15000	Canara Bank, Nasareth
9.	Roja Pengal	10	Cloth merchandise	180000	90000	90000	Tamil Nadu Mercantile Bank, Prakasapuram
10.	Anbu Pengal	12	Palm frond products, palm sugar cake making	240000	120000	120000	Pandian Grama Bank, Srivenkatesapuram
11.	Indira Gandhi	11	Dry fish making	180000	90000	90000	Bharatha State Bank, Punnakayal

Source : DRDA, Thoothukudi.

Table 3.17 : Thiruchendur Panchayat Union.

Sl. No.	*SHG Name*	*Total Members*	*Enterprise*	*Total Amount*	*Subsidy*	*Loan*	*Bank Name*
1.	Senthoor	15	Palm cake making and palm mat making	221000	110500	110500	Indian Overseas Bank, Thiruchendur
2.	Josephin Pengal	13	Palm cake making and palm mat making	161000	80500	80500	Canara Bank, Arumuganeri
3.	Chiristhu Pengal	13	Groceries shop	230000	115000	115000	Canara Bank, Arumuganeri
4.	Annai Bilominal Pengal	14	Palm cake making and palm mat making	161000	80500	80500	Canara Bank, Arumuganeri
5.	Kanthari	11	Groceries shop	200000	100000	100000	Indian Overseas Bank, Thiruchendur

Source : DRDA, Thoothukudi.

Table 3.18 : Udangudi Panchayat Union.

Sl. No.	*SHG Name*	*Total Members*	*Enterprise*	*Total Amount*	*Subsidy*	*Loan*	*Bank Name*
1.	Thalampoo	14	Palm sugar cake making, and palm mat knitting	178400	89200	89200	Tamil Nadu Mercantile Bank, Megnanapuram
2.	Josmin	12	Palm sugar cake making, and palm mat weaving	240000	120000	120000	Tamil Nadu Mercantile Bank, Megnanapuram
3.	Annai Mahalir	16	Palm sugar cake making, and palm mat weaving	161160	80580	80580	Indian Overseas Bank, Paramankurichi
4.	Vaigai Mahalir	12	Palm sugar cake making, and palm mat weaving	216000	108000	108000	Tamil Nadu Mercantile Bank, Megnanapuram
5.	Mahalir	10	Palm sugar cake making, and palm mat weaving	200000	100000	100000	Pandian Grama Bank, Semmarikulam
6.	Mariamman Mahalir	13	Palm sugar cake making, and palm mat weaving	234000	117000	117000	State Bank of India, Udankudi
7.	Bharathi Mahalir Mandram	19	Palm mat weaving	163800	81900	81900	Indian Bank, Kulasekaran-pattinam
8.	Karpagataru Semippu Matrum Kadan Kulu	17	Palm sugar cake making, and palm mat weaving	246600	123300	123300	Bharatha State Bank, Udankudi
9.	Roja Semippu Matrum Kadan Kulu	14	Coconut frond pandal making	153200	76600	76600	Pandian Grama Bank, Semmarikulam
10.	Malligai Pengal Thamaraikulam	17	Coconut frond pandal making	180200	90100	90100	Pandian Grama Bank, Semmarikulam
11.	Star Suya	11	Coconut frond pandal making	126200	63100	63100	Canara Bank, Udankudi
12.	Mullai Mahalir	11	Coconut frond pandal making	126200	63100	63100	Canara Bank, Udankudi
13.	Olimuthu Amman	7	Coconut frond pandal making	180200	90100	90100	State Bank of India, Udankudi

Source : DRDA, Thoothukudi.

A total of 11 SHGs received SGSY loans with subsidy in Alvarthirunagari PU during 2001-2002. The amount of loan ranged from Rs. 1,80,000 to Rs. 3,00,000 for enterprises such as goat rearing, dairy unit, cloth merchandise, palm frond products, palm sugar cake making and dry fish making. The total amount of loan was Rs. 26,73,000. Out of this Rs.12,51,000 was subsidy and Rs. 14,22,000 was repayable loan. The average amount of subsidy for an SHG was Rs.1,29,272.

A total of 5 SHGs received SGSY loans with subsidy during 2001-2002 in Thiruchendur PU. The amount of loan ranged from Rs. 1,61,000 to Rs. 2,30,000 for enterprises such as groceries shop, palm cake making and palm mat making. The total amount of loan was Rs. 9,73,000, of which Rs. 4,86,500 was subsidy and Rs. 4,86,500 was repayable loan. The average amount of subsidy for an SHG was Rs. 97,300.

SGSY loans with subsidy were provided to 13 SHGs in Udangudi PU during 2001-2002. The amount of loan ranged from Rs. 1,26,000 to Rs. 2,46,600 for enterprises such as palm sugar cake making, coconut frond pandal making and palm mat weaving. The total amount of loan was Rs. 24,05,960. Out of this, Rs.12,02,980 was subsidy and Rs.12,02,980 was repayable loan. The average amount of subsidy for an SHG was Rs. 95,536.

A total of 5 SHGs, were benefited from the SGSY loans with subsidy in Sathankulam PU during 2001-2002. The amount of loan ranged from Rs. 2,00,000 to Rs. 2,50,000 for enterprises such as handicraft products, masala powder making, readymade garments and paper bag making. The total amount of loan was Rs. 11,10,000. Out of this Rs. 5,55,000 was subsidy and Rs. 5,55,000 was repayable loan. The average amount of less subsidy for an SHG was Rs. 1,11,000.

SGSY loans with subsidy were provided to 5 SHGs in Kovilpatti PU during 2001-2002. The amount of loan ranged from Rs. 1,80,000 to Rs. 3,00,000 for the traders of dairy unit and goat rearing. The total amount of loan was Rs.11,69,000, of which Rs. 5,59,500 was subsidy and Rs. 6,09,500 was repayable loan. The average amount of subsidy for an SHG was Rs. 1,11,900.

Table 3.19 : Sathankulam Panchayat Union.

Sl. No.	*SHG Name*	*Total Members*	*Enterprise*	*Total Amount*	*Subsidy*	*Loan*	*Bank Name*
1.	Nila Mahalir	11	Handicraft products	230000	115000	115000	Canara Bank, Muthalur
2.	Vidiyal	10	Masala powder making	200000	100000	100000	Canara Bank, Muthalur
3.	Weeds Mahalir	10	Readymade garments	250000	125000	125000	Canara Bank, Muthalur
4.	Annai Therasa Mahalir	18	Handicraft products	230000	115000	115000	Tamil Nadu Mercantile Bank, Kommadikottai
5.	Sri Mutharamman Mahalir	12	Paper bag making	200000	100000	100000	Canara Bank, Muthalur

Source : DRDA, Thoothukudi.

Table 3.20 : Kovilpatti Panchayat Union.

Sl. No.	*SHG Name*	*Total Members*	*Enterprise*	*Total Amount*	*Subsidy*	*Loan*	*Bank Name*
1.	Dr. Muthulakshmi Reddi Mahalir	15	Dairy unit	300000	125000	175000	State Bank of Thiruvankur, Kovilpatti
2.	Durgai Amman	14	Goat rearing	232000	116000	116000	Pandian Grama Bank, Keelaeral
3.	Venkatachalapathi Mahalir	14	Goat rearing	232000	116000	116000	Pandian Grama Bank, Keelaeral
4.	Malaiammal Mahalir	11	Goat rearing	180000	90000	90000	Canara Bank, Ettaiyapuram
5.	Indira Mahalir	10	Goat rearing	225000	112500	120000	Canara Bank, Ettaiyapuram

Source : DRDA, Thoothukudi.

Table 3.21 : Kayatharu Panchayat Union.

Sl. No.	*SHG Name*	*Total Members*	*Enterprise*	*Total Amount*	*Subsidy*	*Loan*	*Bank Name*
1.	Kaliammal Mahalir	17	Goats rearing	255000	125000	130000	Canara Bank, Kalampatti
2.	Thamarai Mahalir	17	Dairy units	340000	125000	215000	Canara Bank, Kayathar
3.	Kalaimahal Mahalir	18	Dairy units	360000	125000	235000	Canara Bank, Kayathar
4.	Roja Mahalir	19	Dairy units	380000	125000	255000	Canara Bank, Kayathar
5.	Perarigar Anna	12	Goats rearing	180000	90000	90000	Canara Bank, Kayathar

Source : DRDA, Thoothukudi.

Table 3.22 : Ottapidaram Panchayat Union.

Sl. No.	*SHG Name*	*Total Members*	*Enterprise*	*Total Amount*	*Subsidy*	*Loan*	*Bank Name*
1.	Kathiroli Mahalir Mandram	12	Crab preserving	150000	75000	75000	Pandian Grama Bank, Tharuvaikulam
2.	Sarojini Mahalir Mandram	18	Crab preserving	225000	112500	112500	Pandian Grama Bank, Tharuvaikulam
3.	Arulosai Mahalir Mandram	17	Crab preserving	212500	106250	106250	Pandian Grama Bank, Tharuvaikulam
4.	Athisayam Mahalir Mandram	16	Fishing net knitting	249920	124960	124960	Pandian Grama Bank, Tharuvaikulam
5.	Vennila Mahalir Mandram	16	Fishing net knitting	249920	124960	124960	Pandian Grama Bank, Tharuvaikulam
6.	Neethi Mahalir Mandram	20	Milch animals rearing	340000	125000	215000	Pandian Grama Bank, Kulathur
7.	Puthir Mahalir Mandram	13	Milch animals rearing	260000	125000	135000	Indian Overseas Bank, Eppothumvendran
8.	Kathir Mahalir Mandram	13	Milch animals rearing	260000	125000	135000	Indian Overseas Bank, Eppothumvendran

Source : DRDA, Thoothukudi.

Table 3.23 : Vilathikulam Panchayat Union.

Sl. No.	*SHG Name*	*Total Members*	*Enterprise*	*Total Amount*	*Subsidy*	*Loan*	*Bank Name*
1.	Gangai Mahalir	12	Charcoal making	250000	125000	125000	Tamil Nadu Mercantile Bank, Vilathikulam
2.	Vaigai Mahalir	11	Charcoal making	250000	125000	125000	Tamil Nadu Mercantile Bank, Vilathikulam
3.	Selvi Mahalir Mandram	12	Goat rearing	270000	125000	145000	Tamil Nadu Mercantile Bank, Vilathikulam
4.	Sirumalar Mahalir Mandram	20	Palm frond products	250000	125000	125000	Pandian Grama Bank, Vembar
5.	Annai Mahalir Mandram	19	Palm frond products	250000	125000	125000	Pandian Grama Bank, Vembar
6.	Vinnoli Mahalir Mandram	19	Palm frond products	250000	125000	125000	Pandian Grama Bank, Vembar
7.	Rose Mahalir Mandram	20	Palm frond products	250000	125000	125000	Pandian Grama Bank, Vembar
8.	Muthukuvial Mahalir Mandram	20	Palm frond products	250000	125000	125000	Pandian Grama Bank, Vembar
9.	Bharathiar Karimootta Kulu	10	Charcoal making	250000	125000	125000	Canara Bank, Ettaiyapuram
10.	Anna Karimootta Kulu	10	Charcoal making	250000	125000	125000	Canara Bank, Ettaiyapuram
11.	Mullai Mahalir Mandram	12	Charcoal making	250000	125000	125000	Thodakka Velanmai Kootturavu Bank, Sakkammalpuram
12.	Thamarai Mahalir	12	Charcoal making	250000	125000	125000	Thodakka Velanmai Kootturavu Bank, Sakkammalpuram
13.	Punitha Thomaiyar Pengal	12	Dry fish making	150000	75000	75000	Pandian Grama Bank, Vembar
14.	Punitha Anthoniyar Pengal	12	Dry fish making	162500	81250	81250	Canara Bank, Ettaiyapuram
15.	Scot Roja Mahalir Mandram	15	Goat rearing	250000	125000	125000	Canara Bank, Ettaiyapuram
16.	Annai Therasa Mahalir	12	Goat rearing	270000	125000	145000	Canara Bank, Ettaiyapuram
17.	Deepam Om Sakthi	20	Basket knitting	260000	125000	135000	Pandian Grama Bank, Vembar
18.	Mullai Mahalir	12	Goat rearing	270000	125000	145000	Bharatha Manila Bank, Vilathikulam
19.	Sri Muthuramman Mahalir	10	Charcoal making	250000	125000	125000	Canara Bank, Ettaiyapuram
20.	Valarpirai Nanbargal	10	Charcoal making	250000	125000	125000	Canara Bank, Ettaiyapuram
21.	Anna	5	Irrigation and fish farming	400000	125000	275000	State Bank of India, Vilathikulam

Source : DRDA, Thoothukudi.

Table 3.24 : Pudur Panchayat Union.

Sl. No.	*SHG Name*	*Total Members*	*Enterprise*	*Total Amount*	*Subsidy*	*Loan*	*Bank Name*
1.	Samuka Sevai Sangam	16	Charcoal making	240000	120000	120000	Tamil Nadu Mercantile Bank, Pudur
2.	Aringar Anna	12	Goat rearing	260000	125000	135000	Indian Overseas, Nagalapuram
3.	Mullai	10	Goat rearing	260000	125000	135000	Indian Overseas, Nagalapuram
4.	Komatha	10	Charcoal making	250000	125000	125000	Indian Overseas, Nagalapuram
5.	Puratchi Thalaivar	10	Charcoal making	250000	125000	125000	Indian Overseas, Nagalapuram

Source : DRDA, Thoothukudi.

Table 3.25 : Thoothukudi Panchayat Union.

Sl. No.	*SHG Name*	*Total Members*	*Enterprise*	*Total Amount*	*Subsidy*	*Loan*	*Bank Name*
1.	Chevandipoo Sahothara Valvu Sankam	16	Palm frond baskets	160000	80000	80000	Pandian Village Bank, Puthukudi
2.	Chevandipoo Sahothara Valvu Sankam	14	Palm frond baskets	140000	70000	70000	Pandian Village Bank, Puthukudi
3.	Pichipoo Sahathara Valvusankam	14	Milch animals	280000	125000	155000	Pandian Village Bank, Puthukudi
4.	Muthamil Mahalir Mandram	20	Palm frond baskets	200000	100000	100000	Tamil Nadu Mercandile Bank, Pudukottai
5.	Santhanam Mahalir Mandram	20	Palm frond baskets	180000	90000	90000	Tamil Nadu Mercandile Bank, Pudukottai
6.	Madathur Suyavelaivayppu Sangam	11	Milch animals	259600	125000	134600	Bharath State Bank Harbor
7.	Gandhinagar Makkal Suyavelaivayppu Nallasangam	11	Milch animals	259600	125000	134600	Bharath State Bank, Harper
8.	Mallihaipoo Sahothara Valvusangam	13	Milch animals	260000	125000	135000	UCO Bank, Mudivaithanedal
9.	Semparuthi Sahothara Valvusankam	13	Milch animals	260000	125000	135000	Syndicate Bank, Harper
10.	Thalampoosuya Sevaikkulu	13	Groceries and flour products	175500	87750	87750	Indian Overseas Bank, Mappillaiyurani
11.	Suriyagandhi Sahathoravalvu Sangam	11	Goat rearing	168700	84350	84350	UCO Bank, Moodivaithanendal
12.	Sirumalar	16	Groceries and masala products	216000	108000	108000	Indian Overseas Bank, Mappillaiyurani
13.	Vaikaraimahalir Mandram	16	Readymade garments	240000	120000	120000	UCO Bank, Mudivaithanendal
14.	Thamarai Mahalir Mandram	12	Readymade garments	150000	75000	75000	Indian Overseas Bank, Mappillaiyurani
15.	Pavalam Mahalir Mandram	14	Dry fish making	226000	113000	113000	Indian Overseas Bank, Mappillaiyurani

Source : DRDA, Thoothukudi.

A total 5 SHGs were benefited from SGSY loans with subsidy in Kayatharu PU during 2001-2002. The amount of loan ranged from Rs. 1,80,000 to Rs. 3,80,000 for enterprises such as dairy units and goat rearing. The total amount of loan was Rs.15,15,000. Out of this, Rs. 5,90,000 was subsidy and Rs. 9,25,000 was repayable loan. The average amount of subsidy for an SHG was Rs.1,18,000.

A total of 8 SHGs received SGSY loans with subsidy in Ottapidaram PU during 2001-2002. The amount of loan ranged from Rs. 1,50,000 to Rs.3,40,000 for the trades of crab preserving, fishing net knitting and milch animals rearing. The total amount of loan was Rs.15,15,000. Out of this, Rs. 5,90,000 was subsidy and Rs. 9,25,000 was repayable loan. The average amount of subsidy for an SHG was Rs.1,18,000.

A total of 21 SHGs received SGSY loans with subsidy in Vilathikulam PU during 2001-2002. The amount of loan ranged from Rs. 1,50,000 to Rs. 4,00,000 for various trades such as charcoal making, palm frond products, goat rearing, dry fish making, basket knitting, irrigation and fish farming. The total amount of loan was Rs. 52,82,500. Out of this, Rs. 10,31,250 was subsidy and Rs. 32,51,500 was repayable loan. The average amount of subsidy for an SHG was Rs. 49,100.

SGSY loans were provided to 5 SHGs in Pudur PU during 2001-2002. The amount of loan ranged from Rs. 2,40,000 to Rs. 2,60,000 was provided for enterprises such as charcoal making and goat rearing. The total amount of loan was Rs. 12,60,000. Out of this, Rs. 6,20,000 was subsidy and Rs. 6,40,000 was repayable loan.The average amount of subsidy for an SHG was Rs. 1,24,000.

SGSY 2000-2001

This part of the discussion deals with the loans provided under SGSY during 2000-2001 for SHGs, in Thoothukudi District. The PU-wise details of SHGs are given hereunder.

A total of 15 SHGs were benefited from SGSY loans with 50 per cent subsidy during 2000-2001 in Thoothukudi PU. The amount of loan ranged from Rs. 1,50,000 to Rs. 2,60,000 for the trades such as making of palm frond baskets, milch animals rearing, groceries and flour products, goat rearing, masala powder making, readymade garments and dry fish making. The total amount of loan was Rs. 31,75,400 of which Rs. 15,87,700 was subsidy and the remaining Rs. 15,87,700 was repayable loan. The average amount of subsidy provided to an SHG was Rs. 1,05,850.

SGSY loan with 50 per cent subsidy was provided to 9 SHGs during 2000-2001 in Karungulam PU for enterprises such as vessels and chairs hiring, goat rearing and milch animals rearing. The amount of loan ranged from Rs. 54,000 to Rs. 2,73,000. The total amount of loan was Rs. 20,42,694, of which Rs. 10,21,347 was subsidy and the remaining Rs. 10,21,347 was loan. The average amount of subsidy for an SHG was Rs. 1,13,480.

Fourteen SHGs were benefited under SGSY loans with 50 per cent subsidy during 2000-2001 in Thiruvaikundam PU. The amount of loan ranged from Rs.21,000 to Rs.3,46,500 for the trades such as fishery, goat rearing, milch animals rearing, fish preservation, readymade garments and coconut frond products. The total amount of loan was Rs. 34,25,500. Out the total amount Rs. 17,12.750 was subsidy and the remaining Rs. 17,12,750 was loan. The average amount of subsidy was Rs. 1,22,340 for an SHG.

A total of 9 SHGs were provided loans with 50 per cent subsidy under SGSY during 2000-2001 in Alvarnagari PU. The amount of loan ranged from Rs. 1,05,000 to Rs. 3,00,000 for enterprises such as goat rearing, mini dairy, readymade garments, dry fish making, groceries shop and pickles production. The total amount of loan was Rs. 16,65,600, of which Rs. 8,32,800 was subsidy and the remaining amount of Rs. 8,32,800 was loan. The average amount of subsidy for an SHG was Rs. 92,530.

A total of 3 SHGs were benefited from SGSY loans with 50 per cent subsidy during 2000-2001 in Thiruchendur PU. The amount of loan was Rs. 1,60,000, Rs. 58,500 and Rs. 2,80,800 for the trades of palm frond products, coconut frond products and milch animals rearing. The total amount of loan was Rs. 4,99,300. Out of this, half of the amount, Rs. 2,49,650, was subsidy and the remaining half of the amount was loan. The average amount of subsidy for an SHG was Rs. 83,216.

Table 3.26 : Karungulam Panchayat Union.

Sl. No.	SHG Name	Total Members	Enterprise	Total Amount	Subsidy	Loan	Bank Name
1.	Annaitherasa Gramodaya Mahalir Mandram	13	Milch animals	273000	125000	148000	Indian Overseas Bank
2.	Indra Gramodaya Mahalirmandram	13	Milch animals	273000	125000	148000	Indian Overseas Bank Vallanadu
3.	Vennila Gramodaya Mahalir	19	Goat rearing	250162	125000	125162	UCO Bank, Karunkulam
4.	Marutham Gramodaya Mahalir	20	Goat rearing	253560	125000	128560	UCO Bank, Karunkulam
5.	Ulaikkumpenkal Munetrasangam	19	Vessels and chairs hiring	54000	27000	27000	Pandian Grama Bank, Thiruvaikundam
6.	Ulaikkumpenkal Munetrasangam	20	Milch animals	252000	125000	127000	Pandian Grama Bank, Thiruvaikunam
7.	Ulaikkumpenkal Munetrasangam	15	Milch animals	273000	125000	148000	Indian Overseas Bank Chokkarakudi
8.	Ulaikkumpenkal Munetrasangam	20	Milch animals	231000	115500	115500	Indian Overseas Bank, Chokkarakudi
9.	Annaitherasa Gramodaya Mahalir	14	Goat rearing	182972	91486	91486	UCO Bank, Karunkulam

Source : DRDA, Thoothukudi.

Table 3.27 : Thiruvaikundam Panchayat Union.

Sl. No.	*SHG Name*	*Total Members*	*Enterprise*	*Total Amount*	*Subsidy*	*Loan*	*Bank Name*
1.	Annai Indra Suyanithimahalir Mandram	17	Milch animals	340000	125000	215000	UCO Bank, mutivaithanendal
2.	Nehru Mahalir	18	Goat rearing	225000	112500	112500	Canara Bank, Eral
3.	Rajiv Gandhi	20	Goat rearing	250000	125000	125000	Canara Bank, Eral
4.	Mutharamman	20	Milch animals	315000	125000	190000	UCO Bank, Mudivaithanendal
5.	Marutham Penkal	20	Milch animals	290000	125000	165000	Pandian Grama Bank, Siakalai
6.	Punitha Elolal Meen Piti Tholilalar	10	Fishery	250000	125000	125000	Thotakkavelanmai Kutturavu Bank, Mukkani
7.	Attaikalamatha Meen Piti Tholilalar	10	Fishery	250000	125000	125000	Thotakkavelanmai Kutturavu Bank, Mukkani
8.	Dowra Kulu	10	Goat rearing	145000	72500	72500	Thotakkavelanmai Kutturavu Bank, Mukkani
9.	Dowcra Kulu	15	Goat rearing	203000	101500	101500	Thotakkavelanmai Kutturavu Bank, Mukkani
10.	Maruthampenkal	20	Goat rearing	290000	125000	165000	Pandian Grama Bank, Sivakalai
11.	Srimutharamman	20	Milch animals goat rearing	346500	125000	221500	UCO Bank, Mutivaithanendal
12.	Dowcra Kulu	14	Readymade garments & coconut frond products	21000	105000	105000	Pandian Grama Bank, Thiruvaikundam
13.	Jyothimahalir Mandram	15	Readymade garments & coconut frond products	250000	125000	125000	Pandian Grama Bank, Palaiyakayal
14.	Paripuranimahalir Mandram	15	Fish preservation	250000	125000	102000	Pandian Grama Bank, Palaiyakayal

Source : DRDA, Thoothukudi.

Table 3.28 : Alvarthirunagari Panchayat Union.

Sl. No.	SHG Name	Total Members	Enterprise	Total Amount	Subsidy	Loan	Bank Name
1.	Sethuguvaithan	11	Goat rearing	204000	102000	102000	Canara Bank, Athur
2.	Srivenkateshwara	11	Mini dairy	259600	125000	134600	Pandian Grama Bank, Srivenkateshwara puram
3.	Karunkadal (Palaniyappa puram)	12	Readymade garments	145000	72500	72500	Pandian Grama Bank, Srivenkateshwara puram
4.	Srivenkateshwara puram	14	Mini dairy	300000	125000	175000	Pandian Grama Bank, Srivenkateshwara puram
5.	Saliputhur	12	Readymade garments	145000	72500	72500	Pandian Grama Bank, Srivenkateshwara puram
6.	Rojapenkal Suyauthavikkulu, Narthankurichi	10	Mini dairy	236000	118000	118000	Pandian Grama Bank, Srivenkateshwara puram.
7.	Punithaarul anandar Penkal Suyauthavikkulu, Punnakkalayal	12	Groceries shop	156000	78000	78000	State Bank of India, Punnakkalayal
8.	Docra Suyauthavikkulu, Kạdaiyanodai	11	Pickles production	105000	52500	52500	Pandian Grama Bank, Nasareth
9.	Udayakala	10	Dry fish making	115000	57500	57500	

Source : DRDA, Thoothukudi.

Table 3.29 : Thiruchendur Panchayat Union.

Sl. No.	*SHG Name*	*Total Members*	*Enterprise*	*Total Amount*	*Subsidy*	*Loan*	*Bank Name*
1.	Mahalir	12	Palm frond products	160000	80000	80000	Tamil Nadu Mercandile Bank, Kayamoli
2.	Mahalir	13	Coconut frond products	58500	29250	29250	State Bank of India, Gurumbur
3.	Sathiyamman Mahalir	15	Milch animal	280800	125000	155800	Indian Overseas Bank, Thiruchendur

Source : DRDA, Thoothukudi.

Table 3.30 : Udangudi Panchayat Union.

Sl. No.	*SHG Name*	*Total Members*	*Enterprise*	*Total Amount*	*Subsidy*	*Loan*	*Bank Name*
1.	Karpagatharu	17	Sugar cakes making, mat weaving	255000	125000	130000	Pandian Grama Bank, Semarikulam
2.	Malar	15	Goat rearing, mat weaving	121500	60750	60750	Canara Bank, Utankudi
3.	Muthuramman	12	Palm sugar cake making, mat weaving	144000	72000	72000	Indian Bank, Gulasekaranpattinam
4.	Karpagatharu Penkal	20	Goat rearing, mat weaving	204000	102000	102000	Indian Overseas Bank, Paramankurichi
5.	Malligai Penkal	20	Goat rearing, mat weaving	204000	102000	102000	Indian Overseas Bank, Paramankurichi
6.	Indramahalir	12	Milch animals	248640	124320	124320	Thottakkavelanmai Kutturavu Bank, Maignanapuram

Source : DRDA, Thoothukudi.

SGSY loans with 50 per cent were provided to 6 SHGs in Udangudi PU during 2000-2001. The amount of loan ranged from Rs. 1,21,500 to Rs. 2,55,000 for enterprises such as sugar cakes making, palm sugar cake making, goat rearing, milch animals rearing and mat weaving. The total amount of loan was Rs. 11,77,140, of which Rs. 5,88,570 was subsidy and Rs. 5,88,570 was loan. The average amount of subsidy for an SHG was Rs. 98,000.

A total of 6 SHGs received loans with 50 per cent subsidy under SGSY during 2000-2001 in Sathankulam PU. The amount of loan ranged from Rs. 1,65,000 to Rs. 3,21,000 for trades such as goat rearing, dairy unit and handicraft products. The total amount of loan was Rs. 19,55,606, of which Rs. 8,87,500 was subsidy and Rs.10,68,100 was loan. The average amount of subsidy for an SHG was Rs.1,10,937.

Loans with 50 per cent subsidy were provided to 5 SHGs under SGSY during 2000-2001 in Kovilpatti PU. The amount of loan ranged from Rs. 2,40,000 to Rs. 3,00,000 for the trade of mini dairy unit. The total amount of loan was Rs.14,00,000, of which Rs. 6,40,000 was subsidy and Rs. 6,20,000 and Rs. 6,72,000 was the loan. The average amount of subsidy for an SHG was Rs.1,24,000.

A total of 9 other SHGs were benefited from SGSY loans with subsidy in Kayatharu PU during 2000-2001. The amount of loan ranged from Rs.1,65,000 to Rs. 3,40,000 for enterprises such as mini dairy unit and goat rearing. The total amount of loan was Rs. 22,75,000, of which Rs. 10,62,500 was subsidy and Rs. 12,12,500 was repayable loan. The average amount of subsidy for an SHG was Rs. 1,18,055.

SGSY loans with subsidy were provided to 17 SHGs in Ottapidaram PU during 2000-2001. The amount ranged from Rs. 1,00,000 to Rs. 3,40,000 for the traders of readymade garments, dairy units, milch animal rearing, and fishing net mating. The total amount of loan was Rs. 42,52,500, of which Rs. 19,51,250 was subsidy and Rs. 23,01,250 was loan. The average amount of subsidy was Rs. 1,14,780 provided for an SHG.

Table 3.31 : Sathankulam Panchayat Union.

Sl. No.	SHG Name	Total Members	Enterprise	Total Amount	Subsidy	Loan	Bank Name
1.	Veetsmahalir	Not available	Goat rearing	210000	105000	105000	Canara Bank, Muthalur
2.	Veetsmahalir	11	Goat rearing	165000	82500	82500	Canara Bank, Muthalur
3.	Veetsmahalir	10	Handicrafts products	230000	115000	115000	Canara Bank, Muthalur
4.	Veetsmahalir	10	Handicrafts products	230000	115000	115000	Canara Bank, Muthalur
5.	Veetsmahalir	14	Goat rearing	210000	105000	105000	Canara Bank, Muthalur
6.	Veetsmahalir	15	Dairy unit	321000	125000	196000	Canara Bank, Muthalur
7.	Veetsmahalir	14	Dairy unit	299600	125000	174600	Canara Bank, Muthalur
8.	Veetsmahalir	20	Goat rearing	300000	125000	175000	Canara Bank, Muthalur

Source : DRDA, Thoothukudi.

Table 3.32 : Kovilpatti Panchayat Union.

Sl. No.	SHG Name	Total Members	Enterprise	Total Amount	Subsidy	Loan	Bank Name
1.	Mahalir & Kualandai Mempattu Thitta Sankam	14	Mini dairy unit	280000	125000	155000	State Bank of India, Thiruvankur, Kovilpatti
2.	Veerachinnammal	15	Mini dairy unit	300000	125000	175000	State Bank of India, Solapuram
3.	Duragadevi Mahalir	15	Mini dairy unit	300000	125000	175000	State Bank of India, Solapuram
4.	Sitar - Madurai Meenatchi	12	Mini dairy unit	240000	120000	120000	Pandian Grama Bank, Kovilpatti
5.	Mahalir Matrum Kulandaikal Mempattuthittam Sangam	14	Mini dairy unit	280000	125000	155000	Pandian Grama Bank, Keelaeral

Source : DRDA, Thoothukudi.

Table 3.33 : Kayatharu Panchayat Union.

Sl. No.	*SHG Name*	*Total Members*	*Enterprise*	*Total Amount*	*Subsidy*	*Loan*	*Bank Name*
1.	Malligaimalar	13	Mini dairy unit	260000	125000	135000	Central Bank of India, Katampur
2.	Kiramapura Mahalir Matrum Kulandaikal Mempattuthittakulu,	14	Mini dairy unit	280000	125000	155000	Canara Bank, Kayathar
3.	Docra	11	Goat rearing	165000	82500	82500	Canara Bank, Kalampatti
4.	Nehruji Narpanimandram	12	Goat rearing	270000	125000	145000	Canara Bank, Kayathar
5.	Annaitherasa Mahalir	17	Mini dairy unit	340000	125000	215000	Canara Bank, Kayathar
6.	Vellai Roja Mahalirmandram,	12	Mini dairy unit	240000	120000	120000	Canara Bank, Kayathar
7.	Mahathma Gandhi Narpanimandram	12	Mini dairy unit	240000	120000	120000	Canara Bank, Kayathaar
8.	Annai IndraGandhi Mahalirmandram	12	Mini dairy unit	240000	120000	120000	Canara Bank, Kayathaar
9.	Annaitherasa Mahalirmandram	12	Mini dairy unit	240000	120000	120000	Canara Bank, Kayathaar

Source : DRDA, Thoothukudi.

Table 3.34 : Ottapidaram Panchayat Union.

Sl. No.	*SHG Name*	*Total Members*	*Enterprise*	*Total Amount*	*Subsidy*	*Loan*	*Bank Name*
1.	Roajamahalir	12	Readymade garments	120000	60000	60000	Bharath State Bank, Savarimangalam
2.	Santhanam Mahalir	15	Goat rearing	217500	108750	108750	Bharath State Bank, Savarimangalam
3.	Rojamahalir	20	Dairy unit	340000	125000	215000	Pandian Grama Bank, Pasuvandanai
4.	Selvam Mahalirmandram	20	Dairy unit	340000	125000	215000	Pandian Grama Bank, Pasuvandanai
5.	Indra Mahalirmandram	20	Dairy unit	340000	125000	215000	Pandian Grama Bank, Pasuvandanai
6.	Docra	13	Dairy unit	221000	110500	110500	Indian Overseas Bank , Ottanatham
7.	Annaitherasa	13	Dairy unit	260000	125000	135000	Pandian Grama Bank, Akkanayakkanpatti
8.	Annai Indra	14	Dairy unit	280000	125000	155000	Pandian Grama Bank, Akkanayakkanpatti
9.	Thiruvalluvar	12	Dairy unit	240000	120000	120000	Central Bank of India, Kadampur
10.	Bharathi Mahalir	13	Dairy unit	260000	125000	135000	Central Bank of India, Kadampur
11.	Indra Ghandhi Mahalir	13	Dairy unit	260000	125000	135000	Central Bank of India, Kadampur
12.	Rajiv Gandhi	13	Dairy unit	260000	125000	135000	Pandian Grama Bank, Akkanayakkanpatti
13.	Gandhiatikal Mempattu Valarchikulu	13	Dairy unit	260000	125000	135000	Pandian Grama Bank, Akkanayakkanpatti
14.	Docra Kulu	12	Dairy unit	204000	102000	102000	Indian Overseas Bank, Ottanatham
15.	Mullaimahalir Mandram	15	Fishing net mating	187500	93750	93750	Pandian Grama Bank, Tharuvaikulam
16.	Malligai Mahalirmandram	20	Fishing net mating	250000	125000	125000	Pandian Grama Bank, Tharuvaikulam
17.	Therasa Mahalirmandram	17	Fishing net mating	212500	106250	106250	Pandian Grama Bank, Tharuvaikulam

Source : DRDA, Thoothukudi.

Table 3.35 : Vilathikulam Panchayat Union.

Sl. No.	*SHG Name*	*Total Members*	*Enterprise*	*Total Amount*	*Subsidy*	*Loan*	*Bank Name*
1	**2**	**3**	**4**	**5**	**6**	**7**	**8**
1.	Thamarai Mahalirmandram	10	Goat rearing	225000	112500	112500	Tamil Nadu Mercandile Bank, Villathikulam
2.	Roja Mahalir	12	Goat rearing	270000	125000	145000	Bharat State Bank, Vilathikulam
3.	Kurunchi Mahalir	12	Goat rearing	270000	125000	145000	Bharat State Bank, Vilathikulam
4.	Nila Mahalirmandram	15	Dry fish making	140000	70000	70000	Pandian Grama Bank, Vembar
5.	Annaitherasa Mahalirmandram	16	Dry fish making	160000	80000	80000	Pandian Grama Bank, Vembar
6.	Vidivelli Mahalirmandram	17	Dry fish preservation	170000	85000	85000	Pandian Grama Bank, Vembar
7.	Jawaharlal Nehru	10	Charcoal	250000	125000	125000	Bharat State Bank, Vilathikulam
8.	Mahatma Gandhi	10	Charcoal	250000	125000	125000	Bharat State Bank, Vilathikulam
9.	Indra	12	Goat rearing	270000	125000	145000	Pandian Grama Bank, Kulathur
10.	Kashduribai	12	Goat rearing	270000	125000	145000	Pandian Grama Bank, Kulathur
11.	Thamarai Mahalir	11	Charcoal	250000	125000	125000	State Bank of India, Vilathikulam
12.	Kalaimahal Mahalir	21	Charcoal	231000	115500	115500	Tamil Nadu Mercandile Bank, Vilathikulam
13.	Sanathuvam Mahalirmandram	20	Milch animal rearing	280800	125000	155800	Pandian Grama Bank, Kulathur
14.	Parasakthi Karimootakulu	11	Charcoal	250000	125000	125000	Thotakka Velanmai Kutturavu Vanki, Kalukasalapuram
15.	Thiruppathy Karimuttakulu, Vellaiammalpuram	10	Charcoal	250000	125000	125000	Thotakka Velanmai Kutturavu Vanki, Kalukasalapuram

(Table Contd. ...)

(Contd. ...)

1	2	3	4	5	6	7	8
16.	Sevamahalir	12	Charcoal	250000	125000	125000	Thotakka Velanmai Kutturavu Vanki, Vellaiammalpuram
17.	Malligai	12	Charcoal	250000	125000	125000	Thotakka Velanmai Kutturavu Vanki, Vellaiammalpuram
18.	Malligai Suyauthavikkulu	12	Charcoal	250000	125000	125000	Thotakka Velanmai Kutturavu Vanki, Sivagnanapuram
19.	Jawahar Mahalir	12	Charcoal	250000	125000	125000	Thotakka Velanmai Kutturavu Vanki, Sivagnanapuram
20.	Allikoti Mahalirmandram	18	Basket weaving	180000	90000	90000	Pandian Grama Bank, Vembar
21	Pavalakodi Mahalirmandram	18	Basket weaving	180000	90000	90000	Pandian Grama Bank, Vembar
22.	Kamaraja	10	Centring work	255000	125000	130000	Tamil Nadu Mercandile Bank, Vilathikulam

Source : DRDA, Thoothukudi.

Table 3.36 : Pudur Panchayat Union.

Sl. No.	*SHG Name*	*Total Members*	*Enterprise*	*Total Amount*	*Subsidy*	*Loan*	*Bank Name*
1.	Malligai Vivasaya	11	Vessels, chairs and pandal hiring	250000	125000	125000	Tamil Nadu Mercandile Bank, Puthur
2.	Malligai Vivasaya Kulu	11	Vessels and pandal hiring	250000	125000	125000	Tamil Nadu Mercandile Bank, Puthur
3.	Mullai Vivasayakulu	11	Vessels and pandal hiring	250000	125000	125000	Tamil Nadu Mercandile Bank, Puthur
4.	Malligai Vivasayakulu	20	Vessels, chairs and pandal hiring	250000	125000	125000	Tamil Nadu Mercandile Bank, Puthur
5.	Tharamarai Vivasayakulu	12	Vessels, chairs and pandal hiring	250000	125000	125000	Tamil Nadu Mercandile Bank, Puthur
6.	Sarojinidevi Dokrakulu	12	Milch animal rearing	250000	125000	125000	ThottakkaVelanmai Vanki, Keelakarandai
7.	Narmadha Dowcra Kulu	10	Decoration of pandals	250000	125000	125000	Thotakka Velanmai Vanki, Nakalapuram
8.	Peraringar Anna Suyauthavi Ulaippalarkulu	12	Goat rearing	270000	125000	145000	Thotakka Velanmai Vanki, Kammathupatti
9.	Puratchi Thalaivar M.G.R.	12	Goat rearing	270000	125000	145000	Thotakka Velanmai Vanki, Kammathupatti
10.	Lakshmi Mahalir	15	Charcoal	250000	125000	125000	Thotakka Velanmai Vanki, Ramachandrapuram
11.	Kurunchi Mahalir	10	Milch animal rearing	250000	125000	125000	Indian Overseas Bank, Nakalapuram
12.	Thirumahal Mahalir	10	Milch animal rearing	250000	125000	125000	Indian Overseas Bank, Nakalapuram
13.	Malar Mahalir	10	Milch animal rearing	250000	125000	125000	Indian Overseas Bank, Nagalapuram
14.	Senduran	10	Milch animal rearing	250000	125000	125000	Indian Overseas Bank, Nagalapuram
15.	Kalanchiyam Mahalir	10	Milch animal rearing	250000	125000	125000	Indian Overseas Bank, Nagalapuram
16.	Roja	10	Milch animal rearing	250000	125000	125000	Indian Overseas Bank, Nagalapuram

Source : DRDA, Thoothukudi.

A total of 22 SHGs received SGSY loans with subsidy in Vilathikulam PU during 2000-2001. The amount of loan ranged from Rs. 1,40,000 to Rs. 2,70,000 for enterprises such as of goat rearing, dry fish making, dry fish preservation, charcoal milch animal rearing, basket weaving and centring work. The total amount of loan was Rs. 51,51,800, of which subsidy was Rs. 25,18,000 and loan Rs. 26,33,800. The average amount of subsidy for an SHG was Rs. 1,14,454.

12. Pudur Panchayat Union

Sixteen SHGs received SGSY loans with subsidy in Pudur PU during 2000-2001. The amount of loan ranged from Rs. 2,50,000 to Rs. 2,70,000 for the trades of vessels, chairs and pandal hiring, decoration of pandals, charcoal, goat rearing, and milch animal rearing. The total amount of loan was Rs. 40,40,000, of which subsidy amount was Rs. 20,00,000 and remaining Rs. 20,40,000 was loan. The average amount of subsidy for an SHG was Rs.1,25,000.

SGSY 1999-2000

Thoothukudi

The SHGs provided with loan under SGSY in Thoothukurin District during 1999-2000 are presented detailed in this part. Union-wise details given hereunder.

SGSY loans ranging from Rs.1,20,000 to Rs. 2,59,000 were provided to 14 SHGs with a subsidy of 50 per cent during 1999-2000 in Thoothukudi Panchayat Union. The enterprises for which the loans were sanctioned were basket weaving, mini dairy, goat rearing, dry fish, and pickle manufacturing, masala products and milch animals rearing.

Seven SHGs were benefited from loans provided for mini dairy, basket weaving, puppet making and goat rearing in Karungulam Panchayat Union under SGSY scheme during 1999-2000. The amount of loan, ranged from Rs. 50,000 to Rs. 3,15,000 with a subsidy of 50 per cent.

Table 3.37 : Thoothukudi Panchayat Union.

Sl. No.	*SHG Name*	*Enterprise*	*Total Amount*	*Subsidy*	*Loan*	*Bank Name*
1.	Subash Mahalirmandram	Basket weaving	120000	60000	60000	Tamil Nadu Mercandile Bank, Pudukottai
2.	Seviyar Mahalirmandram	Basket weaving	140000	70000	70000	Tamil Nadu Mercandile Bank, Pudukottai
3.	Annai Mahalirmandram	Basket weaving	150000	75000	75000	Tamil Nadu Mercandile Bank, Pudukottai
4.	Annaitherasa Mahalirmandram	Basket weaving	150000	75000	75000	Tamil Nadu Mercandile Bank, Pudukottai
5.	Indranagar Makkalvelaivayppu nalachangam	Mini dairy	259600	134600	125000	Bharat State Bank, Duraimugam
6.	Royappar Mahalirmandram	Goat rearing	250000	125000	125000	Tamil Nadu Mercandile Bank, Pudukottai
7.	Annai Indira Grama Abivirithi Sangam	Goat rearing	230000	115000	115000	Pandian Grama Bank, Pudukudi
8.	Rojappu Sahotharavalvu Sangam	Goat rearing	230000	115000	115000	Pandian Grama Bank, Pudukudi
9.	Dowcra Kulu	Dry fish	120000	60000	60000	Indian Overseas Bank, Mappillaiyurani
10.	Lilli Mahalirmandram	Masala products	160000	80000	80000	Indian Overseas Bank, Mappillaiyurani
11.	Anbu Mahalirmandram	Dry fish and pickle manufacturing	140000	70000	70000	Indian Overseas Bank, Mappillaiyurani
12.	Malligai Mahalirmandram	Goat rearing	250000	125000	125000	Indian Overseas Bank, Mappillaiyurani
13.	Meelavittan Makkalsuya Velaivaippu Sangam	Mini dairy	259600	134600	125000	Bharat State Bank, Duraimugam
14.	Madathur Makkal Suyauthavikkulu	Mini dairy	259600	134600	125000	State Bank of India, Duraimugam

Source : DRDA, Thoothukudi.

Table 3.38 : Karungulam Panchayat Union.

Sl. No.	*SHG Name*	*Enterprise*	*Total Amount*	*Subsidy*	*Loan*	*Bank Name*
1.	Ulaikkum Mahalir	Mini dairy	273000	148000	125000	Indian Overseas Bank, Vallanadu
2.	Docra Kulu	Basket weaving	50000	25000	25000	Indian Overseas Bank, Ramanujampudur
3.	Ulakkum Mahalir Nalachangam	Mini dairy	231000	115500	115500	Pandian Grama Bank, Akanayakkanpatti
4.	Ulakkum Mahalir	Mini dairy	250000	125000	125000	Pandian Grama Bank, Thiruvaikundam
5.	Ulakkum Mahalir	Mini dairy	315000	190000	125000	Indian Overseas Bank, Vallanadu
6.	Docra Kulu	Puppet making	50000	25000	25000	UCO Bank, Karunkulam
7.	Indra Mahalirmandram	Goat rearing	238000	119000	119000	UCO Bank, Karunkulam

Source : DRDA, Thoothukudi.

Table 3.39 : Thiruvaikuntam.

Sl. No.	SHG Name	Enterprise	Total Amount	Subsidy	Loan	Bank Name
1.	Dokrakulu	Goat rearing	225000	112500	112500	Indian Overseas Bank Sayarpuram
2.	Dokrakulu	Wire basket weaving	70000	35000	35000	Bharat State Bank, Thiruvaikundam
3.	Dokrakulu	Coconut frond products	162000	81000	81000	Indian Overseas Bank, Sayarpuram
4.	Kurinchipenkal	Goats rearing	270000	145000	125000	Pandian Grama Bank, Sevathayapuram
5.	Suyauthavikkulu,	Brick industry	302000	177000	125000	Canara Bank, Eral
6.	Ambethkar penkal Suyauthavikkulu	Milch animals	440000	315000	125000	Pandian Grama Bank, Sivakalai
7.	Dowcra Kulu	Coconut frond products	50000	25000	25000	Tamil Nadu Mercandile Bank, Siruthondanallur
8.	Annaitherasa Mahalirmandram-1	Vadagam, phenyle, iral pickle making	249600	124800	124800	Pandian Grama Bank, Palaiyakayal
9.	Annaitherasa Mahalirmandram-2	Coffee powder making	268000	143000	125000	Pandian Grama Bank, Palaiyakayal
10.	Doucrakulu	Perfume sticks manufacturing	150000	75000	75000	Canara Bank, Thiruvaikundam

Source : DRDA, Thoothukudi.

Table 3.40 : Alvarthirunagar Panchayat Union

Sl. No.	*SHG Name*	*Enterprise*	*Total Amount*	*Subsidy*	*Loan*	*Bank Name*
1.	Vigaimahalir	Mini dairy	236000	118000	118000	Pandian Grama Bank, Thiruvenkatesa puram
2.	Malligai	Mini dairy	259600	134600	125000	Pandian Grama Bank, Thiruvenkatesa puram
3.	Kopura Mahalir	Mini dairy	236000	118000	118000	Pandian Grama Bank, Thiruvenkatesa puram
4.	Karpagatharu Mahalis	Mini dairy	259600	134600	125000	Pandian Grama Bank Thiruvenkatesa puram
5.	Deepam	Mini dairy	236000	118000	118000	Pandian Grama Bank, Thiruvenkatesa puram
6.	Dokrakulu	Palm frond mat weaving	140000	70000	70000	Pandian Grama Bank, Thiruvenkatesa puram
7.	Paralogamatha	Palm frond mat weaving	104000	52000	52000	Bharath State Bank, Punaikayal
8.	Motcharahini	Fish pickle making	104000	52000	52000	Bharath State Bank, Punaikayal
9.	Punitha Anthoniyar	Fish pickle making	118800	59400	59400	Bharath State Bank, Punnaikayal
10.	Barpara	Fish pickle making	104000	52000	52000	Bharath State Bank, Punnaikayal

Source : DRDA, Thoothukudi.

Table 3.41 : Thiruchendur Panchayat Union.

Sl. No.	*SHG Name*	*Enterprise*	*Total Amount*	*Subsidy*	*Loan*	*Bank Name*
1.	Docra Kulu	Palm frond mat making	100000	50000	50000	Tamil Nadu Mercandile Bank, Kayamoli
2.	Mupitathiamman	mini dairy	236000	118000	118000	Tamil Nadu Mercandile Bank, SonakanVilai
3.	Docra Kulu	Readymade garments	100000	50000	50000	Tamil Nadu Mercandile Bank, Kayamoli

Source : DRDA, Thoothukudi.

Table 3.42 : Udangudi Panchayat Union.

Sl. No.	*SHG Name*	*Enterprise*	*Total Amount*	*Subsidy*	*Loan*	*Bank Name*
1.	Karpagatharu	Mini dairy and palm sugar cake making	190000	95000	95000	Canara Bank, Uttankudi
2.	Karpagatharu	Mat weaving, goat rearing	232680	116340	116340	Pandian Grama Bank, Semmarikulam
3.	Vijayanarayana puram Mahalir		252720	127720	125000	Bharat State Bank, Uttankudi
4.	Paruvam Suyauthavikkulu	Mat weaving, goat rearing	252540	157540	125000	Tamil Nadu Mercandile Bank, Maignanapuram
5.	Karpagatharu	Mat weaving, goat rearing	216060	108030	108030	Pandian Grama Bank, Semmarikulam
6.	Thamarali	Mat weaving, goat rearing	218160	109080	109080	Tamil Nadu Mercandile Bank, Maignanapuram
7.	Docra Kulu	Mat weaving	90000	45000	45000	Canara Bank Uttankudi
8.	Karpagatharu	Palm sugar cake making mat weaving	307000	182000	125000	Tamil Nadu Mercandile Bank, Meignanapuram

Source : DRDA, Thoothukudi.

3. Thiruvaikundam Panchayat Union

Under SGSY scheme during 1999-2000, 10 SHGs received loans for enterprises such as goat rearing, wire basket weaving, coconut frond products, brick industry, milch animals, coffee powder making, vadagam, phenyle, iral pickle making and perfume sticks manufacturing in Thiruvaigundam Panchayat Union. The amount of loan ranged from Rs. 70,000/- to Rs. 4,40,000/- with 50 per cent subsidy.

Loans were provided to 10 SHGs in Alvarthirunagar PU under SGSY during 1999-2000. The amount of loan ranged from Rs. 1,04,000 to Rs. 2,59,600 for the enterprises of mini dairy, palm frond mat weaving and fish pickle making.

Only 3 SHGs were benifited from the SGSY loans in Thiruchendur PU during 1999-2000. The amount of loan ranged from Rs. 1,00,000 to Rs. 2,32,600 for the enterprises of mini dairy, readymade garments and palm frond mat making.The total amount of loan was Rs. 4,36,000, of which Rs. 2,18,000 was subsidy and the amount of repayable loan was Rs. 2,18,000. Subsidy was provided @ 50 per cent per unit.

6. Udangudi Panchayat Union

Eight SHGs were benefited from loans provided under SGSY during 1999-2000 in Udangudi PU. The amount of loan ranged from Rs. 90,000 to Rs. 3,03,000 with subsidy @ 50 per cent. The loans were provided for enterprises such as mat weaving, goat rearing, mini dairy and palm sugar cake making. The total amount of loan was Rs.17,88,760, of which subsidy was of Rs. 8,94,330 and the remaining amount of Rs. 8,94,380 was loan. The average amount of subsidy was Rs. 1,11,797.

The SGSY scheme provided loans to SHGs during 1999-2000 in Sathankulam PU. The amount of loan was Rs. 1,00,000 for 5 SHGs and Rs. 2,14,000 for 3 SHGs with 50 per cent subsidy. The enterprises proposed for the loan were palm products manufacturing and mini dairy. The total amount of loan provided was Rs.11,42,000, of which Rs. 5,71,000 was the amount of subsidy and the remaining amount of Rs.5,71,000 was the loan. The average amount of subsidy was Rs. 71,375 for an SHG.

Table 3.43 : Sathankulam Panchayat Union.

Sl. No.	*SHG Name*	*Enterprise*	*Total Amount*	*Subsidy*	*Loan*	*Bank Name*
1.	Dowcra Kulu	Palm products	100000	50000	50000	Indian Bank, Pattukkapathu
2.	Dowcra Kulu	Palm products	100000	50000	50000	Indian Bank, Pattukkapathu
3.	Dowcra Kulu	Palm products	100000	50000	50000	Tamil Nadu Mercantile Bank, Kommatikkottai
4.	Dowcra Kulu	Palm products	100000	50000	50000	Indian Bank, Pattukkapathu
5.	Dowcra Kulu	Palm products	100000	50000	50000	Tamil Nadu Mercantile Bank, Kommatikkottai
6.	Penkal	Mini dairy	214000	107000	107000	Canara Bank, Muthalur
7.	Mahalir	Mini dairy	214000	107000	107000	Canara Bank, Muthalur
8.	Mahalir	Mini dairy	214000	107000	107000	Canara Bank, Muthalur

Source : DRDA, Thoothukudi.

Table 3.44 : Kovilpatti Panchayat Union.

Sl. No.	*SHG Name*	*Enterprise*	*Total Amount*	*Subsidy*	*Loan*	*Bank Name*
1.	Thirisuli Penkal	Goat rearing	210000	105000	105000	Pandian Grama Bank, Kovilpatti
2.	Docra Kulu	Readymade garments	150000	75000	75000	Pandian Grama Bank, Kovilpatti
3.	Docra Kulu	Mini dairy	224000	112000	112000	Canara Bank, Ettaiyapuram

Source : DRDA, Thoothukudi.

Table 3.45 : Kayatharu Panchayat Union.

Sl. No.	*SHG Name*	*Enterprise*	*Total Amount*	*Subsidy*	*Loan*	*Bank Name*
1.	Annaitherasa Mahalirkulu	Match box making	248200	124100	124100	Bharat State Bank, Therkkukonarkottai
2.	Dokrakulu	Match box making	180400	90200	90200	Bharath State Bank, Therkkukonarkottai
3.	Dokrakulu	Goat rearing	180000	90000	90000	Canara Bank, Kalampatti
4.	Dokrakulu	Mini dairy	265200	140200	125000	Pandian Grama Bank, Kayatharu
5.	Dokrakulu	Goat rearing	285000	160000	125000	Central Bank of India, Kalukumalai

Source : DRDA, Thoothukudi.

Table 3.46 : Ottapidaram Panchayat Union.

Sl. No.	SHG Name	Enterprise	Total Amount	Subsidy	Loan	Bank Name
1.	Annaitherasa Matharsangam	Mini dairy unit	204000	102000	102000	Pandian Grama Bank, Akkayanayakkan Patti
2.	Dokrakulu	Mini dairy unit	272000	147000	125000	Pandian Grama Bank, Pasuvandanai
3.	Malligaimandram	Goat rearing	294500	169500	125000	Bharat State Bank, Savarimangalam
4.	Pasumbon Muthuramalinga thevar Suyauthavikkulu	Mini dairy unit	272000	147000	125000	Central Bank of India, Kadampur
5.	Subashchandraboss Suyauthavikkulu	Mini dairy unit	255000	130000	125000	Central Bank of India Kadampur
6.	Jansi Mahalirmandram	Mini dairy unit	340000	215000	125000	Indian Overseas Bank, Ebothumvendran
7.	Deepaoli Mahalirmandram	Mini dairy unit	322500	197500	125000	Indian Overseas Bank, Ebothumventran
8.	Silambu Mahalirmandram	Mini dairy unit	340000	215000	125000	Indian Overseas Bank, Ebothumventran
9.	Vinmathi Mahalirmandram	Readymade garments	200000	100000	100000	Tamil Nadu Mercandile Bank, Puthiyambuthur
10.	Niraimathi Mahalirmandram	Readymade garments	200000	100000	100000	Tamil Nadu Mercandile Bank, Puthiyambuthur
11.	Vanmathi Mahalirmandram	Readymade garments	200000	100000	100000	Tamil Nadu Mercandile Bank, Puthiyambuthur
12.	Vennila Mahalirmandram	Readymade garments	200000	100000	100000	Tamil Nadu Mercandile Bank, Puthiyambuthur
13.	Koseri Mahalirmandram	Readymade garments	255000	130000	125000	Pandian Grama Bank, Ottapitaram
14.	Kangai Mahalirmandram	Readymade garments	255000	130000	125000	Pandian Grama Bank, Ottapitram

Source : DRDA, Thoothukudi.

Table 3.47 : Vilathikulam Panchayat Union.

Sl. No.	*SHG Name*	*Enterprise*	*Total Amount*	*Subsidy*	*Loan*	*Bank Name*
1.	Roja	Charcoal making	250000	125000	125000	Bharat State Bank
2.	Malligai	Charcoal making	250000	125000	125000	Bharat State Bank
3.	Mullai	Goat rearing	250000	125000	125000	Bharat State Bank
4.	Annaitherasa	Goat rearing	250000	125000	125000	Pandian Grama Bank
5.	Kalukachala Puram	Charcoal making	250000	125000	125000	Canara Bank
6.	Kalukachala Puram aduvalarppukulu	Goat rearing	250000	125000	125000	Canara Bank
7.	Om sakthi Kulu	Charcoal making	250000	125000	125000	Canara Bank
8.	Therkku Pudupatti karimuttam thayarikkumkulu	Charcoal making	250000	125000	125000	Canara Bank
9.	Dowcra Kulu	Palm frond products	150000	75000	75000	Pandian Grama Bank
10.	Vidya Mahalir Kulu	Mini dairy	250000	125000	125000	Pandian Grama Bank

Source : DRDA, Thoothukudi.

Table 3.48 : Pudur Panchayat Union.

Sl. No.	*SHG Name*	*Enterprise*	*Total Amount*	*Subsidy*	*Loan*	*Bank Name*
1.	Tensilar Mahalirmandram	Match industry	220000	110000	110000	Tamil Nadu Mercandile Bank
2.	Fransis Mahalirmandram	Match industry	220000	110000	110000	Tamil Nadu Mercandile Bank
3.	Samuga Nalaiyakkam	Paddy and chilli preservation for sales	240000	120000	120000	Tamil Nadu Mercandile Bank
4.	Jancirani Magalir Mandram	Match industry	220000	110000	110000	Tamil Nadu Mercandile Bank
5.	Samuga Nala Mandram	Charcoal making	240000	120000	120000	Tamil Nadu Mercandile Bank
6.	Annai Therasa Magalir Mandram	Match industry	220000	110000	110000	Tamil Nadu Mercandile Bank
7.	Bharathi Suya Udhavi Kulu	Milch animals	250000	125000	125000	Indian Overseas Bank, Nagalapuram
8.	Balan Suya Uthavi Kulu	Milch animals	250000	125000	125000	Indian Overseas Bank, Nagalapuram
9.	Victoriya Suya Uthavi kulu	Palm frond products	240000	120000	120000	Tamilnadu Mercantile Bank, Pudur
10.	Vennila Suya Uthavi Kulu	Milch animals	250000	125000	125000	Indian Overseas Bank, Nagalapuram
11.	Gandhi Suya Uthavi Kulu	Milch animals	250000	125000	125000	Indian Overseas Bank, Nagalapuram

Source : DRDA, Thoothukudi.

Only 3 SHGs were provided with loan including 50 per cent subsidy under SGSY during 1999-2000 in Kovilpatti PU. The amount of loan were Rs. 2,10,000, Rs. 1,50,000 and Rs. 2,24,000 for the enterprising purposed of readymade garments, goat rearing and mini dairy. The total amount of loan was Rs. 5,84,000 of which Rs. 2,92,000 was the amount of loan. The average amount of subsidy was Rs. 97,300 for a SHG.

Five SHGs were benefited from SGSY loans in Kayatharu PU during 1999-2000. The amount of loan ranged from Rs.1,80,000 to Rs. 2,85,000 with a subsidy of 50 per cent. The enterprises purposed were match box making, goat rearing and mini dairy units. The total amount of loan was Rs.11,58,800. The amount of subsidy was Rs. 5,79,400 and the amount of loan was Rs. 5,79,400. The average amount of subsidy for a SHG was Rs. 1,15,880.

During 1999-2000, 14 SHGs received loans with 50 per cent subsidy under SGSY in Ottapidaram PU. The amount of loan ranged from Rs. 2,00,000 to Rs. 3,40,000 for the enterprising purpose of mini dairy units, normal dairy units. readymade garments, goat rearing and milch animals rearing. The total amount of loan was Rs. 36,10,000. As the subsidy fixed @ 50 per cent, the subsidy amount was Rs. 18,05,000 and the remaining amount of Rs. 13,05,000 was the loan. The average subsidy amount for a SHG was Rs. 1,28,900.

Ten SHGs were benefited from SGSY loans in Vilathikulam PU during 1999-2000. The amounts of loan were Rs.1,50,000 for one SHGs and Rs. 2,50,000 for 9 SHGs. The enterprises proposed were charcoal making, palm frond products, goat rearing and mini dairy. The total amount of loan was Rs. 24,00,000. The subsidy and the loan were Rs.12,00,000 each. The average amount of subsidy for a SHG was Rs.1,20,000.

Eleven SHGs received loans with 50 per cent subsidy under SGSY during 1999-2000 for enterprises such as paddy and chilli preservation for sales, match industry, charcoal making, palm frond products and milch animals. The total amount of loan was Rs. 26,00,000, of which Rs. 12,00,000 was subsidy and Rs. 12,00,000 was loan. The average amount of subsidy for a SHG was Rs. 1,18,200.

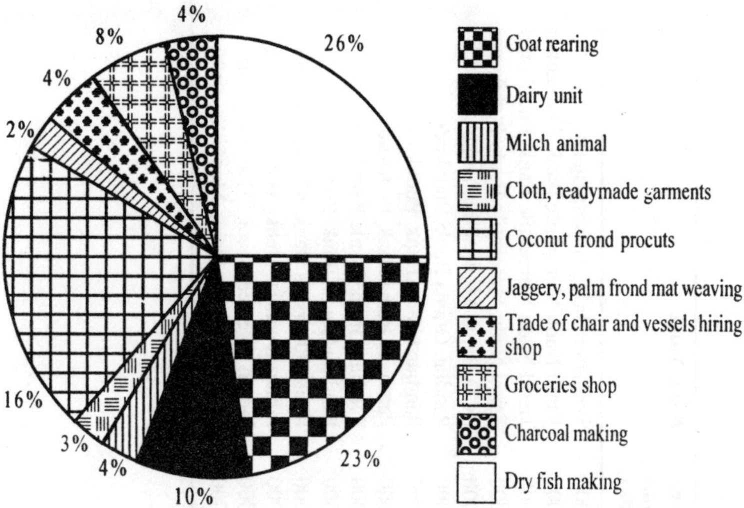

Fig. : Major Trades of SHGs.

REVOLVING FUND

This part of the analysis discuss the details of the SHGs which received revolving fund from various banks such as Syndicate Bank, Tamil Nadu Mercantile Bank, UCO Bank, Pandian Grama Bank, Indian Overseas Bank, Canara Bank and State Bank. The amount of revolving fund for one SHG was Rs.10,000. During 1999-2000, 14 SHGs in Thoothukudi PU, 33 SHGs in Karungalakudi PU, 4 SHGs in Thiruvaikundam PU, 8 SHGs in Alvarthirunagari PU, 10 SHGs in Sathankulam PU, 5 SHGs in Kovilpatti PU, 6 SHGs in Kayatharu PU, 25 SHGs in Ottapidaram PU received revolving fund of Rs.10,000 each. No SHGs in Vilathikulam and Pudur Panchayat Unions had received revolving fund during 1999-2000. The total amount of revolving fund was Rs.13,60,000 for 136 SHGs in Thoothukudi District.

During 2000-2001, 3 SHGs in Thoothukudi PU, 19 SHGs in Karungulam PU and 10 SHGs in Thiruvaigundam PU received revolving fund of Rs.10,000 each. A total amount of revolving fund of Rs.3,20,000 was provided to 32 SHGs. The SHGs in the remaining 9 Panchayat Unions did not receive revolving fund during 2000-2001.

Table 3.49 : 1999 – 2000 (Thoothukudi).

Sl. No.	*SHG Name*	*Revolving Fund (Rs.)*	*Bank Name*
1.	Semparuthi Sakothara Valvu Sangam North Kalankarai	10000	Syndicate Bank, Thuraimugam
2.	Alwin Mahalir Mandram, Siluvaipuram	10000	Tamil Nadu Mercantile Bank, Pudukottai
3.	Thalampoo Sakothara Valvu Sangam, Mangalagiri	10000	Tamil Nadu Mercantile Bank, Pudukottai
4.	Vadamalli Sakothara Valvu Sangam, Ramachandrapuram	10000	Tamil Nadu Mercantile Bank, Pudukottai
5.	Manoranjitham Sakothara Valvu Sangam, Allkulam	10000	UCO Bank, Mudivaithonenthal
6.	Sevanthipoo Sakothara Valvu Sangam, Indira Nagar	10000	Pandian Grama Bank, Pudukudi
7.	Samanthipoo Sakothara Valvu Sangam, Thiraviyapuram	10000	Pandian Grama Bank, Pudukudi
8.	Kanagambrampoo Sakothara Valvu Sangam, Maravanmadam	10000	Pandian Grama Bank, Pudukudi
9.	Pitchipoo Sakothara Valvu Sangam, South Kalangarai	10000	Pandian Grama Bank, Pudukudi
10.	Thamaraipoo Sakothara Valvu Sangam, South Silukkanpatti	10000	Pandian Grama Bank, Pudukudi
11.	Indira Mahalir Mandram, Mela Alagapuri	10000	Indian Overseas Bank, Mappilliayurani
12.	Gopuram Mahalir Mandram, Kothanar Colony	10000	Indian Overseas Bank, Mappilliayurani
13.	Alli Mahalir Mandram, Ganapathy Nagar	10000	Indian Overseas Bank, Mappilliayurani
14.	Alagu Mutharamman Mahalir Mandram, Karuppasami Nagar	10000	Indian Overseas Bank, Mappilliayurani

Source : DRDA, Thoothukudi.

Table 3.50 : Karungulam

Sl. No.	*SHG Name*	*Revolving Fund (Rs.)*	*Bank Name*
1	**2**	**3**	**4**
1.	Ulaikkum Pengal Munnetra Sangam, Pakkapatti	10000	Indian Overseas Bank, Vallanadu
2.	Ulaikkum Pengal Munnetra Sangam, Sethuramalingapuram	10000	Indian Overseas Bank, Vallanadu
3.	Ulaikkum Pengal Munnetra Sangam, Idamaruthan Puliankulam	10000	Indian Overseas Bank, Vallanadu
4.	Ulaikkum Pengal Munnetra Sangam, (Keela Vallanadu)	10000	Indian Overseas Bank, Vallanadu
5.	Ulaikkum Pengal Munnetra Sangam, Navalkattankulam (Vadą Vallanadu)	10000	Indian Overseas Bank, Vallanadu
6.	Ulaikkum Pengal Munnetra Sangam, (Kaliyavoor)	10000	Indian Overseas Bank, Vallanadu
7.	Ulaikkum Pengal Munnetra Sangam, (Vallanadu)	10000	Indian Overseas Bank, Vallanadu
8.	Ulaikkum Pengal Munnetra Sangam, Seetharkulam (Keelavallanadu)	10000	Indian Overseas Bank, Chekkarakudi
9.	Ulaikkum Pengal Munnetra Sangam, Alantha	10000	Pandian Grama Bank, Akkanaickenpatti
10.	Thendral Gramodaya Mahalir Mandram, South karaseri	10000	UCO Bank, Karungulam
11.	Indira Sakothara Valvu Sangam, Keelaputhaneri	10000	Indian Overseas Bank, Vallanadu
12.	Annai Therasa Gramodaya Mahalir Mandram, Keelaputhaneri	10000	Indian Overseas Bank, Vallanadu
13.	Pitchipoo Gramodaya Mahalir Mandram, Mela Thoothukuli	10000	Pandian Grama Bank, Seithunganallur
14.	Ulaikkum Pengal Munnetra Sangam, Singathakurichi	10000	Indian Overseas Bank, Chekkarudi
15.	Ulaikkum Pengal Munnetra Sangam, Deivaseyalpuram	10000	Indian Overseas Bank, Chekkarudi
16.	Ulaikkum Pengal Munnetra Sangam, Kaliyavoor	10000	Indian Overseas Bank, Vallanadu
17.	Ulaikkum Pengal Munnetra Sangam, Nanalkattankulam	10000	Indian Overseas Bank, Vallanadu

(Table Contd. ...)

(Contd. ...)

1	2	3	4
18.	Ulaikkum Pengal Munnetra Sangam, Vallakulam	10000	Indian Overseas Bank, Vallanadu
19.	Ulaikkm Pengal Munnetra Sangam, Seetharkulam	10000	Indian Overseas Bank, Chekkarudi
20.	Ulaikkum Pengal Munnetra Sangam, Athikadu	10000	Indian Overseas Bank, Vallanadu
21.	Ulaikkum Pengal Munnetra Sangam, Manakkarai	10000	State Bank of India, Thiruvaigundam
22.	Ulaikkum Pengal Munnetra Sangam, Udaiyarkulam	10000	Indian Overseas Bank, Vallanadu
23.	Ulaikkum Pengal Munnetra Sangam, Sethuramalingapuram	10000	Indian Overseas Bank, Vallanadu
24.	Ulaikkum Pengal Munnetra Sangam, Pakkapatti	10000	Indian Overseas Bank, Vallanadu
25.	Muneeswarar Gramodaya Sarvodaya Seva Sangam, Kuyavan Colony	10000	Pandian Grama Bank, Seithunganallur
26.	Roja Gramodaya Sarvodaya Seva Sangam, Anna Nagar	10000	Pandian Grama Bank, Seithunganallur
27.	Pitchipoo Gramodaya Sarvodaya Seva Sangam, Muthalankurichi	10000	Pandian Grama Bank, Seithunganallur
28.	Thamarai Gramodaya Sarvodaya Seva Sangam, Muthalankurichi	10000	Pandian Grama Bank, Seithunganallur
29.	Nehru Gramodaya Sarvodaya Seva Sangam, Alikudi	10000	Pandian Grama Bank, Seithunganallur
30.	Natchathiram Gramodaya Sarvodaya Seva Sangam, South Karaseri Colony	10000	Indian Overseas Bank, Ramanujampudur
31.	Thendral Gramodaya Sarvodaya Seva Sangam, Kurukalkottai	10000	UCO Bank, Karunkulam
32.	Marutham Mahalir Mandram, Puliyankulam	10000	UCO Bank, Karunkulam
33.	Annai Therasa Mahalir Suya Uthavi Kulu, Puliyankulam	10000	UCO Bank, Karunkulam
34.	Malligai Pengal Suya Uthavi Kulu, Thiruvarangampatti	10000	UCO Bank, Karunkulam

Source : DRDA, Thoothukudi.

Table 3.51 : Thiruvaigundam.

Sl. No.	*SHG Name*	*Revolving Fund (Rs.)*	*Bank Name*
1.	Mahalir Kulu, Thiruppanichettikulam	10000	Indian Overseas Bank, Sayarpuram
2.	Mullai Pengal Suya Uthavi Kulu, Nattathi	10000	Pandian Grama Bank, Sebathaiapuram
3.	Valarpirai Suya Uthavi Kulu, Soolaivaikal	10000	Canara Bank, Eral
4.	Senthamil Mahalir Suya Uthavi Kulu, Siruthondanallur	10000	Tamil Nadu Mercantile Bank, Siruthondanallur

Source : DRDA, Thoothukudi.

Table 3.52 : Alwarthirunagari.

Sl. No.	*SHG Name*	*Revolving Fund (Rs.)*	*Bank Name*
1.	Annai Mahalir Mandram, Sethukkuvaithan	10000	Canara Bank, Athur
2.	Parvathi Mahalir Suya Uthavi Kulu, Kadambankulam, Karungadal	10000	Pandian Grama Bank, Srivenkatesapuram
3.	Sakthi Mahalir Suya Uthavi Kulu, Mela Puliyankulam	10000	Pandian Grama Bank, Srivenkatesapuram
4.	Pengal Suya Uthavi Kulu, North Elamalkulam, Karunkadal	10000	Pandian Grama Bank, Srivenkatesapuram
5.	Karpagatharu Suya Uthavi Kulu, Sembankudiyiruppu	10000	Pandian Grama Bank, Srivenkatesapuram
6.	Pushpam mahalir Suya Uthavi Kulu, Ganapathy Nagar	10000	Pandian Grama Bank, Srivenkatesapuram
7.	Kalaivani Mahalir Suya Uthavi Kulu, Kattarimangalam Colony	10000	Pandian Grama Bank, Srivenkatesapuram
8.	Karpagatharu Suya Uthavi Kulu, Karuvelampadu	10000	Indian Overseas Bank, Sathankulam

Source : DRDA, Thoothukudi.

Table 3.53 : Thiruchenthur

Sl. No.	*SHG Name*	*Revolving Fund (Rs.)*	*Bank Name*
1.	Anthoniyar Mahalir Suya Uthavi Kulu, Adaikkalapuram	10000	Canara Bank, Arumuganeri
2.	Christhuraja Pengal Suya Uthavi Kulu, Bilomina Nagar	10000	Canara Bank, Arumuganeri
3.	Thamarai Mahalir Suya Uthavi Kulu, Pitchivilai	10000	Indian Overseas Bank, Thiruchendur
4.	Sarojini Mahalir Suya Uthavi Kulu, Melanagakannipuram	10000	State Bank of India, Kurumbur
5.	Bilominarl Suya Uthavi Kulu, Bilomi Nagar	10000	Canara Bank, Arumuganeri
6.	Anthoniyar Mahalir Suya Uthavi Kulu, Sebasthiar Nagar	10000	Canara Bank, Arumuganeri
7.	Joseph B Mahalir Suya Uthavi Kulu, Adaikkalapuram	10000	Canara Bank, Arumuganeri
8.	Santhiamman Suya Uthavi Kulu, Kayamozhi	10000	Indian Overseas Bank, Thiruchendur
9.	Mutharamman Suya Uthavi Kulu, Pitchivilai	10000	Indian Overseas Bank, Thiruchendur
10.	Suryagandhiamman Suya Uthavi Kulu, Ammanpuram	10000	State Bank of India, Udankudi

Source : DRDA, Thoothukudi.

Table 3.54 : Udankudi.

Sl. No.	*SHG Name*	*Revolving Fund (Rs.)*	*Bank Name*
1.	Josmin Mahalir Suya Uthavi Kulu, Latchimipuram	10000	Tamil Nadu Mercantile Bank, Meygnanapuram
2.	Thalampoo Mahalir Suya Uthavi Kulu, Thandavankadu	10000	Canara Bank, Udankudi
3.	Star Mahalir Suya Uthavi Kulu, Karankadu	10000	Canara Bank, Udankudi
4.	Santhanamari Pengal Suya Uthavi Kulu, Vijayanarayanapuram	10000	State Bank of India, Udankudi
5.	Mariamman Mahalir Suya Uthavi Kulu, Vijayanarayanapuram	10000	State Bank of India, Udankudi
6.	Karpagatharu Pengal Suya Uthavi Kulu, Valliammanpuram	10000	Pandian Grama Bank, Semmarikulam
7.	Roja Mahalir Suya Uthavi Kulu, Sathya Nagar	10000	Pandian Grama Bank, Semmarikulam
8.	Karpagatharu Mahalir Mandram-1 Kuthiraimozhi	10000	Indian Overseas Bank, Paramankurichi
9.	Karpagatharu Mahalir Mandram-2 Kuthiraimozhi	10000	Indian Overseas Bank, Paramankurichi
10.	Karpagatharu Mahalir Mandram, Athiyakurichi – Ramasamipuram	10000	State Bank of India, Udankudi
11.	Karpagatharu Mahalir Mandram, Vethakottaivilai	10000	Canara Bank, Udankudi
12.	Karpagatharu Mahalir Mandram, Gnananiar Kudiyiruppu	10000	State Bank of India, Udankudi
13.	Karpagatharu Mahalir Mandram, Thithapuram	10000	State Bank of India, Udankudi
14.	Karpagatharu Mahalir Mandram, Athiyadithattu	10000	State Bank of India, Udankudi
15.	Karpagatharu Mahalir Mandram, Mathavankurichi	10000	Canara Bank, Udankudi
		10000	Canara Bank, Udankudi

Source : DRDA, Thoothukudi.

Table 3.55 : Sattankulam

Sl. No.	*SHG Name*	*Revolving Fund (Rs.)*	*Bank Name*
1.	Weeds Mahalir Suya Uthavi Kulu, Kadatchapuram	10000	Canara Bank, Muthaloor
2.	Weeds Mahalir Suya Uthavi Kulu, Shenbagapuram	10000	Canara Bank, Muthaloor
3.	Weeds Mahalir Suya Uthavi Kulu, Pothakkalanvilai	10000	Canara Bank, Muthaloor
4.	Weeds Mahalir Suya Uthavi Kulu, Athikadu	10000	Canara Bank, Muthaloor
5.	Weeds Mahalir Suya Uthavi Kulu, Chokkalingapuram	10000	Canara Bank, Muthaloor
6.	Mahalir Suya Uthavi Kulu, Anbinnagaram – 1	10000	Canara Bank, Muthaloor
7.	Mahalir Suya Uthavi Kulu, Vellaiammalpuram	10000	Canara Bank, Muthaloor
8.	Mahalir Suya Uthavi Kulu, Athikadu	10000	Canara Bank, Muthaloor
9.	Mahalir Suya Uthavi Kulu, Dharmapuri Colony (Veppankadu)	10000	Canara Bank, Muthaloor
10.	Mahalir Suya Uthavi Kulu, Pothakalan Colony – 2	10000	Canara Bank, Muthaloor
11.	Mahalir Suya Uthavi Kulu, Muthaloor	10000	Canara Bank, Muthaloor
12.	Mahalir Suya Uthavi Kulu, Rajamannarpuram	10000	Canara Bank, Muthaloor
13.	Mahalir Suya Uthavi Kulu, Anbinnagaam – 2	10000	Canara Bank, Muthaloor
14.	Mahalir Suya Uthavi Kulu, Shanmugapuram	10000	Canara Bank, Muthaloor
15.	Selaikkiapuram Mahalir Suya Uthavi Kulu, Sasthavinallur	10000	Canara Bank, Muthaloor
		10000	Canara Bank, Muthaloor

Source : DRDA, Thoothukudi.

Table 3.56 : Kovilpatti

Sl. No.	*SHG Name*	*Revolving Fund (Rs.)*	*Bank Name*
1.	Annai Therasa Mahalir Suya Uthavi Kulu, Nalattinpudur	10000	Pandian Grama Bank, Nalattinpudur
2.	Kalaimagal Suya Uthavi Kulu, Peekkilipatti	10000	Pandian Grama Bank, Kovilpatti
3.	Malaiamman Mahalir Suya Uthavi Kulu, Sinthalakarai	10000	Pandian Grama Bank, Ettaiyapuram
4.	Madathiamman Mahalir Suya Uthavi Kulu. R.Venkateswaram	10000	Pandian Grama Bank, Ettaiyapuram
5.	Ambigai Mahalir Suya Uthavi Kulu, Meenatchipuram	10000	Pandian Grama Bank, Kovilpatti

Source : DRDA, Thoothukudi.

Table 3.57 : Kayathar

Sl. No.	*SHG Name*	*Revolving Fund (Rs.)*	*Bank Name*
1.	Malli Malar Suya Uthavi Kulu, Kappulingampatti	10000	Central Bank of India, Kadambur
2.	Annai Therasa Mahalir Mandram, Akilandapuram	10000	Pandian Grama Bank, Kayathar
3.	Roja Mahalir Suya Uthavi Kulu, Balaiahpuram	10000	Pandian Grama Bank, Kayathar
4.	Annai Therasa Mathar Sangam, Chithambarampatti	10000	Pandian Grama Bank, Kayathar
5.	Annai Indira Mahalir Mandram, Mudukkalankulam	10000	Pandian Grama Bank, Kovilpatti
6.	Kamalam Mahalir Mandram, Mudukkalankulam	10000	Pandian Grama Bank, Kovilpatti

Source : DRDA, Thoothukudi.

Table 3.58 : Ottapidaram

Sl. No.	*SHG Name*	*Revolving Fund (Rs.)*	*Bank Name*
1.	Annai Therasa Mahalir Mandram, Govinthapuram	10000	Pandian Grama Bank, Akkanaickenpatti
2.	Selvam Mahalir Mandram, Keela Mudiman	10000	Pandian Grama Bank, Pasuvanthanai
3.	Indira Mahalir Mandram, Keela Mudiman	10000	Pandian Grama Bank, Pasuvanthanai
4.	Subash Chandrabose Suya Uthavi Kulu, Onamakkulam	10000	Central Bank of India, Kadambur
5.	Pasumpon Muthuramalingathevar Suya Uthavi Kulu, Onamakulam	10000	Central Bank of India, Kadambur
6.	Malligai Mahalir Mandram, S. Pudur	10000	State Bank of India, Savarimangalam
7.	Vinmathi Mahalir Mandram, Puthiamputhur	10000	Tamil Nadu Mercantile Bank, Puthiamputhur
8.	Vennila Mahalir Mandram, Puthiamputhur	10000	Tamil Nadu Mercantile Bank, Puthiamputhur
9.	Vanmathi Mahalir Mandram, Puthiamputhur	10000	Tamil Nadu Mercantile Bank, Puthiamputhur
10.	Niraimathi Mahalir Mandram, Puthiamputhur	10000	Tamil Nadu Mercantile Bank, Puthiamputhur
11.	Jansi Mahalir Mandram, Sinthalakattai	10000	Indian Overseas Bank. Eppothumvendran
12.	Deepaoli Mahalir Mandram, Sinthalakattai	10000	Indian Overseas Bank. Eppothumvendran
13.	Silambu Mahalir Mandram, Ramachandrapuram	10000	Indian Overseas Bank. Eppothumvendran
14.	Avarampoo Suya Uthavi Kulu – 1, South Avarankadu	10000	Pandian Grama Bank, Ottapidaram
15.	Avarampoo Suya Uthavi Kulu – 2, South Avarankadu	10000	Pandian Grama Bank, Ottapidaram
16.	Pengal Suya Uthavi Kulu – 1, North Avarankadu	10000	Pandian Grama Bank, Ottapidaram
17.	Pengal Suya Uthavi Kulu – 2, North Avarankadu	10000	Pandian Grama Bank, Ottapidaram
18.	Pengal Suya Uthavi Kulu – 3, North Avarangadu	10000	Pandian Grama Bank, Ottapidaram
19.	Neithal Mahalir Suya Uthavi Kulu, K. Thalavaipuram	10000	Pandian Grama Bank, Ottapidaram
20.	Marutham Mahalir Suya Uthavi Kulu, K. Thalavaipuram	10000	Pandian Grama Bank, Ottapidaram
21.	Pengal Suya Uthavi Kulu – 1, Melameenakshipuram	10000	Pandian Grama Bank, Ottapidaram
22.	Pengal Suya Uthavi Kulu – 2, Melameenakshipuram	10000	Pandian Grama Bank, Ottapidaram
23.	Pengal Suya Uthavi Kulu – 1, Kulasekaranallur	10000	Pandian Grama Bank, Ottapidaram
24.	Marikkolunthu Mahalir Suya Uthavi Kulu – 1, Kappikulam	10000	Pandian Grama Bank, Pasuvanthanai
25.	Pengal Suya Uthavi Kulu, Kappikulam	10000	Pandian Grama Bank, Pasuvanthanai

Source : DRDA, Thoothukudi.

Table 3.59 : 2000 - 2001 (Thoothukudi)

Sl. No.	*SHG Name*	*Revolving Fund (Rs.)*	*Bank Name*
1.	Arul Mahalir Mandram, Ri.Saveriarpuram	10000	Palanokku Samuka Sevai Sangam, Thoothukudi
2.	Roja Mahalir Mandram, Ri.Saveriarpuram	10000	Palanokku Samuka Sevai Sangam, Thoothukudi
3.	Sivanthi Mahalir Mandram, Kuroospuram	10000	Palanokku Samuka Sevai Sangam, Thoothukudi
4.	Anista Mahalir Mandram, Rajapalayam	10000	Palanokku Samuka Sevai Sangam, Thoothukudi
5.	Redrose Mahalir Mandram, Sameervias Nagar	10000	Palanokku Samuka Sevai Sangam, Thoothukudi
6.	Alphonsa Mahalir Mandram, Matha Nagar	10000	Palanokku Samuka Sevai Sangam, Thoothukudi
7.	Annai Mahalir Mandram, Matha Nagar	10000	Palanokku Samuka Sevai Sangam, Thoothukudi
8.	Jenista Mahalir Mandram, Rajapalayam	10000	Palanokku Samuka Sevai Sangam, Thoothukudi
9.	Selvam Mahalir Mandram, Sameervias Nagar, Thalamuthu Nagar	10000	Palanokku Samuka Sevai Sangam, Thoothukudi
10.	Saraswathi Mahalir Mandram, Siluvaipatti, Thalamuthu Nagar	10000	Palanokku Samuka Sevai Sangam, Thoothukudi
11.	Tensila Mahalir Mandram, Thalamuthu Nagar 3rd Group	10000	Palanokku Samuka Sevai Sangam, Thoothukudi
12.	Anbu Malar Mahalir Mandram, Anthoniyarpuram	10000	Tamil Nadu Mercantile Bank, Pudukottai
13.	Amutham Mahalir Mandram, Anthoniyarpuram	10000	Tamil Nadu Mercantile Bank, Pudukottai
14.	Agal Mahalir Mandram, Anthoniyarpuram	10000	Tamil Nadu Mercantile Bank, Pudukottai

Source : DRDA, Thoothukudi.

Table 3.60 : Karungulam.

Sl. No.	*SHG Name*	*Revolving Fund (Rs.)*	*Bank Name*
1.	Ulaikkum Pengal Munnetra Sangam, Akaram North Street	10000	Indian Overseas Bank, Vallanadu
2.	Ulaikkum Pengal Munnetra Sangam, North Karaseri	10000	Indian Overseas Bank, Sekkarakudi
3.	W.W.T.A. Alwarkarkulam	10000	Pandian Grama Bank, Thiruvaikundam
4.	W.W.T.A. Alwarkarkulam	10000	Pandian Grama Bank, Thiruvaikundam
5.	W.W.T.A. Alwarkarkulam	10000	Pandian Grama Bank, Thiruvaikundam
6.	W.W.T.A. Alwarkarkulam	10000	Pandian Grama Bank, Thiruvaikundam
7.	W.W.T.A. Puthumanai Theru, Konkaraya Kurichi	10000	Pandian Grama Bank, Thiruvaikundam
8.	W.W.T.A. Puthumanai Theru, Konkaraya Kurichi	10000	Pandian Grama Bank, Thiruvaikundam
9.	W.W.T.A. Thiruvalperumal Kovil Street Kongarayakurichi	10000	Pandian Grama Bank, Thiruvaikundam
10.	W.W.T.A. Nadu Theru, Kongarayakurichi	10000	Pandian Grama Bank, Thiruvaikundam
11.	W.W.T.A. Thiruvalperumal Kovil Street Kongarayakurichi	10000	Pandian Grama Bank, Thiruvaikundam
12.	W.W.T.A. Nadu Theru, Konkayakurichi	10000	Pandian Grama Bank, Thiruvaikundam
13.	Kurunchi Gramodaya Mahalir Suya Uthavi Kulu, Santhaiyadiyur, Seithunganallur	10000	Pandian Grama Bank, Seithunganallur
14.	Kurunchi Gramodaya Mahalir Suya Uthavi Kulu, Melathuthukuli	10000	Pandian Grama Bank, Seithunganallur
15.	Beema Gramodaya Mahalir Suya Uthavi Kulu, V. Kovilpathu, Seithunganallur	10000	Pandian Grama Bank, Seithunganallur
16.	Ulaikkum Pengal Munnetra Sangam, Melatheru, Kasilingapuram	10000	Indian Overseas Bank, Sekkarakudi
17.	Ulaikkum Pengal Munnetra Sangam, Alagapuri	10000	Pandian Grama Bank, Sekkarakkudi
18.	Roja Gramodaya Suya Uthavi Kulu, South Karaseri	10000	UCO Bank, Karunkulam
19.	Pavurnami Gramodaya Suya Uthavi Kulu, South Karaseri	10000	UCO Bank, Karunkulam
20.	Ulaikkum Pengal Munnetra Sangam, Akaram North Street	10000	Indian Overseas Bank, Vallanadu
21.	Ulaikkum Pengal Munnetra Sangam, North Karaseri	10000	Indian Overseas Bank, Sekkarakudi

Source : DRDA, Thoothukudi.

Table 3.61 : Thiruvaikundam.

Sl. No.	*SHG Name*	*Revolving Fund (Rs.)*	*Bank Name*
1.	Appanachiar Suya Uthavi Kulu, Appankoil	10000	Pandian Grama Bank, Siakalai
2.	Indira Gandhi Suya Uthavi Kulu, Siruthondanallur (mottathatan vilai)	10000	Tamil Nadu Mercantile Bank, Siruthondanallur
3.	Senthamil Mahalir Mandram, Sakkammalpuram	10000	Tamil Nadu Mercantile Bank, Siruthondanallur
4.	Kamaraj Suya Uthavi Kulu, Siruthandanallur (Savukkai Keela Theru)	10000	Tamil Nadu Mercantile Bank, Siruthondanallur
5.	Rajiv Gandhi Suya Uthavi Kulu, Manalur	10000	Tamil Nadu Mercantile Bank, Siruthondanallur
6.	Sridevi Mahalir Suya Uthavi Kulu, Appankoil, Sivaramalingam	10000	Pandian Grama Bank, Sivakalai
7.	Tholavilli Amman Mahalir Suya Uthavi Kulu, Angunathapuram, Kaspa	10000	Pandian Grama Bank, Sivakalai
8.	Irattai Thiruppathi Mahalir Suya Uthavi Kulu, Mottachikudiyiruppu, Keelpidagai Kaspa	10000	Pandian Grama Bank, Sivakalai
9.	Thevarpiran Mahalir Suya Uthavi Kulu, Mottachikudiyuiruppu	10000	Pandian Grama Bank, Sivakalai
10.	Scott Mahalir Mandram, Kumarapuram, Nattathi Urantchi	10000	Pandian Grama Bank, Sivakalai

Source : DRDA, Thoothukudi.

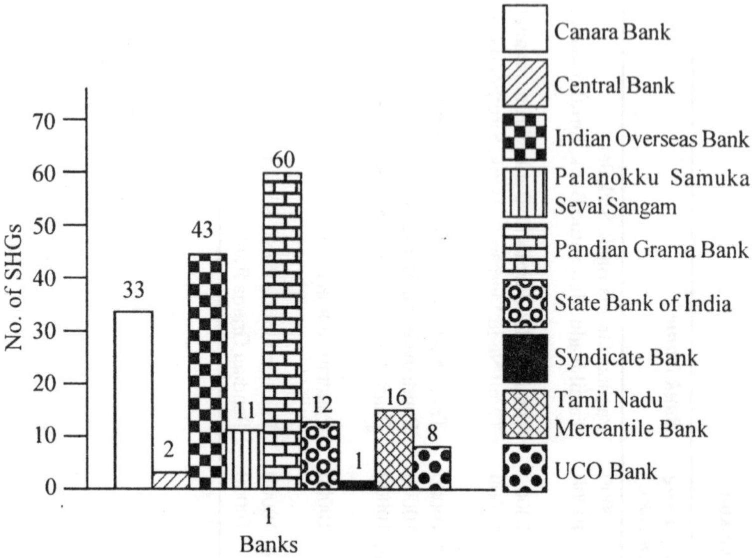

Fig. : Revolving Fund to SHGs.

Revolving Fund to SHGs

Bank Name	*No. of SHGs*
Canara Bank	33
Central Bank	2
Indian Overseas Bank	43
Palanokku Samuka Sevai Sangam	11
Pandian Grama Bank	60
State Bank of India	12
Syndicate Bank	1
Tamil Nadu Mercantile Bank	16
UCO Bank	8
Total	**186**

Source : Computed.

4 STORIES OF SHGs' ENTERPRISES IN THOOTHUKUDI

1. Palm Candies

(Karpagatharu Women Self-Help Groups, Karuvelampatti, Alwarthirunagari – Thoothukudi)

Karuvelmpatti is a remote village situated in Alwarthirunagari Block, Thoothukudi District. Its population depends mainly upon palm trees. Since the income generated from palmyra was considerably low, men and women of Karuvelampatti switched over to employment as migrant coolies. In spite of the migration their monthly income constituted around Rs.750-1150 only. A sudden boon resulted after clubbing the women under a single roof as SHG. This was the best recourse against poverty as they feel now. These SHG women decided to shine from their own land and with the resources available with them. They succeeded in attacking poverty by taking the support of the government.

A prominent NGO, CEDCO, with the support of the District Rural Development Agency, Thoothukudi, brought the women under a single fold towards the target of earning and saving among themselves. These enthusiastic women members were assisted with revolving fund of Rs. 25000 under the SGSY Scheme. This brought the members to the peak of success. The members engaged themselves in full sprit in manufacturing palm candy products and palm jaggery. Special training in preparation was given to them at Marthandam by the District Rural Development Agency, Thoothukudi. Since their previous occupation was wholly dependent on palmyra they had full confidence in their success. Although palm candies are seasonal products, they had learnt to maintain their earnings in non-seasonal periods also.

The decision to launch a new business yielded a monthly income of Rs.1900-4500 per head. Their monthly production of palm candies reached around 150 to 200 kg. and jaggery to around 130 to 150 kg. Their monthly sales reached around 130 to 140 kg and annual sales around 825 kg. This made them hire a building exclusively for production with electrification. The members have decided to construct their own building for their production unit in the near future. At present they have 60 set boxes for palm candies and basement stores with adequate utensils for preparation.

Previously the members were forced to borrow money at high rates of interest and the families struggled for daily meals. But now the entire scene has changed. The members were able to settle their former debts. The living standard of the SHG members has been raised considerably. They are able to educate their children through their earnings. This kindled them to work at full swing increasing their production and widening their market upto Thiruppur and Coimbatore. There is a high demand for palm candies because people have begun to realize the medicinal value of palm candies and jaggery.

Apart from this work, the SHG members are also engaged in social activities. They have streamlined the delivery of services. Observing the activities of their members a "Certificate of Appreciation" was given to them by the Indian Overseas Bank, Sattankulam, in the year 2000 – 2001 in order to recognize their success and to appreciate their prompt settlement of loans. Everybody is confident that they would solve all their problems. They are in a mood to share the excitement of their struggle and success. They recognize that opportunities are abundant and they have to be utilized by the needy.

If an analysis is made on the factors which are responsible for the success three can be listed immediately. They are: aspiration to earn and make achievements; the new venture that they have undertaken on their traditional work for their livelihood; and hardwork to bring success and repay the loan as they have repayment ethics to protect their self-dignity. The hope raised by the NGO with the support of the DRDA worked in the minds of the SHG women.

2. Palm Leaf Productions
(Mutharamman Women Self-Help Group, Sivaloor of Udangudi)

Palm products have their value even today. The members of the Fathima Women Self-Help Group, Kolasai, the India Women Self-Help Group, Kayamozhi, the Mutharamman Women Self-Help Group, Sivaloor of Udangudi, Jeva Oli Mahalir Mandram Nagala-puram Pudur and the Women Self-Help Group, Kayamozhi, Tiru-chendur, of Thoothukudi District are engaged in processing palm leaf products.

The moment women are united functionally their aspiration to achieve has increased tremendously. They are conscious of their self-dignity and they want to raise their social status. They found out self-employment in the only way and, hence, they pursued the option of taking up some works which are known to them. Using the united power the members decided to purchase the dried palm leaves in bulk at a cheap rate. In order to assist them the District Rural Development Agency granted them a revolving fund of Rs. 25, 000. The total fund was invested in purchase of raw materials and building. Some utilized the fund for repaying their old debts.

The DRDA arranged for a technical training programme. The members have benefited by the training programme. As a result the members were able to make toys, plates, garlands, baskets and a few other products. Being professionally trained the members produce mats, boxes and baskets as per orders received from marketing agenices.

The members were encouraged to exhibit their produces at trade fairs held at Chennai, Kanniyakumari, Delhi, Mysore by the DRDA. Their efforts were properly recognized and appreciated. A bank loan of Rs. 2,00,000 has been sanctioned to the groups. A portion of the loan was utilized for their personal needs and the rest was invested in their development. The groups maintain daily accounts and earn a net profit of Rs. 6,450 per month. The group members earn an average net income of Rs.1,000 – 1,500 per month. With bulk orders from Monday Market and Kanniyakumari, their income increases accordingly. The members are seen with self-confidence and contentment with the job. They put in their creativity to produce new products. The group had succeeded in setting up a business unit. Their children are able to continue their studies without any disruption. To keep up the morale of the groups, DRDA has taken earnest efforts by building up their skill and self-confidence. Project Officer, DRDA has set a target for himself and moved accordingly. DRDA is not only involved in training but also in enabling them to place their products in a profitable way. The women had visited many places and participated in exhibitions. By visiting various places and participated along with other groups they picked up the trade. They have been brought to the competitive mode. Since they owned the unit and enjoyed the profit, they started doing innovations in producing new articles.

3. Pickle Preparation

(i) Annai Women Self-Help Group, Vilathikulam

Though people change their life style to suit this ultra modern society we find them still smacking their lips at tasty pickles. Pickle is considered an ideal side dish even today. Idle women club together and succeed in a business venture which depends wholly upon pickle preparation. To illustrate the above statement, this SHG's story is presented. The craze for pickles never goes down, and nothing can beat this ideal side dish. Women know the treasure behind it and they start working tirelessly fixing upon a target. The women of Vilathikulam in Thoothukudi District have traced a path of success in pickle preparation.

With the ultimate aim of thrift, the idle women members gathered under one roof engaging themselves in preparing pickles, squash and jam on a small scale. This made them move a step forward by seeking technical guidance and training. The community Polytechnic, Ettayapuram, guided the members in preparing a variety of pickles including lime, mango, onion, tomato, mixed vegetables, etc. A revolving fund of Rs. 25,000 was given by the DRDA to assist their activities. The members invested the revolving fund in preparing pickles on a large scale. The District Supply and Marketing Society,

Thoothukudi in a tie up with the DRDA is assisting the SHG to market their pickles and other products in the local market and some selected market at Madurai, Trichy and Salem.

The members of the SHG participate in the pickle preparation with utmost care and for this purpose they have hired a building for establishing a production unit exclusively for pickles equipped with needed utensils and adequate store room. The members work in shifts from 10.00 a.m. to 1.00 p.m. and from 1.00 p.m. to 4.00 p.m. Their average preparation reaches from 15 to 20 kg. of pickles per day. They earned a net profit of Rs.17,182 for the months of January and February 2004. The SHG members schedule their work and act on it. The members also engage themselves in, canvassing the local market and households. They expect an increase in production from 20 to 25 kg. per day. Above all, the members have increased their earnings and repaid their previous loans. We can see the pride filled faces of members who have succeeded in launching a new business. Here one has to notice the support of District Supply and Market Divisions in finding out market chain for the pickles produced by the women groups. This is constantly monitored by the DRDA office. Their training needs were attended to by the Community College. To make them professionally fit DRDA had taken efforts to link them with Community College and District Supply and Market Division.

(ii) Kadayanodai Self-Help Group Kadayanodai, Alwarthirunagari

Having realized the market potential of pickles, the women of Kadayanodai, Alwarthirunagari Block, Thoothukudi District, are engaged in pickle preparation. Their main reason for forming SHG was to come out from the force of money-lenders.

Alwarthirunagari Union gathered such members and encouraged them to start a new business in order to increase their income. The steps taken by the DRDA along with the Union succeed. After a series of discussions, the members began to prepare pickles without much training. They started to prepare them with their SHG savings and, after six months of SHG activities, they were assisted with

Rs. 25,000 as revolving fund. The fund was invested to back up the business. Adequate utensils and furniture were purchased. In addition a bank loan of Rs. 1,05,000 was sanctioned for this group with a subsidy of Rs. 52,500 on 07.01.2000. By their rapid development this group was able to repay the bank loan within two years.

The members opened an outlet for their product in the local market and in nearby areas. The members were engaged in canvassing and selling their product. They were able to sell around 400 bottles of 500 gm. per week. They increased their product variety from three to eight varieties. The production volume of each variety stood up to 50 kg. per week. They attracted the consumers by elegant packages—bottles and pouches.

An average income of Rs. 2,000, Rs. 2,500 is earned by the members. Their efforts were rewarded by the District Collector's appreciation. This group picked up the skill fastly. They stood on their own and then only they got the support of the Government. The moment they have decided to start producing pickles, they ventured into a big trade. Marketing was done by the group members by making all out efforts.

4. Wafers

There is yet another opportunity provided by DRDA to women is to train them in wafers and pappads preparation. Home made wafers and pappads are preferred by people in all seasons. Knowing the treasure behind it, the Annai Kasthuribai Mahalir Mandram, Chenamareddipatti, Pudur, the Gokulam Mahalir Mandram, Sankaraligapram, Pudur, the Bismi Women Self-Help Group, Arampatti, Karungulam, and the Bharathiyar Women Self-Help Group, Sivagnanapuram, started preparing a variety of wafers and pappads attracting customers. The groups were stabilized and graded by the SGSY District Committee. As a result, a revolving fund of Rs. 25,000 was granted by District Rural Development Agency for initial investment for the production of wafers. The members produce sixteen kinds of wafers and four kinds of pappads. A monthly production of 120 kgs. of each variety is being done. Their net profit has reached Rs. 6300 per month. The members earn Rs. 35 per day and the net profit gets accumulated as their savings. The District Supply and Marketing Society had placed a bulk order for 240 kg. of selected varieties. All the members of the group work together from 11.00 a.m. to 2.00 p.m. With their tireless work the groups have repaid their dues within 10 months of receipt. Apart from bulk orders the members go in for doorstep sales and visit retail stores for regular canvassing and supply. They have almost covered the whole locality and industrial centers such as cement factories, and spinning mills employees. The groups have invested their savings in setting up production units with grinders, electronic weighing machines, hand and pedal sealers and necessary utensils for production.

This occupation allows the ladies from the villages to be uplifted and develop the village considerably. They are settled with safe and secure daily earnings. Their children are educated and, as a result, their living standard has improved. The members are keen on the development of the village and have taken part in sanitation programme and solved various problems relating to village activities. Thus the women have secured a prominent place and are playing a vital role in village and local development.

5. Stone Quarry

The entrance to Padmanabhamangalam and Servaikaanmadam, receives us with the sound of hammering and the bursting of rocks. The women labourers toiling in the stone quarries illustrate their hard effort for the daily meals. The families of the Suyam Siddha Vinayagam Self-Help Group, Padmanabhamangalam, the Annai Velankanni Self-Help Group, Chettikurichi, and the Everest Self-Help Group, Karisalkulam, of Thoothukudi District had been working as bonded labourers in stone quarries. Their earnings were enough only for one square meal and the debts went on increasing considerably. None of them could run their family well. But the birth of the SHGs comprising of 20 members each was a relief from such torture.

The members approached the District Collector for acquiring the same quarry on lease. In the midst of stiff competition the SHGs took the quarry on lease for three years. The SHGs were allowed to remit the initial lease installments from the revolving fund given by the DRDA. The SHG members are now employed in the quarry. Compressors, trucks and tractors have been rented but they have decided to purchase them after the sanction of loan. The daily earnings of members come to Rs. 40 per day. The SHG members engage 6 to 9 males for the job. The monthly sales of stones comes to Rs. 86,000 by packing 3 to 4 loads of stones of 3 kinds at rates of Rs. 450 to Rs. 900 per day. Their net profit for the month stands at Rs. 20,000 and is transferred to their savings.

The leased quarry has fed them with confidence and happiness. The members are happy working in their own quarry. A feeling of self-employment surrounds them. The livelihoods of the families is secure and safe. Their effort is recognized by their own family members and the community. In societal development activities the members' participation is high. They have extended their full cooperation and support to family welfare, family planning, and sanitation campaigns. This is because of the constant drive by the Government departments, the SHG women are participating in many of the programmes. While attending such meeting they put turn duty. Otherwise their work will suffer.

6. Crab Rearing Straightens the livelihood of Women *(Nala Mahalir Self-Help Group)*

The coastal fishers of Periyathalai of Sattankulam Block are busily engaged in fishing activities. Among the roaring waves the SHG building stands erect, challenging the waves. The 11 BPL members of Nala Women Self-Help Group entered the field of crab rearing tirelessly striving to enhance the habit of savings and achieve prosperity. By the moral support extended by District Rural Development Agency, 11 women formed a strong group. Speaking about employment opportunities these women chose crab rearing. For this purpose the Block Development officials directed them to attend a training programme on the above said process at Punnakayal,

Authoor and Vellapatti crab rearing centers. A building with motor and adequate electrification was realized. A bank loan of Rs. 35,000 was sanctioned. Crabs of 3 varieties were put in for growth. 1 kg. of fully grown crab is worth Rs. 200 based on the variety. The earnings of the ladies comes to Rs. 30 Rs. 35 per day, working for just 5 hours. The earnings of the ladies balance the uncertainties of the family. The entire village is appreciative of the success of the SHG members. They take interest in the sanitation complex and render assistance to the poor and the needy. They are doing this work not as their full-time work. They have other traditional work in fish vending.

7. Lobster Rearing
(Vairam Mahalir Mandram)

The ocean satisfies hunger with its enormous gifts. One among the gifts is the lobsters. Lobster fishery is a boon to fishers. Since large sized lobsters are of high value, they are trained in rearing undersized lobsters to add value for sale. This task is taken up by the SHG women of Tharuvaikulam.

Fishing is the primary occupation of this coastal village. To utilize the natural resources of the sea, the women of Tharuvaikulam village turned to lobster rearing by NIOT through the Department of Fisheries, Government of Tamil Nadu. Twelve BPL family women joined together to form Vairam Women Self-Group' in June 2000 to ensure a steady source of income to the families. The members decided to approach the Government department for training in lobster rearing and were encouraged by the block officials. The members successfully attended the training programme and made arrangements for launching cages for the rearing process on 14th May, 2003. At first only 12 lobsters were stocked and fed with clams, a fish trash, mollusc flesh and deep sea with crabs. Regular monitoring, within 6 months of mariculture the price of the lobsters increases from Rs. 800 to Rs. 3000, depending on the species and the season. The total unit cost of the cages works out to Rs. 2,46,000. The amount was sanctioned by the Pandian Grama Bank, Tharuvaikulam. With a subsidy Rs.1,23,000, 6 cages for maricuture are being used by the members. They rear the lobsters from 100 gm. to 1 ½ kg.

They purchase the juvenile lobsters for just Rs. 5 per lobster and rear them into big lobsters. The members are proud of being employed and secure. This lobster rearing fetches a minimum of Rs.100 for a person as income for their families. They are directed to various orientations and EDP programmes. As a result, during the off season, the members are engaged in other productive avenues like tailoring and pickle production. The SHG's successful programme has helped in popularizing the efforts of the women in the coastal community. The morale and self-confidence of the women have gone up.

8. Fish Farming

The ocean has no limit. Our women SHGs have moved forward beyond the limit. They had taken keen interest in farming and reproducing fish in a pool. The members of the Nehru Gramodaya Women Self-Help Group, Karungulam, and the Muthumalaiamman Women Self-Help Group of Thottiyankudieruppu, Alwarthirunagari, decided to seek an alternative source of employment through fish.

The women formed a prominent SHG on 1st June, 2003. They have previously engaged in agriculture and, due to continuous drought, they were encouraged to choose a different track for livelihood. With the moral support extended by the District Rural Development Agency and the Union officials the members of both the groups were sent for training. They were also assisted with a revolving fund of Rs. 25,000.

With this economic assistance the members selected the land for setting up a pool for Rs. 4000 per year for 5 years. They set up an engine for sucking bore water from 4 foot depth. To safeguard the motor, a motor room was constructed for Rs. 5000. An additional bank loan of Rs.1,67,300 was sanctioned with a subsidy of Rs. 83,750. The pool was set for farming with the help of the Fisheries Department and 7500 fish of four varieties were installed for the first 22 days. The fingerlings we kept in nets for safeguarding and later they were left open. The groups commence their work at 6.00 a.m. and close by 7.00 p.m. They work in two shifts of 2 members for each shift. Their participation gets recycled every 5 days. The members fenced the pool for protection with 15 x 15 feet nets. It takes 6 months for complete growth. The selling rate rises upto Rs. 200 per kg. The initial investment is comparatively very low. The members earned Rs. 2000 to Rs. 4000 per week.

The BPL members were under stress for earning their daily meals and now they experience the feeling of contentment as they are secure with a job. Besides this occupation, the members utilized their loan amount for purchasing cows. Three cows were purchased and a building worth Rs. 35,000 was constructed for their protection. As a highlight the excreta of the cows is used as chow for the fish. Thereby the savings on feed is being increased. The participation of the members in social activities is notable. The self-esteem of the members has increased. The societal status of the group has considerably risen among the inhabitants.

9. Muscoth HALWA

(Thendral Women Self-Help Group, Nila SHG, Muthaloor, Sattankulam, Thoothukudi District)

Teasing the taste buds of people, SHG members have brought in a new flavor to halwa. This mouth watering and lip smacking halwa is exclusively prepared by the SHG members. The BPL members of the groups were previously employed in mud block making and snacks making. With the formation of group the members are pepped up with a new opportunity.

The District Rural Development Agency with its ultimate aim of turning the village women to self-employment, the SHG of Mudaloor gave training in producing muscoth halwa at their doorsteps. Apart from a revolving fund of Rs. 25,000 sanctioned by the District Rural Development Agency, a bank loan of Rs.1,10,000 was given for assisting them. The amount was spent on the purchase of utensils and packaging materials. As the product is perishable within 20 to 22 days of production, the movement of packed halwa is speeded up. An average of 50 to 75 kgs. Halwa is prepared every day. All the members participate in the preparation. They market the products to retail outlets and households in Erode, Chennai, Chengalpat and in local areas. The sales volume reaches up to 60 – 75 kgs. per day. A vehicle has been arranged for prompt delivery of the packs. The net profit of the SHG stands at Rs. 5245 per month.

The earnings and the savings of the members have increased. The members have received a good response from the retailers and households. The loan has been repaid. The members have divided the work equitably among themselves. They have scheduled the task for preparation, packing, canvassing and transporting the packed halwa. A daily earning of Rs. 50 per day is taken by them and the rest is deposited as savings. They want to become proud owners of this establishment and business.

10. Energy – Gasifier
(Vanavil Women Self-Help Group, Melathattaparai, Thoothukudi District)

"The sky is the limit"—this famous saying is being proved by the women of Melathattaparai SHG. The 20 BPL members selected a cluster of activities for improving their standard of living. They have energy under their control. Previously the 20 members were engaged in quarry work and wood work which yielded them only one square meal. This made them work tirelessly to encourage the habit of thrift. They formed a group named Vanavil Women Self-Help Group on 28.8.2000 to prove their power. The savings from their group was the only means of income initially. With the urging of the DRDA they were given a 10 day training in gasifier by a Gujarat team. It was conducted by the DRDA. They launched the gasifier unit and handed over the operating to the group.

A revolving fund of Rs. 25,000 was sanctioned to them. The members changed their occupation from quarry to dairy farming. Now the members own 5-6 goats each. They repaid the revolving fund within 6 months. Appreciating of their activities of bank loan Rs.1,00,000 was sanctioned to them. The members actively took part in the training in operating the gasifier. The gasifier converts wood pieces to electrical energy. The members found it easy as they were previously engaged in wood work. The members schedule their work in 2 shifts engaging 3 members in each shift, from 8.00 a.m. to 1.00 p.m. and from 1.00 p.m. to 5.00 p.m. The members earn Rs. 250 to 300 per week.

11. Non-Vegetarian Pickles
(Annai Therasa Fish Pickle Unit, Vellapatti)

The group effort of women has proved that eradication of poverty through women is possible. The Annai Therasa fish pickle unit in Vellapatti in Thoothukudi District covers the whole village in the form of 11 SHG members. The members targeted the sky and started marching ahead.

One member from each SHG was chosen for the Annai Therasa fish pickle unit, which was formed under the M.S. Swaminathan Foundation. A unit worth Rs. 20.00 lakhs was constructed with adequate infrastructure and machinery worth Rs. 3.49,000, including 4 electronic freezers, 1 electronic weighing machine, hand and pedal sealing machines, necessary utensils, dressing table, aprons, head caps and a well equipped laboratory. The members were trained in preparing fish pickles, prawn pickles, sangu chips, coony etc. All the 11 ladies involved in pickle preparation underwent training at Navam Pickles, Nagercoil. The working hours are from 2.00 p.m. to 5.00 p.m. They engage in preparation of fish and prawn pickles in large quantities varying from 50 kgs. to 150 kgs. per day. Their hygienic preparation attracted various wholesalers and retail units and the local public. They have entered in to an agreement with a private marketing company of Thoothukudi for continuous supply of fish and prawn pickles.

About Rs. 1,63,000 worth of fish and prawn pickles have been sold through the marketeers from August 2003. Apart from this, the members are involved in personal selling of their marine products, which has fetched Rs. 1,33,000. The members of the fish pickle unit are paid Rs. 750 per month. As the income of fishermen is seasonal the members once found it difficult to continue their children's education but this employment allows them to continue their education. Besides the women society extends a helping hand to economically distressed students and encourages the top scorers in their village materially. The Annai Therasa fish pickle unit keenly maintains its books of account well and submits it for auditing every accounting year. The activities of the team have been recognized by the District Collector, the DRDA and the DIG of Police and certificate of merit have been issued to this group.

12. District Maket Complex Thoothukudi

The Thoothukudi District Market Complex was constructed under the SGSY scheme at an estimate of Rs. 28.00 lakhs on at 8th Street, Doovepuram. There are 28 shops and 16 well equipped toilets in the complex. The shops are exclusively allotted for SHGs for the establishment of selling units. At present there are 8 Self-Help Groups occupying the stalls.

The 20 members of the Sharon Roja Women Self-Help Group were brought under a single roof on 20.05.2001. Contributing from their earnings, the members used it on a turn basis for personalizing the amount at a rate of interest. The main goal of the members was to save them from usurious interest rates.

Learning that the District Rural Development Agency rented the stalls to SHG members, the animator, along with the first member, approached the DRDA for applying for the stalls to establish an STD booth, for facilitating a regular stream of income for the members. Fortunately the SHG was allotted a shop for setting up an STD booth. The members invested Rs. 30,000 contributing from their group savings. Now the members are found brisk and active, participating in the management of the business.

The income comes to Rs.17,295 per month (for the past 4 months) and the members feel contented with the profit of Rs.1200- 2500 per month. The member taking charge of the shop is paid Rs. 25 per day. They are settled with a profitable occupation. The members are prepared to expand their business to stationery and xerox facilities.

13. Departmental Store
(Mani Vinayagar Women Self-Help Group)

The Mani Vinayagar Self-Help Group of Thoothukudi had entered the enterprise of setting up a departmental store covering three stalls. The members decided to utilize their savings for establishing a unit covering all categories of products. They decided to set up a departmental store with their savings. The members learnt the tactics of attracting customers by attractive and colourful window display. The layout and quality of the products stood as a plus point for their success. The price of the articles was updated now and then according to the current market rate.

The customers are received with a smile and their pleasing manners earns more customers for the SHG. They provide door delivery too. The average sales for a month has reached Rs. 96,244. The members taking charge of the store are paid Rs. 600 per month. In course of time they have decided to have computerize the billing system and to extend the supply of products in and around Thoothukudi District at a reasonable cost.

14. Fancy Store
(Alaimagal Women Self-Help Group)

To eradicate the pain of toiling as daily coolies, the women of a locality grouped themselves as Alaimagal Women Self-Help Group, with 20 members. Initially the contribution towards the savings itself was difficult for the members but after the completion of 6 months, they applied for a stall allotment at the District Market Complex through the DRDA. For running a fancy store the SHG was allotted a stall. With great expectation the members began the stall with Rs. 15,000 as initial investment. Fancy articles were ordered and purchased wholesale to suit the customers as per fashion and price. Since they make bulk purchase the price is reasonable compared to their competitors. The average sales for a month is 25,000. For expansion and purchase of cosmetics they expect a bank loan to be sanctioned in the near future. The members taking up the responsibility are paid Rs. 20 per day and all the members take part on a shift basis.

15. Canteen
(Kurinji Women Self-Help Group)

To come out of severe financial difficulties the 20 members of the Kurinji Women Self-Help Group, Kurinji Nagar chose on activity previously known with determination and solidarity. They tried to attract the public by their home made food with taste and professional presentation. The members are found busily functioning in full swing, preparing food and serving the customers. The aim of forming the SHG was to increase the savings, but this occupation has not only increased their earnings, but also their prominence among women. The ladies are engaged in preparation of food stuff according to their assigned shifts. There are 5 members to a shift and they work for 7 hours from 7.00 a.m. to 2.00 p.m. and from 2.00 p.m. to 9.00 p.m. The SHG was encouraged by DRDA by giving orders to this canteen. Their prompt and delicious service conquered the hearts of the customers. An average of Rs. 600 per day is earned as profit by the members. The SHG has become popular in the locality and this has made the people come for their home meals. This had added credit to the whole market complex. The District Collector and bankers have appreciated their work.

16. Solid Waste Management
(Muthu Vidiyal Self-Help Group)

The women of Muthaiahpuram, Thoothukudi, inhale salted breeze, working for 8 – 9 hours a day in salt pans. But the introduction of the Solid Waste Management scheme created a garden of pleasures.

Challenging the polluted environment, the 12 BPL members of the Muthu Vidiyal SHG, Muthaiahpuram, were ready to take up the job of operating the solid waste management unit. With the solid encouragement of the DRDA, the members took up the management of solid waste in February 2004. The necessary training was conducted by the DRDA. The members scheduled their programme of work wisely. The time of work was fixed from 7.00 a.m. to 2.00 p.m. The Municipality provided them with a vehicle for the collection of wastes. Specified members were allotted tasks relating to gathering wastes, sorting, processing, collecting, etc.

The members are able to cover two areas located nearby. They start their work from 7.00 a.m. collecting the wastes in the vehicle. The wastes are sorted by 5 members in a separate building. The work schedules of the members are recycled once a week. The members are trained to operate the plastic grinding machine and they grind up to 10 kgs. of plastics a day. They watch the 8 waste compartments and regularly inspect the decomposition status. The grinded plastic granules are purchased by the Government for laying plastic roads. They have earned Rs. 33,500 through waste and plastics materials in the past two months. The daily earnings of members are comparatively high. The involvement of the members in social activities is also up. They engage in sanitation campaign and medical campaign. For the work undertaken by them they have received valuable appreciation from the local public for maintaining the environment clean and tidy.

17. Soda Manufacturing
(Denzila Women Self-Help Group, Thalamuthu Nagar, Thoothukudi)

Though MNCI have spread a wide variety of munchies, the Denzila Women Self-Help Group Thalamuthu Nagar of Thoothukudi District, has put up its own range of products successfully. A group of 20 workers of salt pans joined together to form a SHG under the TMSSS on 10.09.1999. The main objective of forming the SHG was to put up a full stop to their previous tiresome work with poor earnings. Training in soda water preparation was arranged for the 20 members. A revolving fund of Rs. 25,000 was issued to the members for launching the unit. In addition, a bank loan of Rs. 2,50,000 was sanctioned with a subsidy of Rs. 1,25,000. They purchased machinery for Rs. 26,350 and packing materials for Rs. 19,200. The building for the production unit cost Rs. 30,000.

The daily earnings of the members is Rs. 25-30 per day. Self belief and reliance has sprouted their work. They cover the area in and around Thoothukudi—households and retail units. The members work in two shifts. The members are able to prepare 100 bottles in just two hours. Delivery is handled by the members themselves. To tease the taste buds of the customers they launched diversification of flavours like orange, mango and black currant. The members have studied the market. They sell 500-950 bottles on an average every a week. The net profit stands at Rs. 8,950 (for 8 months). Since soda is a seasonal product the members engage themselves in broadening the horizons with their savings in jaggery preparation and pickle preparation. They concentrate much on stabilizing their business. They wanted to repay the loan in time and want to gain the confidence of the bankers and the officials. The profit which they show is after remitting the dues to the bank. Moreover they have to compete with other big companies. As of now they are able to compete them as they are slowly stabilizing their business. Since it is a seasonal work, they have rely on other trades also. Against this background they have relied on pickle and jaggery preparation. They are known works for them.

A stage of self-sustainability has been reached by the members. The spirit of entrepreneurship runs them but still their concentration on social activities never comes down. They extend their valuable participation to medical campaign and economic assistance to the needy.

18. Banana Cultivation
(Kamarajar Women Self-Help Group, Siruthondanallur, Srivaikundam)

The cool breeze of the banana tree clusters brought in a tune of pleasantness. The women of Kottaikadu, Srithondanallur, Srivaikundam of Thoothukudi District, invest their energy in cultivating banana in cooperative climate. The green fields of banana capture the mind of the viewer and sing the praises of the human effort involved.

The 20 BPL families were actively engaged as coolies working in fields. With the push given by the District Rural Development

Agency and the Panchayat Union the members gathered for a single purpose of encouraging and developing the habit of thrift. With a loan assistance of Rs. 2,10,000 and a subsidy of Rs. 1,05,000, the members were guided towards cultivation of banana trees. For this purpose an area of 3 acres was leased for cultivation. Since the members were knowledgeable in this field there was no need for training. About 3,600 banana seedlings were planted with two special varieties. The land was equipped with a motor engine. The total investment was Rs. 1,60,000 and the rest of the loan amount has been shared among the members to settle their previous debts.

The members are able to attain a remarkable social status among their fellows. The feel of entrepreneurs had made them move up their living standards. They have settled their old debts and their children continue to be educated. The members' daily earnings come to Rs. 40 per day. Apart from being employed they feel proud to work on their own land. They work from 8.00 a.m. to 1.00 p.m. During seasons their daily earnings increase from Rs. 40 to Rs. 65 per day. The members are able to repay the loan without any difficulty. The yield is about Rs. 3,15,000 to Rs. 3,60,000 per term. Now the 20 members have increased their earnings and savings. They divert their concentration to societal benefits through assistance for poor school children and aged persons. They take part in eye camps and other public programmes.

19. Stationeries (File Pad and Envelopes)
(Jeyabarath Women Self-Help Group, Savariyarpuram, Thoothukudi)

The Savariyarpuram people of Thoothukudi District are able to learn with pride in their faces, as they have succeeded in the stationery field. Sunk in the salt pan, the life of the members was miserable. The members were given a new stream of life in a new business. The 17 members of the Jeyabarath Women Self-Help Group were trained by the Union officials for 7 days in the production of file pads and envelopes. Assisted by a revolving fund of Rs. 25,000, they began to produce file pads and envelopes on a small range. To encourage them, a bank loan of Rs. 2,22,000 with a subsidy of Rs. 1,11,000 was given. The members were pepped up with confidence and invested the loan in machinery. The whole production unit was mechanised.

Success roots sprouted the member's way. They set up the production unit with a building worth Rs. 79,000 and machinery worth Rs. 1,37,000. They run the machine with a challenge to face orders for office covers, file pads, envelopes from Madurai and Sivakasi. They purchase the paper material in bulk so as to reduce the cost of the product. They supply the goods at a cheaper rate compared to their competitors thanks to the spinning mills in Thoothukudi. They encourage the women to win the race courageously. They produce 1000 envelopes of 8 sizes per day and 1000 file pads per day. The members earn Rs. 340 to Rs. 450 per week. Compared to their previous occupation they feel content with this job. Their sales reached Rs. 2,58,680 in the months of January and February 2004. We find pleasure on the faces of those who are tirelessly working to achieve their object. The members are enthusiastically striving to obtain more orders. Their canvassing spirit indicates the same.

20. Nose Filters

(Kurinji Mahalir Mandram, Pallivasalpatti, Pudur, Thoothukudi)

Scanning the environmental pollution the women of Pallivasalpatti courageously stepped out into the field of nose filters, a protective shield from dust as Kurinji Mahalir Mandram. The seventeen members were previously trained in tailoring by the Pudur Union. Based on it, they were busily engaged in canvassing orders for uniforms and household. Their earnings merely matched expenses. To control this situation and increase the habit of thrift they decided to diversify to a competitive field. With the help of EDP training arranged by the DRDA they were able to select the filed of stitching cotton nose filters. A bank loan of Rs. 1,50,000 with a subsidy Rs. 75,000 was sanctioned for the expansion of the business. The loan was utilized for purchasing 12 sewing machines and securing a building for the production unit with adequate store room. The members divide their work in 2 shifts from 10.00 a.m. to 1.00 p.m. and from 2.00 p.m. to 5.00 p.m.

Monthly sales of cotton nose filters has gone up to 700 – 900 pieces per month. The members come out canvassing for orders to cement and spinning industries. RAMCO Cements and two spinning mills have placed orders for the SHG products. The average income of the members comes up to Rs. 210 –250 per week. For the past 4 months they have earned a net profit of Rs.14,050 per month. The savings of the members have considerably increased. The members are capable of stitching 200 pieces a day. The DRDA, in co-ordination with the DSMS, has encouraged their efforts and placed orders for cotton nose filters. The members, apart from production activities, also engage in social activities by participating in environment cleaning and economic assistance for purchasing school chairs and plates for poor students.

21. Rented Utensils

In Keelanalumoolaikinaru Village of Tiruchendur Block, Thoothukudi District, families were striving hard for their meals with their income from the dry wood. Then the women of the poor families were blessed by the formation of SHGs to cultivate the habit of savings. The Dr. Ambedkar Self-Help Group was successfully formed on 20.10.1999, with the ultimate aim of launching a new business and increasing the standard of living.

After the successful completion of 6 months of savings, the SHG members looked for a suitable means of employment. The Union officials directed them to purchase of utensils, gas lights, decoratives, chairs, table, and water drums essential for celebration. They could earn their living by hiring them for rent. Sanctioning this project the District Rural Development Agency assisted the women with a revolving fund of Rs. 25,000 and in addition a bank loan of Rs. 2,40,000 was sanctioned. The 18 BPL members invested Rs. 1,30,000 in the business and the rest was shared among them to repay their old debts. With a new enthusiasm a building was arranged for storage of utensils and other articles.

During festive seasons the earnings of the ladies go up to Rs. 50 per day. They have covered the entire locality by advertising their services through posters, circulars and notices. They have created awareness among the public. To attract various ranges of customers they have fixed competitive prices compared to their competitors. A three-wheeler vehicle is used by the members for the supply of utensils and decoratives. The members engage in creative decoration, attracting the viewers. Males are drafted for assistance. On work they are paid Rs. 50–60 per day. The rental amount realized in a month during seasons is Rs. 5,000–6,000 per month. They have earned Rs.1,15,000 in a period of 3 months. The successful run of this project has induced other SHGs in various areas to follow their track. As a result MGR SHG, Indira SHG and Chandragiri SHG of Alwarkarkulam, Karungulam Block of Thoothukudi District have commenced this project.

The women were able to educate their children without any hesitation. As this project does not need human labour, the members are free to continue with their commitments along with secured earnings. The members' participation in social activities has gone up. All the 18 members actively participated in contributing economically towards education of poor people and the welfare of aged and physically disabled persons.

22. Rasi Maiyam

(Ganga Women Self-Help Group)

A fervent team of 16 rural women are seen in the Panchayat building of Melathattaparai, zealously striking the keys of the computer key board for the core cause of assisting the rural populace of Melathattaparai, Thoothukudi Block. The technological benefit is now being reflected in the rural areas, as an outcome of the establishment of RASI Maiyam. With the help of Block officials 16 ladies were guided in forming a valid SHG. They were successfully grouped on 19.03.2003. Their focus was mainly on self-employment and increasing savings. After the completion of six months of functioning, various orientation programmes were given to the members.

In course of time the RASI Maiyam was allotted to the Ganga Women Self-Help Group of this village. The block officials encouraged them and the District Rural Development Agency arranged for computer education for the members. Four members who had completed their studies up to 8th standard were sent for computer training. They were trained technically for a period of 4 months at APTECH Computers. Through the installation of computers, the rural public were informed about issues regarding

(a) Ration stock list and prices
(b) Forwarding Monday Petitions
(c) Stock and Share details
(d) Price details of various goods and articles
(e) Reservation of tickets etc.

The members pooled their efforts in creating awareness among the people in utilizing the RASI Maiyam effectively and efficiently. The rural people are served at their doors steps. This created an attitude of being self employed in their home.

23. Paper Cups
(Solid Resources of Fertility)

Thoothukudi is known as an industrial area. Adaikalapuram and Athimarapatti of Tiruchendur Block and Thoothukudi Block set up a unit for manufacturing paper cups. Right at the entrance of Adaikalapuram we are able to spot the manufacturing unit by the rustic music produced by the paper cutting machines.

Adaikalapuram families earn their meals through the benefits extended by palm trees and on the other side Athimarapatti is wholly dependent on salt pans. The urge created by officials of the Union and the DRDA offices made them convert to high risk takers. Their decision was exactly right. For the accomplishment of self-employment benefits, the women grouped together for the formation of a SHG. Initially they had problems in savings due to their poor income and the interest payable for their borrowings. The DRDA assisted them with Rs. 25,000 as revolving fund and in addition they availed of a bank assistance of Rs. 2,79,000 with a 50 per cent subsidy component through the DRDA.

The Block officials guided them towards the track of success. Among the alternatives put up for the SHG's choice, they confidently chose the manufacture and trading of paper cups. The members utilized the economic assistance for the setting up of a new manufacturing unit with adequate machinery worth Rs. 1,91,000. As the members got trained in the activity they made use of this opportunity. Fortunately they were allotted a building under the SGSY scheme in their locality. The members are now running the unit successfully with sufficient orders. The members are engaged in work from 9.30 a.m. to 6.00 p.m. The ladies are capable of producing 3,500 cups per day. All the members feel relived from the clutches of torturous money-lenders since the monthly income, apart from the savings, has increased from Rs. 300 to Rs. 1,500. This has induced the members to canvass for more orders.

They are able to find a market for more than 900 cups per week. The stock maintained in the units is sold at various selling points at Thoothukudi by canvassing and collecting orders. The members are supported by the DRDA and the DSMS by the giving orders for their official requirements. Apart from sufficient income, a series of good events happening in their village has created an excellent image of the SHG members in the area. They extend a helping hand by assisting the disabled, marriages and students economically. The members have been recognized well in the family and society.

24. Power Tiller

(Tholavilliamman Women Self-Group, Sunganathapuram, Srivaikundam)

We have come across the daily saying, "Men and Women are equal". To realise the above concept the SHG from Sunganatha-puarm, Srivaikundam chose an entirely different employment. The women power brought in miracles and made eyebrows rise in astonishment. Yes, the iron ladies turned the hand bars of the power tiller under their control.

Being an agricultural area, the ladies of Sunganathapuram decided to concentrate on agricultural activity. For reaching their goal they formed a SHG named Tholavilliyamman Women SHG on 15.05.2000. For the first six months the members' savings were utilized for the preparation of washing powder, since a member already possessed the knowledge of such preparation. The members tried to increase their savings through personal selling of the preparation, covering the locality and nearby places. After the completion of six months, the members leaped up on a better opportunity. They approached the District Rural Development Agency and with the help of the block officials various orientation programmes were given to them. Training on power tiller was given by the TV, Srinivasan Trust, Chennai. To put it into practice a revolving fund of Rs. 25,000 and a bank loan of Rs 1,25,000 with a subsidy of Rs. 62,500 was given to the ladies. With the assistance they purchased a power tiller. As the entire area is based on agriculture, power tiller is being hired by the landlords for making their farming easier. They charge Rs. 20 per acre. The members have created employment opportunities. For the tiller operators are engaged for daily wages up to Rs.100.

During the past nine months they have earned a profit of Rs. 53,000 and this has enabled them to repay the loan amount and the revolving fund within the stipulated period. Since the power tiller is a seasonal occupation the members never stay idle. They switch on to an alternative task of cable network in their villages. The Tholavilliamman SHG has been crowned with laurels in their pioneering the cable network connection activities also. Apart from it during their leisure hours they engage in preparing incense sticks, washing powder, blue, omam water, phenyle and readymade clothes.

25. Groceries

A group of 22 women SHG formed for a common purpose definitely reaches its target. A solid cluster of 22 SHGs have brought miracles with groceries. This group of women are working for women's empowerment in their village. CEDCO, a prominent NGO, clubbed them together. To reduce the miseries of poverty and unemployment the 396 ladies of the 22 SHGs approached the block officials for getting their guidance in establishing a unit.

To uplift the members 14 SHGs were assisted with a revolving fund of Rs. 15,000 under the SGSY Scheme Rs. 5,000 was contributed by each SHG and a total investment of Rs. 1,10,000 was pooled for setting up a shop. A centrally located building was rented for Rs.700 per month with adequate space for packaging and sorting the stores. Adequate infrastructure with 7 steel racks for product display and storage and electronic weighing machine was arranged. The members scheduled their job and divided their responsibilities as purchase, packaging, sales and canvassing orders. They kept alert of the current market price of articles.

Changing the entire scene of poverty and famine in families, the 396 members made a brisk march towards success. They adopted the following aids to attract the local customers: poster advertising, pamphlets, cable TV advertisements and special offers during festive seasons. The monthly earnings of the members stands at Rs.1,500–2,000. The total sales of the stores has increased from Rs. 3,000 to Rs. 4,200 per day. The 2 members assigned to the stores commence their work by 9.00 a.m. and end by 9.00 p.m. Prompt repayment of funds has made the bankers sanction further loans. All the members are content with the earnings and ready for further achievements.

26. Readymade Garments
(Annapoorani Women Self-Help Group)

Kayamozhi Readymade Garments unit received us with the music of sewing machines. Annapoorani Women Self-Help Group consisting of 15 BPL women is busily engaged on sewing machines and with packages of garments. The village itself stays calm and quiet engaging in their traditional occupation of dealing with palms. Due to drought, the villagers started migrating to urban areas seeking better employment to earn their livelihood. This migration made the members approach the block officials. Under their guidance the 15 women formed a SHG on 10.11.1999.

Various EDP and orientation programmes were given to them through the District Industries Center. One among the members set up a unit based on tailoring. Among them one member extended her backyard by covering the sewer. The activity began in a thatched shed containing 5 sewing machines and 2 iron boxes, purchased with the help of a revolving fund of Rs. 25,000 from the DRDA and a bank loan of Rs. 50,000.

The members engaged themselves in stitching nighties, inskirts, blouses and chudithars. In addition they purchased saris in bulk and sold them for installments. The members work in twins for sales and production. Rs. 30 per day is being paid to each member, and the monthly sales amount of the SHG has reached upto Rs. 5,000 to 15,000 per month. During festive seasons they reach Rs. 25,000 sales per month.

The problem of migration is being tackled through the efforts of the SHG. Now their income through this earning is sufficient and sustainable. Above all, the members are self-employed in their homes. They are able to manage the family as before because they are engaged in work only for 3– 4 hours a day. Through the income raised the members have repaid their debts and loans. For their social involvement they actively participate in environmental cleaning and assisting the poor students economically.

27. Sibi Cool Park
(Thirumagal Women Self-Help Group)

Setting an apt environment for snacks lovers is not an easy task today. Despite this risk, the Thirumagal SHG created the atmosphere of a compact cool bar in the small space allotted to them in the District Market Complex. The members put in their joint effort in establishing an ideal and cool tone suitable for customers.

Previously, before the allotment of stalls, the members were involved in dried flowers processing and snacks making. Since the earnings were meager, the members decided to start a new business.

Fortunately, the District Rural Development Agency allotted the stalls for the Ice Cream Parlor. The 20 members at full swing started working for the establishment of the parlor with a professional look. The members applied for a bank loan of Rs.1,00,000 from Pandian Grama Bank. After the sanction of the loan the members utilized it for investing in interior decoration and infrastructure. The cool bar was equipped with electronic freezers and refrigerators, and 12 varieties of ice creams from Lazza were displayed in their parlor. In addition to the soft drinks like Lehar and Coke, fresh juices of five varieties of fruits are available. For the sake of attracting and creating awareness among the public, poster advertisements and pamphlets distribution strategy were followed.

Now the sales of ice creams and juices has increased from Rs. 150 to Rs. 1,500 per day. This made the members increase the number of snacks items on their menu. Since snacks making is their traditional profession, it was easy for them to attract the customers by preparing hot and delicious cutlets, vegetable and non-vegetarian rolls and mouth watering samosas. This added more goodwill to their stalls. Now the members are satisfied with their earnings. The daily earnings of the members has increased to Rs. 50 per day.

28. RASI Two-Wheeler Driving School

Nowadays women are trying to control the handle bar of two-wheelers. To quench the thirst of driving curiosity, the members of RASI Vidiyal Women Self-Help Group engaged in setting up a driving school exclusively for ladies. They approached the District Rural Development Agency for guidance. As a result, they were allotted a stall on the first floor of District Market Complex for their office. All the 13 members of the SHG belonging to the Municipal area unanimously inaugurated the driving school in February 2004. They possessed two two-wheelers for coaching. Since all the members are well trained in driving they train the trainees in four hours in four batches.

They induce all the idle women seated at home to come out with flying colours by conquering them at their homes through local cable advertisements and pamphlets. They even train the trainees at their doors on phone booking. They have covered even the rural ladies by training them at their homes. The members are proud to introduce themselves to the masses as trainers on two-wheelers. The income of the school reaches up to Rs. 1,750 to Rs. 5,000 per week. The personal earnings of the members has risen from Rs. 50 to Rs. 250 per day.

29. Rural Sanitary Marts

The Rural Sanitary Mart is an outlet dealing with the sanitation requirements of the construction industry and provides technical assistance for household latrine and other environmental sanitation in rural areas. In Thoothukudi District 12 Rural Sanitary Marts have been established as a commercial enterprise. The Rural Sanitary Marts functioned and extend their services to provide sanitation materials and guidance needed for constructing difference types of latrines and other sanitary facilities suitable to the rural areas. The RSMs should be set up as an information center and should have different models and they should be sanitation related. IEC materials are also to be displayed in these centers along with sanitation products, with rates to be made available. It should go for bulk purchase of other products not produced in their production center. The list of masons and their address are to be displayed at the center. The RSMs should be run by suitable SHGs. The SHGs should go in for monitoring and evaluation of the RSMs.

The production centre is established to improve the production of "less-water" sanitary pans and cost effective portable sanitary materials. Two production centres have commenced work in Thoothukudi Block (Melathattaparai) and Ottapidaram Block (Ottapidaram Panchayat). The production centres have produced Methinapur model "less-water" sanitary pans. The production centres should have a marketing outlet attached to it and it should be opened everyday during working hours. The price list should be displayed and competitive prices are to be fixed. The production centre should have a working shed and a room for storage and different working models of toilets can be displayed in the production centre. It should have provision to manufacture other sanitation related items like bathrooms, soaps, brushes, ash and powders. The production centre should be run by selected and suitable SHGs. The SHGs should undertake and monitor and evaluation of the production centre. The production centre should be run by a women self-help group. The SHG of 20 members has been trained in the production of "less-water" sanitary pan in Melathattaparai and Ottapidaram.

30. Extraction of Bio-Diesel from Pungan Oil Seeds *(Sriparangusanallur Panchayat – Srivaikuntam Panchayat Union)*

In Thoothukudi District the SHGs are engaged in various economic activities. In Srivaikuntam Panchayat Union, some of the villages are benefited by the Tamirabarani River, especially Sriparanguanallur Panchayat, as the Village Panchayat lies in the river belt, and all the villages are surrounded by the pungan trees. Initiated by the SUTRA (Sustainable Transformation of Rural Areas) Agency, it is planned to erect a Bio-Diesel Extracting Unit at Sriparangusanallur. Hence the Agency is contacted for erecting a 5 HP Seed-Breaking Machine and 15 HP Oil Rotary Unit and both are erected at an estimated cost Rs. 2.10 lakhs. Moreover, due to necessity one room was constructed with a roof of 40 feet length x 20 feet breadth at an estimated cost of Rs.1.50 lakhs.

The trial running is being made by the DANWA Pannai SHG, which was selected to run this unit. Large quantities of pungan seeds were purchased at the rate of Rs. 5 per kg. and stored in the shed. The seed-breaking machine was used for breaking pungan seeds and the Oil Rotary Unit was used for crushing the oil seeds. This unit can be used to grind 40 kg. pungan seeds in one hour and has the capacity to run 5 hrs. continuously. However, this unit cannot be used for more than 5 to 6 hrs. daily. It was ascertained that, if we run this unit 5 hours continuously, we can produce 50 kg. bio-diesel and 150 kg. of oil cakes by using 200 kg. of pungan oil seeds.

The SHG members said that the seeds-breaking machine was being run by bio-diesel, which was produced in this unit during the trial running period. The rough statement showing the expenditure details of this unit is as follows:

Duration	*Quantity of seeds required*	*Quantity of bio-diesel produced*	*Money earned from the sales of bio- diesel*	*Quantity of oil cakes produced*	*Money earned from the sales of oil cakes*
1 hour	40 Kg.	10 Kg.@Rs. 20	Rs. 200	30 Kg.@Rs. 4	Rs. 120
5 hour per day	200 Kg.	50 Kg.	If we fix the rate of Rs. 20 per one Kg. of bio-diesel (Rs. 22 per 1 Kg. is market rate) we will earn Rs.1,000	150 Kg.	As per the current market rate, we fix Rs. 4 per 1 Kg. of oil cake, we will earn Rs. 600

The SHG members are provided with training and technical guidance through The District Rural Development Agency. Moreover, Canara Bank, Srivaikuntam, has been approached for giving economic assistance to the SHG.

31. Power Generation through the Treatment of Night Soil

A pilot project has been launched in Melathattaparai Village of Thoothukudi District to generate power from the night soil from the women and children sanitary complex. The District Authority is promoting individual toilets and women children sanitary complexes under the Total Sanitation Campaign and other schemes. Because of the awareness created, people are coming forward to use the sanitary complexes and the septic tanks are getting filled very quickly. They have to be cleared periodically and the disposal of night soil is a major problem. To dispose of the night soil in an environment friendly way, the District Authority has introduced the novel idea of power generation through anaerobic digestion. A one tonne capacity fixed dome type bio-gas plant has been installed in the sanitary complex where about 300 persons are using the toilets.

The bio-gas produced from the 10 cum size plant is utilized to run a 1 KW generator and a 1.5 HP water pumping device. The power obtained from the 1 KW generator can be utilized to illuminate 25 lights of 40 watts each for 4 to 5 hours per day. The 1.5 HP water pumping device can pump water for five hours to meet the water requirements of the sanitary complex.

After producing the bio-gas the slurry of the night soil coming out of the bio-gas plant serves as good nutrient for the promotion of vermin-composting. Through the vermin-composting, other solid wastes can be converted to value added organic manure. Thus the night soil is converted to value added organic manure during the process of power generation. A Self-Help Group can undertake an income generation activity through the vermin-composting, by making use of the digested slurry obtained from the night soil fed into the bio-gas plant. The cost of the project is Rs.1.85 lakhs (Rupees one lakh eighty five thousand) and the pay back period is about eight years.

32. Solar Fish-Drier
(Periathalai Panchayat–Sattankulam Panchayat Union)

In Thoothukudi District there are 27 coastal villages in which the people engage themselves only in fishing. Being a healthy and delicious food, fish is preferred to any other edibles by the masses. Dry-fish occupies a major part in this diet. Nowadays it is marketed both within the country and abroad. The leading agencies in Thoothukudi District are engaged in exporting dry-fish to foreign countries. In coastal areas the fish is being dried through different natural process in two or three days. Hence there is a chance of rotting in these processes and, at the same time, the dry-fish cannot be kept for more than two or three months. For hygienic preparation of dry-fish, solar fish-drier, a wonderful unit, is erected at Periathalai Village, Sattankulam Panchayat Union, at an estimated cost of Rs. 5.51 lakhs by Madurai Solsen Equipments and Consultants. In Periathalai Village, Annai Therasa, Vinnarasi and Jeyamatha Women SHGs are selected to run this unit jointly. The unit is erected under consultancy with the officials of the Fisheries Department after visiting Gangavaram Unit, Vishakhapattinam along with the SHG members. With the help of this unit we can dry 300 kg. of fish per day from which we can get 100 kg. of dry-fish. The fish dried under the solar energy can be kept fresh for more than a year and it is also considered to be hygienic.

In this process the fish are cleaned properly and they are kept in boxes with 1/3 quantity of salt for a full day. The very next day they are cleaned three times and then kept in the trays inside the fish-drier to be dried. For small fish it will take five hours to dry and if big, it will take ten hours. Finally, when it is found to have 10–15 per cent of humidity, it is well packed and marketed.

5 ANALYSIS AND INTERPRETATION OF FIELD DATA

Empowerment of women cannot be achieved by fixing target. Government officials have been oriented in achieving targets. Hence when a target in given to the officials, they try their level best achieve the target. In many of the occasions they have achieved the targets but there will not be any sustainability of the achievements made through targets. SHGs had been organized by many NGOs but they took a longer time and the process had been studied. Over a period of time SHG leaders and members have been oriented on many socio-economic issues of the society. They had been oriented to develop perspectives on issues. The now the trend of the formation of SHGs in Thoothukudi District is shown in Table No.5.1.1.

1. Background of the Selected SHGs

Table 5.1.1 : Year of Origin of the SHG.

Sl. No.	*Year*	*No. of SHG*	*Percentage*
1.	Before 2000	09	22.5
2.	2000	05	12.5
3.	2001	05	12.5
4.	2002	14	35.0
5.	2003	06	15.0
6.	2004	01	2.5
	Total	40	100

Source : Computed.

The year of origin of the SHGs is enumerated in Table 5.1.1, which indicates the trend of formation of groups by the Government officials. The above table reveals the speed in formation of groups. In the same speed trades were also organized. In normal circumstances embarking in business or trade will take longer time as ground realities have to be studied thoroughly otherwise the individuals have to lose heavily. Unless individuals gain hope of winning, they will not try the business and invest money. Whereas in the case of SHGs, as the officials evinced keen interest in formation of groups, they continue to evince interest in pursuing them to start trade also.

Table 5.1.2 : Year of Origin of SHG's Trade/Enterpreneurship.

Sl. No.	*Year*	*No. of SHG*	*Percentage*
1.	Before 2000	04	10.0
2.	2000	NIL	
3.	2001	NIL	
4.	2002	01	2.5
5.	2003	15	37.5
6.	2004	20	50.0
	Total	40	100.0

Source : Computed.

According to Table 5.1.2, after 2001, the SHGs have entered in to micro enterprises which are a source of economic growth and a social identity against poverty. After 2001, the growth of entre-preneurship ability among SHGs has increased 2.5 per cent, 37.5 per cent and 50 per cent during the years 2002, 2003 and 2004 respectively.

Table 5.1.3 : Background of Blocks of Selected SHGs.

Sl. No.	*Name of the Block*	*No. of SHG*	*Total No. of Members*
1.	Thoothukudi	8	131
2.	Karukkulam	7	134
3.	Thiruvaikundam	4	73
4.	Alwarthirunagari	7	128
5.	Thiruchanthur	4	74
6.	Udankudi	6	97
7.	Kovilpatti	3	47
8.	Kayatharu	1	12
	Total	40	696

Source : Computed.

Except Chandankulam, Ottapidaram, Vilathikulam and Pudur Blocks, the SHGs are selected for this study from all the other blocks. The Kayatharu Block comes under the lowest category since it has only one SHG consisting of 12 members. Thoothukudi Block has 8 SHGs with 131 members enrolled. Karunkulam and Alwarthirunagari Blocks have 7 SHGs each and Thiruvarankulam and Tiruchendru Blocks have 4 SHGs each. Udankudi Block has 6 SHGs. The total number of SHGs selected are 40 with a membership of 696 women.

Table 5.1.4 : Age of SHG Members.

Sl. No.	*Age*	*No. of SHG*
1.	Below 20	NIL
2.	21-30	130
3.	31-40	315
4.	41-50	216
5.	51-60	45
6.	Above 60	Nil
	Total	696

Source : Computed.

Table 5.1.4 presents the age-wise distribution of the SHG members. As high as 315 members are in the age group of 31-40 years and as low as 45 in the age group of 51-60 years. None of the members are below 20 years and above 60 years.

Table 5.1.5 : Marital Status of SHG Members.

Sl. No.	*Status*	*No. of Members*
1.	Married	585
2.	Widow	96
3.	Separated	15
	Total	696

Source : Computed.

According to Table 5.1.5, all the members are married but 15 are separated and 96 are widows. In Indian context, widows and separated are facing plethora of problems. In normal course, poorest of the poor cannot join in these groups. The widows and separated are considered specifically in the group formation. It is a welcome sign. Nearly 20 per cent of the members of the groups are separated and widows.

Table 5.1.6 : Educational Status of SHG Members.

Sl. No.	*Educational Status*	*No. of Members*
1.	Illitrate	75
2.	Upto 5	333
3.	6 to 8	167
4.	9 to 10	48
5.	11 to 12	48
6.	Technical	05
7.	Degree	20
	Total	696

Source : Computed.

Table 5.1.6 presents the educational status of the SHG members, according to which, illiterates are 75 and graduates are 20. The number of members is high (333) who have attended school up to 5th standard. The number of members who have studied between 6th and 8th are 167, which is moderate. Technically qualified members are very low, i.e., only 5. The number of members who have studied 10th and 12th are 46 each.

Table 5.1.7 : Community Status.

Sl. No.	*Name of the Community*	*No. of Members*
1.	OBC	579
2.	SC	117
3.	ST	NIL
	Total	696

Source : Computed.

As for the community status of the SHG members, Table 5.1.7 579 belong to OBC and 117 belong to SC. The members from ST community are not members of the SHGs. The members from SC have their representation as one fifth.

Table 5.1.8 : Occupational Status of the SHG Members.

Sl. No.	*Status*	*No of SHG Members*
1.	House Wife	177
2.	Agricultural Cooly	336
3.	Non-Farming Sectors	183
	Total	696

Source : Computed.

According to Table 5.1.8, 336 members of SHGs are serving as agricultural coolies and 183 are working in the non-farm sector, while 177 are house-wives.

Table 5.1.9 : House Status.

Sl. No.	*Status*	*No. of SHG Members*
1.	Huts	188
2.	Tiled Houses	209
3.	Pucca Houses	99
	Total	696

Source : Computed.

As for the type of houses where in the members of SHGs are living, Table 5.1.9 shows that 188 are living in huts, 209 are living in tiled houses and only 99 are living in RC pucca houses. Really the targeted members were poor.

Table 5.1.10 : Land-holding Status.

Sl. No.	*Land Status*	*No. of SHG Members*
1.	Land Holding (Hut)	271
2.	Land Not Holding	425
	Total	696

Source : Computed.

The land-holding particulars of the members of SHGs are presented in Table 5.1.10; 271 members of SHGs are holding own lands and 425 are not holding any land. The majority of the members of SHGs are non-landholders. In India owning land is not only income to the family but also a social recognition. It is proved beyond doubt that wherever land is distributed, there people are assertive and increased food production. They lead a life with self-dignity. They targeted only the landless women.

Table 5.1.11 : Religious Status.

Sl. No.	*Religious Status*	*No. of SHG Members*	*Percentage*
1.	Hindus	558	
2.	Chiristians	118	
3.	Muslims	20	
	Total	696	

Source : Computed.

Table 5.1.11 presents the religion of the SHG members is out of 696 members, 558 are Hindus, 118 are Christians and 20 are Muslims. Representation of Muslims is very low in SHGs.

Table 5.1.12 : Individual Monthly Savings in SHGs.

Sl. No.	*Saving Status*	*No. of SHG Members*	*Percentage*
1.	Less than 50	25	62.5
2.	50-100	15	37.5
	Total	40	100

Source : Computed.

As for the monthly savings by the members of SHGs, Table 5.1.12 shows that 62.5 per cent of SHG members save less than Rs. 50 and 37.5 per cent save Rs. 50 to Rs.100. The lowest money savers are high since their income meets several needs of the family. However, the ability and the attitude for saving money have emerged since they realized the necessity for saving money.

The Repurcusions faced by Women members from Money-lenders prior to joining the Women SHG

This study brought out the repercussions faced by women members from money-lenders prior to joining the group. Fishing was the main occupation of the ***Nalmagalir* group**. They faced lots of hardships from money-lenders as the money-lenders blocked them from fishing when they were not able to repay their loan. Moreover they confisticated their fish net which led to depression. Almost all the money-lenders used to come by motorcycle to collect the money. A woman belonging to ***Sridevi* SHG** was driven to madness whenever she heard the sound of any motorcycle. It was an evidence to understand how far they had been affected by money-lenders' atrocities. The tale of ***Marutham* SHG** was very pathetic and painful. On many days they gave up their food as they used their daily wages to pay the interest for the amount they got from the money-lenders. Kanagu was not able to pay the loan of Rs. 10,000 in time as she had promised, which resulted in the money-lenders capturing her house. She faced lots of agonies. Now she is a member of ***Karpagadharu* SHG**.

The traditional occupation of Ponnamal was palm related business. When her business was not up to the level of satisfying her family's livelihood needs, she was forced to get money from the money-lenders. When she was not able to repay the amount the money-lender along with 20 escorts forcibly locked her house and went away with the key. This was not a rare phenomenon. The same story was repeated in Sermakani's case also. She was forced to change the ownership of her house to the money-lender. Now these women are members of the ***Indra, Mariammal and Senthamarai* SHG.** The ***Muthumariamman* SHG** member Anandhi sold her only precious property, i.e., her gold chain to repay the loan got from the money-lender. The money-lenders took away the TV, fan and other valuable belongings of a member of ***Fathima* SHG.**

Table 5.1.13 : Total Savings of SHG.

Sl. No.	*Saving Status*	*No. of SHG Members*	*Percentage*
1.	Less than 50,000	31	77.5
2.	50,000-1,00,000	03	7.5
3.	1,00,001-1,50,000	04	10
4.	1,50,001-2,00,000	02	5
	Total	40	100

Source : Computed.

According to the Table 5.1.13, as high as 77.5 per cent of SHGs saved less than Rs.50,000 and as low as 5 per cent of SHGs saved Rs.1,50,000 to 2,00,000. The largest amount of money was saved by only 5 per cent of the SHGs. However, the capability of mobilizing capital through savings has increased among the members of SHGs rather than non-numbers and this may be an economic activity against poverty.

Capability to Create Assets

A lady belonging to ***Sarojan Roja* group** got loan to purchase an autorickshaw for her husband. Now her husband treats his wife as to be the *kuthuvillagu* (light lamp) of their family as they get daily income from the autorickshaw. Her husband is proud of being an owner of his wife's autorickshaw. Every year the ***Marutham* group** purchase jewels for about Rs. 10,000 whenever they sold their goats reared by their group members. A member in ***Marriammal* group** buys adequate utensils and other household articles to give to her daughter at her marriage time. A ***Kurinji* group** member has purchased furniture, mixie and other domestic items. A ***Manivinayakar* group** woman purchased ear rings and other jewels. ***Vinayakam Suyam Siddha* group** women constructed their own houses. ***Thol Valliyammai*** an SHG woman purchased milch animal *for income generation activity*.

10 members of ***Kamarajar* SHG** purchased cot, fan and ear rings.

(Contd.)

(Contd.)

> 20 members of ***Fatima*** **SHG** bought ear rings, anklets. Fishing was the main occupation of the ***Nalmahaleer*** **SHG** group. The group members also purchased fish nets. The SHG group members purchased many more articles like this. Even though the jewels did not help them to improve their business, they felt very happy as they got uplift in their social status. Many group members acknowledged that their membership in their respective groups paved a significant way for their children's especially girls education.

Table 5.1.14 : Status of Revolving Fund.

Sl. No.	*Status of RF*	*No. of SHG Members*	*Percentage*
1.	Received	38	95
2.	Not Received	02	5
	Total	40	100

Source : Computed.

Table 5.1.14 presents the details of SHGs which received the revolving fund. Out of 40 SHGs, 38 have received it and only 2 are yet to receive the revolving fund.

2. Increasing Capability to visit Government and other Institutions for Development

Table 5.2.1 : Experience of Visiting the Police Station.

Sl. No.	*Particulars*	*No. of SHG*	*Percentage*
1.	Experience	16	40.0
2.	Don't have experience	24	60.0
	Total	40	100.0

Source : Computed.

The experiences in visiting the police station for various cases are presented in Table 5.2.1. Out of 40 SHGs, 16 SHGs have the experience of visiting the police station to get solutions for their problems and 24 SHGs have no such experience since they did not meet any serious problems so far. It is inferred from their statement that they are able to visit police stations for solutions whenever they meet any serious problem.

Table 5.2.2 : Experience of Visiting the DRDA Office.

Sl. No.	*Particulars*	*No. of SHG*	*Percentage*
1.	Experience	39	97.5
2.	Don't have experience	01	2.5
	Total	40	100

Source : Computed.

The DRDA is the main outlet of development programmes in any district. District Rural Development Agency is a registered society with the District Collector is the Chairperson and the Project Officer is the Secretary. All development programmes are being carried out only through DRDA. Even the Panchayat Presidents do not know much about the programmes and schemes. It is only the political parties representatives constantly maintain contact with the officials and do brokerage. It is only after the formation of SHGs and conduct of the Panchayat elections, the grassroots level leaders visit DRDA frequently and get to know what are the programmes and schemes are available for the poor. The establishment of linkage with DRDA will provide a lot of information about development programmes and schemes. The SHGs have several opportunities for their economic activities in DRDA where the Government schemes are triggered down to the grassroots level. According to Table 5.2.2, 39 SHGs expressed their experiences in obtaining programmes and assistance from DRDA. Only one SHG said that they have no such experience so far but they know how to approach the DRDA. This indicates the capability of women in obtaining programmes and assistance from the DRDA has increased.

Table 5.2.3 : Experience to visit Gram Sabha.

Sl. No.	*Particulars*	*No. of SHG*	*Percentage*
1.	Experience	37	92.5
2.	Don't have experience	03	7.5
	Total	40	100.0

Source : Computed.

The capability of attending Gram Sabha meetings has increased among the members of SHGs as against their inability before entering as members in SHGs. This is proved in Table 5.2.3 which presents 92.5 per cent of the SHGs as attending Gram Sabha meeting and catching main role in decision-making. When Gram Sabha attendance was poor in Tamil Nadu, the Chief Minister of Tamil Nadu appealed to the SHG members to attend Gram Sabha meeting. But now Gram Sabha meetings are dominated by the members of SHG. Well oriented se!f-help group members used to take part in the meetings seriously. It is yet another devise for the members to gain confidence to participate in public meetings by the women.

Capability to Participate in Gram Sabha

SHG members thought that participating in the Gram Sabha meeting is their obligation and duty. Almost in all the villages, it seems that the Gram Sabha meeting will not be conducted if there is no participation from the SHG women.

***Marutham* SHG** women responded that the discussion regarding the allocation of cluster houses was the major agenda in the Gram Sabha meeting. Moreover when a grievance or issue was focused on in a Gram Sabha meeting, it should, in the next meeting, be informed whether that grievance was redressed or not. At least out of to fear of answering the constant queries posed by SHG women, panchayat members take adequate action.

***Karpaka Tharu* SHG** women assured that their participation in the Gram Sabha meeting is assured. Their role of intervention while the panchayat leader faced economic crisis was immense. SHG women suggested to the leader to collect Rs. 5 from each house as water levy which tremendously helped the leader to solve the monetary problem. Many times he heartfully appreciated the SHG women's timely intervention and for having given their valuable suggestions. He requested them to participate in all the Gram Sabha meetings.

The television allotted for the colony had been kept in the panchayat president's residence.for his personal use for years.

(Contd.)

(Contd.)

No one noticed it but the ***Olivelakku* SHG** women fought for it and now the whole colony is watching the television by the stern efforts taken by the SHG women.

***Indra* SHG's** role in the installation of hand pump and mini tank was unforgettable and remarkable.

The whole village knows very well about the significant participation of the ***Annai Vellankanni* SHG** women and ***Nehru Karmayoga* SHG** in the installation of pumps and getting infrastructure facilities like making new roads etc.

***Kamarajar* SHG** highlighted the urgent necessity of toilet, sanitary complex, library, OHT at the meeting.

Innovative discussion on bio-gas and vermicompost utilization was held by ***Nanmahalir* SHG** members.

The village was grateful to ***Nalmahalir* SHG** for its enduring effort to acquire street lights the adequate drinking water.

Table 5.2.4 : Experience of Visiting Mahalir Thittam Office.

Sl. No.	*Particulars*	*No. of SHG*	*Percentage*
1.	Experience	39	97.5
2.	Don't have experience	01	2.5
	Total	40	100.00

Source : Computed.

The Mahalir Thittam (Women Development Project) is a separate scheme for women and it concentrates mainly on the women SHGs. Table 5.2.4 presents the experience in visiting the Mahalir Thittam office for obtaining women development schemes. Out of 40 SHGs 39 are approaching the Mahalir Thittam office. This is a source for enriching their confidence and capability to get their due place in the society.

Table 5.2.5 : Experience of Visiting Village Panchayat.

Sl. No.	*Particulars*	*No. of SHG*	*Percentage*
1.	Experience	38	95.0
2.	Don't have experience	02	5.0
	Total	40	100.0

Source : Computed.

Table 5.2.5 presents the experiences of SHGs in visiting Village Panchayats for requesting various common facilities and attracting the notice of Village Panchayat members and Presidents for the development of villages. Out of 40 SHGs, 38 have such experience. It is found that the capability of approaching Village Panchayats for various facilities such as drinking water, street lights, road for burial ground, etc., and to alert the Panchayat to protect environment and the sanitation in the village has increased.

Table 5.2.6 : Experience of Visiting Panchayat Union Office.

Sl. No.	*Particulars*	*No. of SHG*	*Percentage*
1.	Experience	38	95.0
2.	Don't have experience	02	5.0
	Total	40	100

Source : Computed.

Experiences in visiting the Panchayat Union office is presented in Table 5.2.6: 95 per cent have visited and 5 per cent have not visited. The majority of the SHGs have opportunities to visit the Panchayat Union office to get approval for the locations they select to build sanitary complex, overhead tanks, etc. This indicates the increasing capability of getting sources and opportunities from higher level government authorities.

Table 5.2.7 : Experience of Visiting Municipality Office.

Sl. No.	*Particulars*	*No. of SHG*	*Percentage*
1.	Experience	00	0.0
2.	Don't have experience	40	100.0
	Total	40	100.0

Source : Computed.

None of the SHGs have experience in visiting municipalities since their living areas come under the jurisdiction of Village Panchayats.

Table 5.2.8 : Experience to visit the Collector Office.

Sl. No.	*Particulars*	*No. of SHG*	*Percentage*
1.	Experience	38	95.0
2.	Don't have experience	02	5.0
	Total	40	100.0

Source : Computed.

As per Table 5.2.8, 95 per cent SHGs have experience in visiting the Collector's office for submitting applications requesting facilities, assistance, infrastructure, etc., to the Collector and also applying for assistance in social welfare department and DRDA. In India, especially in Tamil Nadu Collector office is considered as power centre and all officials derive powers from the District Collector and administration. Even MLAs and MPs make complaints that they are not able to meet. In such a circumstance meeting the Collector by the SHGs is important. It will remove the fear from the minds of the women and poor. This indicates the increasing capability of women for struggling against poverty through approaching the district administration and higher officials for requesting assistance.

3. Increasing Personal Capability

Table 5.3.1 : Capability to speak.

Sl. No.	*Particulars*	*No. of SHG*	*Percentage*
1.	Yes	40	100.0
2.	No	00	0.0
	Total	40	100.0

Source : Computed.

All the members of the SHGs said that they are able to talk with any authority for obtaining assistance to overcome the bitterness of poverty and social discrimination. Table 5.3.1 shows the increasing capability of women to speak out their problems and needs in Panchayat meetings, in front of higher authorities, etc.

Table 5.3.2 : Increasing Self-confidence.

Sl. No.	*Particulars*	*No. of SHG*	*Percentage*
1.	Yes	40	100.0
2.	No	00	0.0
	Total	40	100.0

Source : Computed.

According to Table 5.3.2, self-confidence among individual women members of SHGs has developed. All the members of SHGs said that they have self-confidence to live and to function at multi-level, achieving goals and ambitions of development and poverty elimination.

Increasing Capability, Self-confidence

Women have got empowerment, confidence, autonomy and reliance through their group formation. It can be seen through their vivid conversation and candid actions. Their expressions of their development are given below:

Vinayagam **SHG** women responded that they had the confidence to confront any untoward incidents in their life.

Saron Raja **SHG** women told that they were once afraid to come out of their houses at night and sought help from their males. But now they run their own STD booth which remain opened until nine o' clock in the night.

Marutham **SHG** women developed the confidence that they could cater their family's economic and other needs.

Karpakatharu **Women SHG** realized that as they successfully run their grocery shop they could definitely manage their family without the support of their males. In fact they felt it would be much better than the males' management.

Indira **SHG** members had confidence that they could mobilize money for their urgent needs from the group.

Marriammal **SHG** women told that they had a feeling of belonging to a mass movement and that in their SHG and its

(Contd.)

(Contd.)

moral support, they could travel anywhere in the state without any money in their hand.

Senthamarai **SHG** believed that they could live with unity.

Annai Vellankani **SHG** women felt that they were equal to their males.

Kurinji **SHG** realized that women can perform well in any field if they were given proper training.

Olivillaku **SHG** was convinced that they could fight against women injustice through women's mass movement and social action.

Tholvalliyammai **SHG** women felt that they have developed confidence enough to inform others about their demands without any hesitation.

Fatima **SHG** felt that even Muslim women were equal to the males.

Satya **SHG** women hoped that they could sort out any problem and they believed that they could resolve any conflict in the family and even in the village.

Table 5.3.3 : Experience of participating in Household Decision-making Process.

Sl. No.	*Particulars*	*No. of SHG*	*Percentage*
1.	Experience	38	95.0
2.	Don't have Experience	02	5.0
	Total	40	100.0

Source : Computed.

Table 5.3.3 presents the part of SHG women in the decision-making process at home regarding investments, children's education, marriage, solving the disputes, etc., as 95 per cent SHGs have opportunities to take part in family decision-making and contribute useful ideas and suggestions to take important decisions. This indicates that the capability of women in decision-making has increased.

Increasing Capability – Participation in Household Decision-making Process

This study shows that all the group members actively participated in the decision-making process of their household. Before joining the group, the family related decisions were taken by either their husbands or by their sons. But there was a drastic change in their life style as they developed the capacity to mobilize resources on their own and got proper education through various training programmes.

It is virtually understood that women had a pivotal role in decision-making, employment, children's education, son's/daughter's marriage, asset creation and health related issues in their household.

When Theresa's husband drifted without any income source, she got a loan of Rs. 40,000 to buy an autorickshaw. Now he is the owner of an autorickshaw and is proud of having his own employment.

When the husbands of Febin of ***Karpakatharu*** **SHG**, and Lakshmi of ***Marriammal*** **SHG** found no way to perform their daughters' puberty ritual, the decision was taken by the mothers and they themselves led the functions.

Many women took self-decision or participated in their husbands' decision's regarding their children's marriage. When the marriage of Sermakani of ***Indira*** **SHG** and Kattithankam of ***Satya*** **SHG** was about to be stopped without proper patronage these women took the initiative with the assistance of their concerned groups. When Ms. Rathinam's son fell in love with a girl, Rathinam never bothered about her husband's rude mentality and solemnized her son's love marriage successfully without her husband's support.

The women's role in taking decisions pertaining to their children's education was immense. When Mankaneshwari of ***Kurinji*** **SHG's** daughter wanted to study B.Sc. she was opposed by her father as he thought that women's education was a sheer

(Contd.)

(Contd.)

wastage. Mankaneshwari, in consultation with her SHG, stubbornly sent her daughter to college. It influenced Jeyalaxmi also, as she sent her son and daughter to study B.Sc. and B.E. respectively.

Ms. Ramalakshmi of ***Thirumakal* SHG** came to know that her husband decided to put a full stop to their son's convent education on account of poor economic condition. She got a loan from her group and sent her son to the convent school.

It is virtually shown that women's contribution towards asset creation and protecting the existing properties is significant.

Rajapupathi of ***Marriammal* Group** saved money in the group and purchased jewels. Thankabai got a loan to construct her hut on her own with electricity. Ms. Mallika of ***Kamaraj* SHG** used the group loan to extend her husband's shop. Vijalakshmi of the same group upgraded her hut house to a brick one.

It is a well known fact that lot of changes have happened in women's life in matters of autonomy, decision-making process, patronizing their family and assisting their spouses to be empowered in their own life. SHG women replied that all these were possible only through the training they got from their group.

Table 5.3.4 : Interested to understanding Government Development Programmes.

Sl. No.	*Particulars*	*No. of SHG*	*Percentage*
1.	Interested	37	92.5
2.	Don't have interest	03	7.5
	Total	40	100.0

Source : Computed.

The interest of SHG members to understand the development programmes of the Government is presented in Table 5.3.4, according to which, the members of 92.5 per cent SHGs said that they are interested to be aware of and to understand the development programmes of the Government. As low as 7.5 per cent SHGs have no such interest. This indicates that their self-motivation is functioning well to search for development programmes and results in increasing capability for searching and receiving opportunities against poverty.

Table 5.3.5 : Opinion on Womens Marriage Age.

Sl. No.	*Marriage Age*	*No. of SHG*	*Percentage*
1.	Below 20	00	0.0
2.	20-25	40	100.0
3.	25-30	00	0.0
•		40	100.0

Source: Computed.

Marriage is an essential part of each women's life and the age at marriage determines the capability of functioning as change agents for development. The members of all the SHGs said that the age at marriage should be between 20 and 25. This indicates that the women are aware of the demerits of early marriage.

Table 5.3.6 : Enjoying Freedom for Physical Mobility.

Sl. No.	*Particulars*	*No. of SHG*	*Percentage*
1.	Yes	40	100.0
2.	No	00	0.0
	Total	40	100.0

Source : Computed.

Table 5.3.6 presents the freedom enjoyed by women for moving out of home for the purpose of development activities and earning. All the members of the SHGs said that they are allowed to move out of home for development activities, SHG meetings, trainings, trading and earning, etc. It is evidence of the capability of the women to convince their family for moving out of the house in connection with their development activities, earning, meetings, meeting officials, participating in Gram Sabha meetings, visiting police station, Panchayat offices, etc.

4. Increasing Capability to Participate in Development Activities

Increasing Capability to Work for Gender Development

Some women shared their experience of having got women empowerment by becoming members of SHG groups.

Marutham **SHG** said that they could easily get access to loans from their group. They felt that they could freely move with the males in their village which was unimaginable in earlier days. Gone are the days when they hesitated to talk boldly.

Saron Roja **SHG** felt that they have forged unity among the women in the village by forming the groups. They shared that once *Thankapushpam* house was damaged by a track and almost the whole house collapsed. All the group members went to the police station to fight for justice. Finally they got compensation from the truck owner. The police station never threatened them. Ironically police personnel are now frightened upon seeing them *en masse*.

Karpatharu **SHG** felt that nowadays women have also started owning properties in their own names, which, they felt, bloomed with their self-reliance. Many of the group members bought houses and lands in their own name.

Indira **SHG** stated that the women were not expecting money from outside —money-lenders. They felt that their self-esteem is protected by avoiding them.

Senthamarai **SHG** went one step ahead by protecting the honour of the women by paying the outside loan from the savings of the group. Now the village women sigh in relief.

Vinayakam Suyam Sidda **SHG** felt that SHGs provided employment to unemployed women and helped to generate income to their household. They have their own crusher where the husbands of the group members were provided with employment.

Tholevalliyammami **SHG** showed their gratitude to the government and the banks as they were ready to provide loans to the group members which was not at all possible for them as individuals.

(Contd.)

(Contd.)

> ***Nalmahalir* SHG** thought that to have bank account was a great achievement, which made significant inroads towards women autonomy in the economic decision-making of the family.
>
> ***Thendral* and *Vasantham* SHG** groups said that women's caliber, skills and potentialities could be enhanced by forming the groups.
>
> ***Annai Sivakami* SHG** reiterated that women who were SHG group members acquired sufficient status in the society.
>
> ***Parvathiyammal* SHG** group believed that they got collective strength by evolving as a group.
>
> ***Mahalir Kulanthaikal Mempattu Kulu* (women and child development group)** learnt the health and sanitation awareness only by becoming members of the group.

Table 5.4.1 : Experience of Solving Women Problems.

Sl. No.	*Particulars*	*No. of SHG*	*Percentage*
1.	Experience	28	70.0
2.	Don't have Experience	12	30.0
	Total	40	100.0

Source : Computed.

Out of 40 SHGs, 28 have experience in solving the problems of women such as natural disaster, law, harassment, discrimination, indebtedness, sudden accidents resulting in wounds, sudden loss of assets, houses, etc. and only 12 SHGs have no such experience since such situations have not arisen. However, all the members of the SHGs said that they are able to extend a helping hand to the common victims of natural disaster, harassment by money-lenders, discrimination, etc.

Table 5.4.2 : Experience of Solving Village Common Problems.

Sl. No.	*Particulars*	*No. of SHG*	*Percentage*
1.	Experience	29	72.5
2.	Don't have Experience	11	27.5
	Total	40	100.0

Source : Computed.

Women members of SHGs participated in problem solving occasions in the villages concerned. According to Table 5.4.2, 29 SHGs expressed their experiences in solving the common village problems; 11 SHGs have not had such experience since they did not find any serious common problems in the villages concerned. The capability of women has increased to take efforts for solving the common problems such as drinking water, street lights, road facilities, conveyance facilities, conflicts, etc.

Increasing Capability to Solve the Village Common Problems

When there was not enough water taps in the village, ***Marutham* SHG** initiated action to meet the panchayat leader and asked him to provide adequate taps in the village. Moreover they fought to get proper weirs in the water supply channel as the water was always leaking out. When they had no other way to go to the graveyard and had to carry the body through water they organized a social action and engaged in road roko (blocking the road), which eventually led to them getting a proper bridge. The women group initiated action to renovate the tank as it was full of silted soil for more than ten years. They have organized rallies for getting sufficient roads and for public toilets. The overhead tank was not opened to public as the politicians did not allot a particular day to inaugurate it. ***Karpakatharu* Group** members met the Collector and gave a petition to open it for public use. It worked out well as the Collector ordered to open it forthwith and appreciated the women for their efforts.

When the community did not find a proper place to run its anganwadi, the ***Olivillaku* SHG** provided its own place to run the anganwadi.

Some families in the village encroached on the Amman temple properties and enjoyed them. ***Mutharamman* SHG** women members met the Thoothukudi District Superintendent of Police to give a petition and got them back with his efforts.

***Kamaraj* SHG** women were appreciated by the District

(Contd.)

(Contd.)

Collector as they bravely protested against the illicit liquor prepared by local influential persons. Now there is no illicit liquor in that area.

Annai Sivakami **SHG** added one more feather to its cap when its fight for house *patta* for fifty households was successful.

Mahalir Kulanthaikal Mempattu Kulu found that the main cause for many diseases was people polluting the drinking well water. It organized health and sanitation related meetings to make people aware of their bad practices.

Even though the public tap is meant for all, people allowed taking water only after the influential persons took the water for their houses. That inadequate water created an artificial water scarcity in the village. It was first protested by ***Sankamam*** **SHG** giving a petition to the Village Panchayat. Now all are equally treated and water is being distributed to all.

The village panchayat leader got signatures from all the village people on a blank white paper during the *Grama Shaba* meeting and later wrote that they did not need a water tank for their village and that it could better be allotted to the next village. ***Sangamam*** **SHG** came to know of this plot and immediately met and explained to the District Collector. The Collector appreciated the group and warned the panchayat leader.

Their successful tales have no full stop. They have solved many more problems with the assistance of the village panchayat, bureaucrats and others. And their endeavour to attain empowerment is still going on without bothering about the obstacles they face here and there.

Table 5.4.3 : Experience of Collective Action.

Sl. No.	*Particulars*	*No. of SHG*	*Percentage*
1.	Experience	36	90.0
2.	Don't have Experience	04	10.0
	Total	40	100.00

Source : Computed.

Collective action and team efforts always result in fruitful solutions to any problem. This is proved in Table 5.4.3 as 36 SHGs said that they took collective action against problems and poverty. Collective entrepreneurial ability has increased among the members of the SHGs. About 4 SHGs have no experience of collective action but they are capable of collective action.

Table 5.4.4 : Experience of Participating in Conference/Meeting.

Sl. No.	*Particulars*	*No. of SHG*	*Percentage*
1.	Experience	29	72.5
2.	Don't have Experience	11	27.5
	Total	40	100.0

Source : Computed.

Out of 40 SHGs, 29 have experience of participating in conferences, meetings, training programmes, etc., and 11 SHGs have no such experience, as Table 5.4.4 presents. It is inferred that the SHG women have opportunities to enhance their capability for multi-functioning as change agents of self, family and national development.

Table 5.4.5 : Experience of Participating in Village Planning.

Sl. No.	*Particulars*	*No. of SHG*	*Percentage*
1.	Experience	29	72.5
2.	Don't have Experience	11	27.5
	Total	40	100.0

Source : Computed.

Table 5.4.6 presents the experience of SHG members of participating in village planning: 72.5 per cent of the SHGs are regularly participating the village planning and 27.5 per cent do not participate. It is evident that the capability of women is enhanced since they have started to participate in the village planning and they are able to contribute their views for effective planning.

Table 5.4.6 : Experience of Participating in Village Panchayat Budget.

Sl. No.	*Particulars*	*No. of SHG*	*Percentage*
1.	Experience	15	37.5
2.	Don't have Experience	25	62.5
	Total	40	100

Source : Computed.

According to Table 5.4.7, 15 SHGs are participating in Village Panchayat budget meeting while 25 SHGs said that they have no experience of participating in village budget meetings. Budget meetings are an important part of the Village Panchayat and the women have to be allowed since they are capable of contributing to effective budgeting.

Table 5.4.7 : Experience of Selecting Place to Implement Development Programme.

Sl. No.	*Particulars*	*No. of SHG*	*Percentage*
1.	Experience	21	52.5
2.	Don't have Experience	19	47.5
	Total	40	100.0

Source : Computed.

Table 5.4.8 presents the experience of SHGs of the selection of places for group houses, drainage, hand pumps, overhead tanks etc., in their village's. Out of 40 SHGs, 21 have such experience and 19 SHGs have not. However, it is observed that all the members of the SHGs are able to suggest appropriate location for building and installation of hand pumps and water taps.

Table 5.4.8 : Experience of Evaluating Development Programme.

Sl. No.	*Particulars*	*No. of SHG*	*Percentage*
1.	Experience	13	32.5
2.	Don't have Experience	27	67.5
	Total	40	100.0

Source : Computed.

Increasing Capability to Select Locations for implementing Development Programmes

The experience of Executing Rural Development and Rural Panchayat Schemes.

It was decided by the panchayat to construct the drainage in front of the houses, but, as ***Jeyabarathi*** **SHG** women got awareness about health and sanitation, they consulted the Panchayat leader and asked him to change the place from the front yard to the back yard. It was accepted and executed in the same way.

There was a dispute over the location of some group houses. Finally the ***Marutham*** **SHG** selected the ideal place to construct the group houses which was unanimously accepted. Now the construction is in progress in the same area.

Karpagatharu **SHG** selected the location for constructing the overhead tank in their village which was appreciated by all the village people.

The decision to install the hand pump and street pump was left with ***Annai Vellankanni*** **SHG.**

Olivillaku **SHG** selected the place for the installation of street lamps. ***Satya*** **Group's** decision regarding street construction in the village was unanimously endorsed.

According to Table 5.4.9, 32.5 per cent of the SHGs have experience of evaluating development programmes and 67.5 per cent SHGs have no such experience. Evaluation of the development programmes is essential for identification of the gap between benefits and beneficiaries, quality of the benefits, gap in delivery system of development programmes, etc. All the members should be aware of evaluating development programmes since their capability has increased for other relevant activities.

5. Increasing Political Capability

Table 5.5.1 : Experience of Participating in Local Body Election.

Sl. No.	*Particulars*	*No. of SHG*	*Percentage*
1.	Experience	18	45.0
2.	Don't have Experience	22	55.0
	Total	40	100.0

Source : Computed.

Providing due place in politics and democracy for women is in the nation's interest. Table 5.5.1 shows the experience of SHGs of participating in Panchayat elections: 18 SHGs participated in local body elections and 22 SHGs did not participate. Participation of SHGs in local body elections is very low and this may be due to inability to find time and opportunities. However the field observation showed that they are good alternatives for men in democratic representation if they get the opportunity to take part in local body elections.

Table 5.5.2 : Experience of Participating Protest Activities.

Sl. No.	*Particulars*	*No. of SHG*	*Percentage*
1.	Experience	17	42.5
2.	Don't have Experience	23	57.5
	Total	40	100.0

Source : Computed.

Table 5.5.2 presents the experience of SHGs of participating in protest activities. Out of 40 SHGs, only 17 have such experience and 23 have not. It is contradictory since other SHGs take part in all the activities as we have seen in the previous tables, and so let us assume that the women are capable of taking part in protest or public activities.

According to Table 5.5.3, members of 12 SHGs registered their membership in various political parties. The members of the remaining 28 SHGs have not registered but they morally support the political parties which they perceive as good. However, they are able to be transparent in supporting and being members of political parties. It is assumed that the capability of women has increased to take part in political parties.

Table 5.5.3 : Membership in Political Party.

Sl. No.	*Particulars*	*No. of SHG*	*Percentage*
1.	Having membership	12	30.0
2.	Don't have membership	28	70.0
	Total	40	100.0

Source : Computed.

6. Increasing Capability to Receive Assistance from various Institutions for Entreperneurship

Table 5.6.1 : Experience of Receiving Assistance from NGOs.

Sl. No.	*Particulars*	*No. of SHG*	*Percentage*
1.	Experience	34	85
2.	Don't have Experience	06	15
	Total	40	100.0

Source : Computed.

Table 5.6.1 presents the experience of SHGs of receiving assistance from NGOs. Out of 40 SHGs, 34 SHGs received assistance from NGOs and 6 have not received such assistance. The NGOs are extending opportunities for increasing the capability of women and it is assumed that the capability has increased to associate with NGOs for development.

Table 5.6.2 : Experience of Receiving Assistance from Banks.

Sl. No.	*Particulars*	*No. of SHG*	*Percentage*
1.	Experience	29	72.5
2.	Don't have Experience	11	27.5
	Total	40	100.0

Source : Computed.

According to Table 5.6.2, 29 SHGs received loans from banks with subsidy and 11 SHGs are yet to receive loans from banks. This indicates that the members of SHGs have learnt the procedures for obtaining financial assistance with subsidy from banks and developed their capability to launch enterprises as the sources of income.

Table 5.6.3 : Experience of Receiving Assistance from Village Panchayat.

Sl. No.	*Particulars*	*No. of SHG*	*Percentage*
1.	Experience	15	37.5
2.	Don't have Experience	25	62.5
	Total	40	100.0

Source : Computed.

Table 5.6.3 presents the experience of SHGs in receiving assistance from the Village Panchayat concerned. Out of 40 SHGs, 15 SHGs received and 25 SHGs did not receive assistance from the Village Panchayat such as place, building, permission, approach, support, etc., for their enterprises. It is inferred that the capability of women has increased to approach the Village Panchayat for assistance.

Table 5.6.4 : Experience of Receiving Assistance from DRDA.

Sl. No.	*Particulars*	*No. of SHG*	*Percentage*
1.	Experience	31	77.5
2.	Don't have Experience	09	22.5
	Total	40	100.0

Source : Computed.

With reference to Table 5.6.4, out of 40 SHGs, 31 SHGs received assistance and aid from the DRDA and 9 SHGs are yet to receive assistance from the DRDA. The DRDA is the grassroots outlet of the State Government delivering benefits to the rural areas through schemes and projects. It is interested that the women members of SHGs learn to contact the DRDA and propose their plans/projects for assistance and aid. These experiences increased the capability of women to receive assistance from the government.

Table 5.6.5 : Experience of Receiving Assistance from Mahalirthittam.

Sl. No.	*Particulars*	*No. of SHG*	*Percentage*
1.	Experience	28	70
2.	Don't have Experience	12	30
	Total	40	100.0

Source : Computed.

Table 5.6.5 presents the experience of SHGs of receiving assistance from Mahalirthittam, according to which, 28 SHGs received assistance and 12 SHGs are yet to receive assistance from Mahalirthittam. Receipt of assistance from Mahalirthittam by SHGs is less when compared with assistance from the DRDA.

Table 5.6.6 : Experience of Receiving Assistance from District Collector.

Sl. No.	*Particulars*	*No. of SHG*	*Percentage*
1.	Experience	32	80
2.	Don't have Experience	08	20
	Total	40	100.0

Source : Computed.

Out of 40 SHGs, 32 SHGs received assistance from the District Collector directly and 11 SHGs have no such experience, says Table 5.6.6. It is evident that the capability of women has increased to meet the District Collector for development assistance.

Table 5.6.7 : Experience of Receiving Assistance from Panchayat Union.

Sl. No.	*Particulars*	*No. of SHG*	*Percentage*
1.	Experience	21	52.5
2.	Don't have Experience	19	47.5
	Total	40	100.0

Source : Computed.

With reference to Table 5.6.7, 21 SHGs received assistance from the Panchayat Union and 19 have not received such assistance. However, it is learnt that the women are able to approach of Panchayat Union for assistance and aid.

Table 5.6.8 : Experience of Receiving EDP Loan.

Sl. No.	*Particulars*	*No. of SHG*	*Percentage*
1.	Experience	22	55
2.	Don't have Experience	18	45
	Total	40	100.0

Source : Computed.

Out of 40 SHGs, 22 SHGs received Entrepreneurship Development loans and 18 SHGs have not received such loans, says Table 5.6.9. However, the women are able to take up entrepreneurship with financial assistance.

Increasing Capability—Achievements in spending and repaying the loan amount

A widow belonging to ***Sri Devi*** **SHG** recorded an achievement in spending her loan fruitfully. After the sudden demise of her husband, life became deserted for her and her two children. If anyone heard her tales of suffering they could not restrain their eyes from becoming wet. She underwent such unbearable hardship as to find no way to collect money for her sons' education. At that time ***Sri Devi*** **SHG** came forward to extend its helping hand to her. She got a loan of around three and half lakh rupees to meet the first son's B.Pharm. course expenditure and she successfully repaid the amount. Now her first son has become the breadwinner of the family and the second one is studying first year B.Pharm. course. So far she has got sixty-four thousand rupees for her second son's education. Furthermore, as people came to know about her honest repaying habit, banks and other financial institutions voluntarily came forward to provide loans to her. She bought milch animals with the help of a bank loan which she repaid periodically.

The tale of successful repayment is not a closed process. A woman by name Rajive got a loan for her daughter's delivery, another woman, Lakshmi by name, used the group loan to purchase milch animals and to meet her daughter's maiden

(Contd.)

(Contd.)

deepavali expenditure. Uttharam, another lady, got a loan to renovate her damaged house. All these women belonged to ***Marutham*** **SHG.**

Saron Roja **SHG** women utilized the group loan amount to fund their children's education, to repay the amount borrowed at high rates of interest from money-lenders, to buy autorickshaw, to meet their children's wedding expenditures and to perform social and religious rituals.

Sermakani was heavily injured falling from a palm tree while she was climbing it. Her life was saved by the loan given by the group. She felt it was her second life, given by the group. Many women belonging to ***Indira, Mariaamal, Senthamarai*** **SHGs** got loans to renovate their damaged huts, to get power supply to their households, to repay loans got from money-lenders and to purchase jewels. ***Jeyalakshmi*** got a loan to fund her daughter's BCA course from ***Kurinji*** **SHG.** Shanthi mortgaged her mother-in-law's jewels to meet some urgent expenditure which created a lot of chaos in her family. So she got a loan of about Rs.10,000 from ***Olivillaku*** **SHG** to redeem her mother-in-law's jewels. Rathinam could never forget the timely assistance rendered by ***Olivillaku*** **SHG** as she got a loan for her husband's cardiac treatment.

It is a well known fact that many women got loans to repay loans got from others. The striking thing is that all repaid their loan from the group in time.

Sum Up

- Organizing SHGs has considerably increased after the year 2000. 35 per cent of the SHGs were organized during the first year (2001) and 2.5 per cent were organized during the year 2004. The growths of entrepreneurship ability has increased among the SHGs after the year 2001. As high as 50 per cent of the SHGs were engaged in various trades during 2004. The trades of the SHGs are super market, ready-made garments, canteen, honey merchandize, ice cream parlor, telephone booth, driving school, paper cup making, file pad and envelope making, fisheries, halva making, utensils hiring, goat rearing, stone quarry, stone drilling, pickles making, palm mat weaving, palm leaf products, grocery shop, detergents manufacturing, rearing milch animals and banana cultivation.

- Out of 696 members of 40 SHGs, 579 belong to OBC and 117 belong to SC. No members from the ST community were found in any of the selected SHGs. 315 is the highest number of SHG members in the age group of 31-40 and 45 is the lowest number of SHG members in the age group of 51-60. None of the members are below 20 years and above 60 years. Out of 696, 96 members of SHGs are widows and 15 are separated. The number of illiterates 75, graduates 20, technically qualified 5 and all others have studied at school and high school level. Out of 696 members of SHGs, 336 are agricultural coolies, 183 are working in the non-farm sector, and 177 are housewives. 99 members of SHGs are living in pucca houses, 188 are living in huts and 209 are living in tiled houses. The majority of the members of SHGs are non-landholders. Representation of Muslim members in SHG is very low against Hindus and Christians who are the highest and moderate respectively. The ability for and attitude of saving money has been ignited among the members of SHGs.
- The highest amount of money (Rs.1,50,000 to 2,00,000) was saved by 5 per cent of the SHGs and smallest amount of money (less than Rs. 50,000) was saved by 77.5 per cent of the SHGs. It is found that the capability of mobilizing capital through savings exists among the members of SHGs. As for the capability of going to the police station without fear to get solutions for problems faced by all the SHG members 16 SHGs have the experience of visiting the police station. 97.5 per cent of the SHGs have experience of approaching the DRDA and other Government offices for programmes and assistance. This indicates the awareness and capability of

approaching government sources among SHG members for their development. 38 SHGs received revolving fund from government sources and 2 of the SHGs have yet to receive it. 92.5 per cent of the SHGs attend Gram Sabha meetings and play the main role in decision-making. The capability of participation and decision-making has increased among all the members of the SHGs. 39 SHGs have experience of visiting the Mahalir Thittam office for obtaining women development schemes. The remaining one is yet to visit the Mahalir Thittam office. 38 SHGs have experience of visiting Village Panchayats for various common facilities and to alert the Panchayat on protecting environment and sanitation in the villages.

- 95 per cent of the SHGs have experience of visiting the Panchayat Union office for getting approval and permission for their plans for village development. None of the SHG members have experience of visiting a municipality. 95 per cent of the SHGs have experience of visiting the Collector's office for various purposes. This indicates their increasing capability to approach the district administration and higher officers for requesting assistance. All the members of the SHGs are capable of speaking out their problems and needs in any relevant place and in front of higher authorities. The self-confidence of all the SHG members has been enhanced through the team and collective efforts to be responsible citizens. The members of 95 per cent SHGs have opportunities to take part in the family decision-making process at home and have contributed timely and helpful suggestions. This indicates that the capability of women in decision-making has increased. The members of 97.5 per cent SHGs have interest in and are eager to know and understand the development programmes of the government. It is inferred that they are self-motivated to search for and members of avail opportunities for development. Members of all SHGs stated that the age at marriage should be between 20 and 25. This indicates the awareness of women about the disadvantages of early marriage.

- All members of the SHGs have freedom to move out of home for various purposes such as economic and social activities. It is evident that the women are capable of convincing their family about moving out of home in connection with the economic and social activities. 28 SHGs have experience of solving the problems of women and 12 SHGs have no such experience. It is found that all the women members are capable of extending their assistance in terms of money, team effort, etc. to those who are struggling against harassment and discrimination etc. 29 SHGs have experience of solving the common problems of the village and 11 SHGs have no such experience. However, the members of the SHGs are capable of participating in solving common village problems. 36 SHGs have experience of collective action against social problems and poverty. Only 4 SHGs have no such experience. However, all the members of the SHGs are capable of participating in their team's collective efforts and actions against all kinds of problems, including poverty and unemployment. 29 SHGs have experience of participating in conferences, meetings, training programmes, etc. and 11 SHGs have no such experience. However, all the members of the SHGs have opportunities to enhance their capability. 34 SHGs have experience of participating in Gram Sabha meetings and 6 SHGs have no such experiences. The capability of women has increased to take effective part in Gram Sabha meetings.
- 72.5 per cent of the SHGs have experience of participating in village planning and 27.5 per cent have no such experience. However, all the women members of the SHGs are capable of participating in and contributing their views and ideas on village planning. Only 15 SHGs have experience of taking part in Village Panchayat budget meetings. 25 SHGs have no such experience since they are not aware of the budget. 21 SHGs have experience of selecting locations for development work like constructing group houses, overhead tanks, drainages, installation of hand pump and water taps while 19 have no such experience. But all of them are capable of locating

appropriate places for buildings and water sources in their village. Only 32.5 per cent of the SHGs have experience of evaluating the development programmes and the remaining 67.5 per cent have no such experience. All the women are motivated to bring out their capabilities for evaluating the development programmes. 18 SHGs have experience of taking part in local body elections and the remaining 20 SHGs have no such experience. However, the experience gained through being SHG members extended their capability to take effective part in elections and in democratic institutions. Out of 40 SHGs, 17 have the experience of taking part in protest activities and the remaining 23 SHGs have no such experience. But, the women suggested several public activities appropriate for development.

- Out of 40 SHGs, 12 SHGs have registered their membership in various political parties and the remaining 28 SHGs have not. But the field observation reveals that the women of the SHGs are able to take part in politics whenever necessity arises. 34 SHGs has received assistance from various institutions and 6 are yet to receive it for the purpose of entrepreneurship development activities. It is inferred that the women are capable of bringing out their entrepreneurial skills as traders. 22 SHGs have received loan with subsidy from various banks and 18 SHGs have not received any loan from banks for the purpose of entrepreneurship. But all the SHG women have learnt to draft their plan for business and understand the procedures for obtaining loan with subsidy from banks for entrepreneurial purpose. Out of 40 SHGs, 15 SHGs have received assistance from the Village Panchayat such as space, building, permission, approval support, etc., and 25 SHGs are yet to receive such assistance. However, we learn that the women are capable of approaching the Village Panchayat for assistance. Out of 40 SHGs, 34 SHGs have received assistance from NGOs and 6 have not received such assistance. The NGOs are extending opportunities for increasing the capability of women and it has assumed that the capability is increased to attach themselves with NGOs for development. Out of 40 SHGs, 31 SHGs have received assistance and aid from the DRDA and 9 SHGs are yet to receive assistance from the DRDA. The DRDA is the grassroots outlet of the State Government delivering benefits to the rural areas through schemes and projects. The women members of the SHG have learnt to contact the DRDA and propose their plans/projects for assistance and aid. These experiences have increased the capability of women to receive assistance from the government. 28 SHGs have received assistance and 12 SHGs are yet to receive assistance from the Mahalirthittam. Receipt of assistance from the Mahalirthittam by the SHGs is less when compared with assistance received from the DRDA.

- Out of 40 SHGs, 32 SHGs have received assistance from the District Collector directly and 11 SHGs have no such experience. It is evident that the capability of women has increased to meet the District Collector for development assistance. 21 SHGs have received assistance from the Panchayat Union and 19 have not received such assistance. However, it is learnt that the women are able to approach the Panchayat Union for assistance and aid. 29 SHGs have experience of self-support and 11 SHGs have no such experience. Self-support for poverty eradication is one of the major factors increasing multi-dimensional capability to struggle against the poverty. The SHG women have done it. None of the SHGs has experienced problems in receiving assistance from the DRDA. Out of 40 SHGs, 14 have experienced problems in receiving loans from banks and 26 SHGs have no such experience. It is inferred that the women are capable of tackling the problems with banks to receive assistance. Out of 40 SHGs, 13 have experience of using their group money for business/entrepreneurship development while 27 SHGs have no such experience. It is learnt that the women should be guided to identify better suitable businesses to invest their group money in since their capability has increased to become entrepreneurs. 36 SHGs do not have the experience of mobilizing capital from others such as money-lenders, private sources, etc. and only 4 SHGs have such experience. This indicates that the women are wary of money-lenders and other private sources of money in order to escape from the hardships of indebtedness. 27 SHGs have earned profits from the business/entrepreneurship and 13 SHGs said that they have no such experience since the business is yet to be started by them. It is inferred that the women are capable of running their business successfully. In the beginning of the business, 21 SHGs experienced a little loss and 19 were not experienced. However, the women who met with loss identified the reasons for the loss, rectified the defects and developed their business. These experiences have increased the capability of the women to develop the business. 29 SHGs received and 11 SHGs did not receive marketing assistance from NGOs.

- Out of 40 SHGs, 29 received marketing assistance from the DRDA and 11 SHGs did not. The marketing assistance of DSMS was received by 26 SHGs and 14 SHGs did not receive it. 29 SHGs received assistance from the Panchayat Union for marketing and 11 SHGs did not receive such assistance from the Panchayat Union. 31 SHGs did not receive marketing assistance from the Village Panchayat but 9 SHGs said that they received marketing assistance from the Village Panchayat. 20 SHGs said that they received marketing assistance from other sources such as wholesalers etc. and 20 SHGs said that they did not receive marketing assistance from other sources. All the SHGs received marketing assistance through their own efforts. 26 SHGs said that they required financial assistance for the sustainability of their business and 14 SHGs did not want such assistance for the sustainability of their business. 18 SHGs reported that they face the problem of getting raw materials but 22 SHGs said that they do not have any problems in getting raw materials. 34 SHGs said that they are willing to extend their business and 6 SHGs said that they do not want to extend their business.

EXPECTATIONS

THOOTHUKUDI BLOCK

Sl. No.	*Name of the Women SHG*	*Enterprise*	*Present Status*	*Required Assistance*	*Reason*
1.	Saranaaroja	Supermarket	Good	Loan	Like to extend the enterprise
2.	Kurinji	Readymade garments, canteen	Good	Loan	Bank Loan not received
3.	Oolivelukku	Honey sales	Very good	Training	Extend the Honey Business
4.	Thirumakal	Ice cream parlour	Good	Loan	Bank Loan not received
5.	Maniveenayagam	STD both	Good	Marketing	Marketing facility not available
6.	Rasiveediyal	Driving center	Good	Advertisement, Loan	Not aware of Advertisement. Like to purchase Car and Auto
7.	Sathiya	Paper cup	Very poor	Marketing	TASMAC lack of marketing facility
8.	Jeyabharath	File pad. Envelope	Very poor	Marketing	Not aware of cost fixation and marketing facility

Source : Computed.

KARUNGULAM BLOCK

Sl. No.	*Name of the Women SHG*	*Enterprise*	*Present Status*	*Required Assistance*	*Reason*
1.	Nehru Gramodaya	Fish farming	Good	Loan	Like to do other business also
2.	Nalmakalir	Crab rearing	Very good	Loan	Like to do other business also
3.	Thendral	Halva	Very good	Training in other enter-prise also	Like to do other business also
4.	Vasantham	Halva	Very good	Training in other enter-prise also	Like to do other business also
5.	M.G.R.	Renting utensils	Very good	Training in other enter-prise also	Like to do other business also
6.	Indira	Renting utensils	Very good	Training in other enter-prise also	Like to do other business also
7.	Chandaragri	Renting utensils	Very good	Training in other enter-prise also	Like to do other business also

Source : Computed.

SRIVAIKUNDAM BLOCK

Sl. No.	*Name of the Women SHG*	*Enterprise*	*Present Status*	*Required Assistance*	*Reason*
1.	Marutham	Goat farming	Very good	Loan	Extend the business
2.	Sugam Siddtha Venayagam	Stone quarry	Good	Government should use for building construction	Heavy competition
3.	Tholavelli-yamman	Power tiller	Very poor	Alternative employment	Power tiller already sold
4.	Kamarajar	Banana cultivation	Good	5 acre cultivation land	Extend the business

Source : Computed.

ALWARTHIRUNAGARI BLOCK

Sl. No.	*Name of the Women SHG*	*Enterprise*	*Present Status*	*Required Assistance*	*Reason*
1.	Ponvela Dowcra	Pickles	Very good	No need	Sustainable
2.	Annai Sivagami	Jute	Very good	No need	Sustainable
3.	Kamarajar	Jute	Very good	No need	Sustainable
4.	Karpagatharu	Palm candy Jaggery	Very good	Alternative business	Seasonal work only three month in the year
5.	Muthumaalai-amman	Fish farming, milch animals	Very good	No need	To protect fish and vegetable cultivation in wasteland
6.	Sridevi	Milch animals	Very good	Alternative business	To extend
7.	Dowcra	Palm mat wearing	Good	Alternative business	Poor income

Source : Computed.

THIRUCHENDUR BLOCK

Sl. No.	*Name of the Women SHG*	*Enterprise*	*Present Status*	*Required Assistance*	*Reason*
1.	Sangam Makalir kuttuaamaippu	Grocery Shop	Very good	No need	Sustainable
2.	Annai	Paper Cup	Very poor	Marketing	Marketing facility not available
3.	Christhuraja	Provision Store	Very poor	No need	Not interested to continue the business
4.	Parvathiyammal	Washing detergents	Good	Marketing	To extend the business

Source : Computed.

UDANDKUDI BLOCK

Sl. No.	*Name of the Women SHG*	*Enterprise*	*Present Status*	*Required Assistance*	*Reason*
1.	Karpagatharu	Grocery Shop	Good	Loan	Heavy competition. To extend
2.	Indira	Palm leaf products	Very good	Loan	To extend the business
3.	Mariyammal	Palm leaf products	Very good	Loan	To extend the business
4.	Santhanamery	Palm leaf products	Very good	Loan	To extend the business
5.	Fathima	Palm leaf products	Very good	Loan	To extend the business
6.	Muththalamman	Palm leaf products	Very good	Loan	To extend the business

Source : Computed.

KOVILPATTI BLOCK

Sl. No.	*Name of the Women SHG*	*Enterprise*	*Present Status*	*Required Assistance*	*Reason*
1.	Vinayagam	Stone quarry	Very poor	No need	Not interested to continue
2.	Suyachitta Everest	Stone quarry	Very poor	No need	Not interested to continue
3.	Annaitherasa	Stone quarry	Very poor	No need	Not interested to continue

Source : Computed.

KAYATHARU BLOCK

Sl. No.	*Name of the Women SHG*	*Enterprise*	*Present Status*	*Required Assistance*	*Reason*
1.	Annaivelankanni	Stone quarry	Very good	Lorry	To save money and time

Source : Computed.

SHG women members over a period of time have learnt about the nuances of running an enterprise and most of them felt that presently they are in good status and likely to extend their business activities in the future. Moreover, those who found difficulty in running their chosen enterprise do not want to waste their money and seek alternative employment. They also found problems in marketing their products since no training was given to them in this particular area. SHGs who have undertaken quarrying of stone were in a critical situation and they are not interested to continue their activity since they are not benefited much. If they are trained properly and explore the marketing opportunities, perhaps, they can elevate their status. They required assistance in the form of:

- Loan,
- Advertisement and marketing facilities,
- Training for alternative employment, and
- Infrastructure facilities to run their business.

While observing the activities of the SHG one would find quick emergence of the women's movement in the name of SHG. Behind this scheme, however, there are District Collector and project officials. The officials have moved in the project mode to achieve the target. In the same way they moved into trade also. In our observation we find that for the success of all these ventures, both Collector and project officials were responsible as they pushed them to training and organize groups and trades. The women have made use of this opportunity and emerge victoriously. It's success depends on its sustainability. It requires R and D, support facilitation by the Collector and the project officials and the enthusiasm of the women. In the absence of all, this is just another cooperative exercise.

6 MAJOR FINDINGS AND CONCLUSIONS

Major Findings

This study shows that Self-Help Groups (SHG) of women have created a far reaching consequence in the lives of women by exploring the opportunities to lead a life they value. Women can be no longer seen as the passive recipients of welfare activities; rather they are becoming active agents of change and the dynamic promoters of social transformation who alter the lives of both women and men. From the analysis of the study, the following aspects of women's transformative role emerge.

(1) More Economic Opportunity and Economic Security

Women work longer hours than men but at home and this work does not produce any remuneration and its often ignored in accounting and contributions of women to the family's prosperity. But the economic activity performed by these SHG women earns them money and now their contribution to the family's prosperity is more visible. Their freedom to work in a group and to earn income has contributed to the reduction of their poverty. Their freedom of economic activity has led to economic security. This also leads to ownership rights over the assets created by them through their own income. The presence of claims of property amplifies the voice of women, and it makes it easier for women to enter and flourish in economic, commercial and social activities. Ultimately it releases them from the clutches of money-lenders.

(2) Increased Self-confidence

Activity through the SHG has increased the self-confidence of women by making them stakeholders of the project they have chosen.

Since they realize their responsibility they tend to act in an accountable manner, which raises their self-confidence ultimately. The repayment of loan, the activity they perform, increased household prestige have moulded these women. The economic upliftment through their income has motivated them psychologically and their exposure to the world outside their family has given them the opportunity to understand the society they live in better. The recognition given by the family members and neighbours for their contribution to the prosperity of the family has made their prestige high and strengthened them making them more effective.

(3) Status and Decision-making Power within the Household

When women earn income outside the household it enhances the relative position of women even in the power distribution within the household. She also has a respectable position because of being less dependent on others. The ownership of property also makes women more powerful in family decisions. Their economic activity not only generates income but also provides the social benefits that come from women's enhanced status and independence. The economic participation of women is, thus, both a reward on it own with associated reduction of gender bias in the treatment of women in family decisions, and a major influence for social change in general.

(4) Social Mobility

These women, before joining the SHG, were restricted to the house. But, after joining the group, they have come outside their house. Their physical mobility from house to their work station has created a significant impact. Now, as a group of women, they frequently move outside their village. They frequently visit the DRDA and the Collectorate without any male accompany. Regarding their trade activities also they move long distances on their own, which creates opportunities for them to visit various places, introduce themselves to different persons and also helps them to learn the nuances of trade and commerce. This helps them to know the world outside their home.

(5) Ability to Interact Effectively in the Public Sphere

The opportunity to move in the public sphere has increased their efficiency to interact with others. Their trading skill and their negotiation skill have increased through this. These women, without any hesitation, meet officials, political leaders and other professionals in order to get their task fulfilled or for any other common cause for the benefit of the people. This has enhanced their ability to make purchases and sell their products.

(6) Community Involvement

This study also shows that SHG women have made their endeavour in community activity also by participating in the Gram Sabha and helping the Village Panchayat President in many activities. In the Gram Sabha, they occupy a major role and take part in social auditing. Several studies have shown that SHG women form the quorum of the Gram Sabha. This has given them the opportunity to participate in group, community and civic activities. They have collectively achieved many things like putting an end to illicit liquor, water crisis, conducting medical camps and so on. Their role as change agents of the society is more visible through their achievement. It has also increased their opportunity to participate in political activities. Some of these women have contested and got elected in the local body elections and a few others are willing to contest in the coming local body elections. They also involve themselves in preparing village development plan. This shows that, given the opportunity, women have been able to play roles at diverse levels of political activities and social initiatives.

These women have carried out the activities they value most and in turn they are benefited by increasing their own well-being and well-being of others through their commitment to the community. They have become active promoters and facilitators of social transformation. Such transformation influences the lives and well-being of not only women, but also those of men and all children—boys as well as girls. This is a momentous enrichment of the reach of the women's movement (Amartya Sen, 2005[b]). It is a major question whether the initiatives taken by the Government officials in forming groups and initiating trades will sustain and whatever activities they carry out now will go on further without interruption. It has been noticed in many places that the activities and ideas imposed on the community have not succeeded and sustained after the withdrawal of the Government from the assignment. In this case all the initiatives were taken by the Government departments and more particularly the District Collector and the Project Officer of District Rural Development Agency. All positive aspects which we have seen in the project are the inputs of the District Collector and Project Officer. Both the District Collector and the Project Officer are known for their commitment and sincerity. One cannot expect the same commitment from the new Collector who is going to replace the present Collector.

Conclusion

Participation in economic activities is the women's key to their personal advancement and their status in the society. After women started associating themselves in SHGs many changes have taken place in all spheres of life. SHGs have paved the way for the emergence of a new awakening in women by giving them an opportunity to come out of their house, making them associate with others and providing them loan for their economic activity and also a ground to realize and practice their social and political responsibility. Their interactional position in the society has been elevated and they tend to involve themselves in community work, which was once considered men's sphere, and they have got a hold on decision-making both in the household and outside. It also enables them to acquire knowledge, develop self-esteem and take responsibility for their own lives. Moreover activities through SHGs will bring an end to the gender disparities in economic power-sharing, which is an important factor of the poverty of women. Feminization of poverty has become a significant problem, and the experience through the SHGs shows that setting up of micro enterprises at grassroots level will help to cope with this problem. Women contribute to the economy and eradication of poverty through their micro enterprises. In this way, empowerment of women proves to be critical factor in the eradication of poverty. Since women's poverty is directly related to the absence of economic opportunities, lack of access to economic resources and their meagre participation in the decision-making process, the opportunity and the freedom created through the SHGs will meet their requirement. SHGs enhance the access of disadvantaged women in remote rural areas and also strengthens their links with the formal banks and increases the availability of credit. The participation of women in the economic activity not only reflects on the economic development but also has certain other implications for fertility and population growth, access to educational opportunities, health care and so on. The study shows that women play a significant role in the socio-economic as well as political development of a country and their contribution through the process of empowerment cannot be ignored as such. Opportunity and freedom have to be given to the women to exhibit their full potential for the all round development of the country. The need of the hour is the total integration of women in all developmental activities.

APPENDICES

APPENDIX - I

TAKING STOCK OF WOMEN'S PROGRESS

by Lori Ashford

The advancement of girls and women has been on many governments' agendas in the last decade and was central to the plan of action of the Fourth World Conference on Women, held in Beijing in 1995. Gathering data about women—especially about their health, education, political and economic status—is a critical part of efforts to monitor progress toward achieving the goals of Beijing and other international conferences.

The data provide reasons for both optimism and concern, according to the Population Reference Bureau's *Women of Our World 2005.*[1] On the positive side, girls and women have seen steady gains in a number of areas over the past decade. In most developing countries, girls' school enrollments have risen markedly, more couples are using modern contraception, and women are choosing to have fewer children. In addition, women's share of the non-farm workforce and of seats in national parliaments has edged up slightly.

But women everywhere, particularly those in the poorest countries, still face social and economic disadvantages relative to men. For example, girls' literacy and schooling lag well behind boys' in much of sub-Saharan Africa and South Asia, and childbearing begins early in these regions. Deaths related to pregnancy and childbirth, though preventable, show no signs of abating. Women's political leadership may be critical to tackling these issues, but women hold less than one-fifth of seats in national parliaments around the world.

Advances in Girls' Education

Perhaps the best news of the last decade has been the increase in girls' access to education at all levels. The Beijing Platform for Action and the Millennium Development Goals (developed at the

United Nations Millennium Summit in 2000) call for universal primary education for boys and girls and for closing the gender gap in secondary and higher school enrollments. Neither goal has been achieved worldwide yet, but the progress made in the past five to 10 years makes clear that governments are promoting girls' education.

Girls' school enrollments are up nearly everywhere in developing regions: About 91 girls were enrolled per 100 boys at the secondary level in the early 2000s, compared with 84 girls per 100 boys in 1995. The level of literacy among young women (ages 15 to 24) in developing countries was also about 90 per cent of young men's literacy in the early 2000s.

Progress in closing the gender gap in school enrollments has been impressive in some of the countries where girls lagged farthest behind boys, such as Bangladesh, Ghana, Nepal, Uganda, and Yemen (see Figure 1). In Bangladesh, gains in girls' education may be attributed to special interventions such as community schools for girls and the large-scale training of women teachers[2]. In Uganda, the government eliminated school fees as part of an effort to boost girls' education. Still, gaps remain between girls' and boys' schooling, and overall enrollments need to increase, especially in sub-Saharan Africa and South Asia. In Bangladesh, where gender parity has been achieved in secondary school enrollments, only about one-half of all secondary school-aged children are enrolled.

Moreover, enrolling girls in schools does not guarantee that they will receive a quality education or even graduate. It is an important first step, and other indicators of educational attainment, such as completion rates—currently not available for all countries—should be gathered more systematically.

Women's Gradual Gains in the Workforce

Reducing gender inequality in the workforce is viewed as key to increasing women's earnings and promoting economic development more broadly. Over the last decade, women's participation in the global labour force has gradually increased (reflected in economic activity rates). Of all wage earners in the non-farm sector, which includes industry and services, women accounted for 38 per cent in the early 2000s, up from 35 per cent in 1990. Increases in women's share of this sector were modest but fairly consistent across countries in Asia and the Pacific and in Latin America and the Caribbean. In sub-Saharan Africa and the Middle East and North Africa, fewer and less recent survey data are available. Yet even where women have made significant gains in paid employment, labour markets remain segregated, and "female" jobs pay markedly less than "male" jobs[3]. For example, for 15 countries in Latin America and the Caribbean, the average women's income per working hour was 78 per cent of men's in 2000, up from 68 per cent in 1990[4]. While the increases are welcome, gender equality in the workforce is still far from reality.

Women's Political Representation Rising but Still Low

Women's gains in political representation parallel those made in the workforce: The trends are positive but the levels are still low. While women's share of seats in national parliaments has increased nearly everywhere, in only a handful of countries has women's representation reached more than one-fourth of seats (see Figure 2). The Beijing Platform for Action called for women to hold a "critical mass" of 30 per cent of parliamentary seats—a level believed sufficient to bring about change in national political processes[5]. As of late 2004, only 14 countries out of 183 surveyed had reached or exceeded the 30 per cent mark of women's representation in the single or lower house of parliament.

Countries often establish affirmative action measures, such as reserved seats or quotas, to overcome men's historical advantages in electoral systems. Of the 38 countries that held elections in 2003, one-half had some type of mechanism to improve women's chances of being elected[6]. An example of the success of such measures is Rwanda, where women hold the world's record of 49 per cent of seats in the lower house of parliament.

Monitoring one indicator, such as share of parliamentary seats, clearly has limitations in revealing the degree to which women participate equitably at all levels of decision-making. Data are not available worldwide on women's share of all leadership positions, nor do the data reveal how fully women participate when they are elected or appointed. As with school enrollments and other indicators of women's status, the indicators should be viewed as benchmarks or starting points for measuring gender equality.

Declining Family Size and Increasing Contraceptive Use

Throughout the developing world, women are having fewer children than a decade ago (3.0 children per woman in 2005, compared with 3.4 in 1995). This is good news, reflecting the increasing ability of women and couples to act on their preferences. For decades, survey data have shown that women in developing countries have more children on average than they desire.

An estimated 57 per cent of women in developing countries (excluding China) use some form of contraception in 2005, compared with 51 per cent in 1995. Still, a large unmet need remains for contraception: More than 120 million women worldwide say they would prefer to avoid a pregnancy but are not using any method[7]. Unmet need tends to be highest in the poorest countries and among the poorest women within countries.

Adolescent childbearing is also high in the poorest countries and among the poorest women. In India, about one in every 10 adolescents ages 15 to 19 gives birth each year, and in Somalia and Liberia, one in every five adolescents gives birth each year. In most countries, teen fertility is lower than a decade ago because young women are marrying later. But the wide disparities in teen births among and within countries are cause for policy concern: The poorest adolescents are three times more likely than the wealthiest adolescents to give birth in their teens, according to a recent analysis[8]. And these teen births have serious implications for the health of mothers and their babies and for the life prospects of both.

Maternal Deaths: No Drop Yet

The complications of pregnancy and child-birth remain a leading cause of death and disability among women in developing countries.

Whereas women in developed countries face a 1 in 2,800 chance of dying from pregnancy-related causes, women in developing countries face a 1 in 61 chance. The vast majority of maternal deaths occur in just two regions: sub-Saharan Africa and South-Central Asia (see Table 1).

Trends in maternal deaths are hard to assess. Measuring maternal mortality is difficult and complex, resulting in a wide margin of uncertainty in the estimates. In general, however, it appears that mortality rates did not decline over the 1990s and that the *numbers* of deaths may have increased due to population growth (more women of childbearing age)[9].

The percentage of births attended by skilled personnel is a key indicator used to monitor progress toward reducing maternal deaths. If a pregnant woman receives assistance during labour and delivery from a medically trained person—doctor, nurse, or professional midwife—she is more likely to receive the appropriate medical care in the event of a life-threatening complication.

Improvements in this area from the mid-1990s to around 2000 were only slight, and survey data from some countries show a drop in skilled assistance (see Figure 3). Unfortunately, the declines in skilled birth assistance occurred in countries that have had high maternal death rates. Renewed political commitments and funding will be needed to overcome issues such as a shortage of trained personnel and weak health infrastructure—particularly a shortage of facilities for emergency obstetric care. Involving men in maternity care is also key, as they are often in a position to make decisions about medical care.

The Impact of HIV/AIDS on Women

One of the many tragic consequences of the AIDS epidemic has been its effect on women. Women make up almost one-half of HIV infections worldwide and 58 per cent of infections in sub-Saharan Africa. In that region, the virus is spread predominantly through sex between men and women and is prevalent in the general population. Women's low status relative to men puts them at heightened risk of contracting the disease: Women are often unaware of their husbands' or partners' HIV status, may be unable to refuse sex, or may have difficulty negotiating the use of a condom. The risk is particularly high for young women, who are biologically more susceptible to the virus and often have relationships with older men who have previously been exposed to HIV.

Women also account for one-half of HIV infections in the Caribbean, but they account for a smaller share in other regions where the infections are concentrated among high-risk populations such as injecting drug users, sex workers, and men who have sex with men. Policy-makers are paying close attention to the pandemic in Asia and Eastern Europe, where the numbers of infections transmitted heterosexually are increasing rapidly[10].

Data that Address Inequality

The data in *Women of Our World 2005* provide a snapshot of women's situation in those areas that are most easily recorded and quantified in most countries of the world. The data do not capture all aspects of women's position relative to men, nor do they cover other issues such as the exploitation of, abuse of, and violence against women. Data on these issues are limited to a relatively small number of countries or to sub-groups of women within countries.

Data on women's situation can be powerful in demonstrating that discrimination against girls and women is pervasive and merits attention. Addressing all forms of discrimination, whether legal, social, or cultural, can contribute to improving the health, rights, and opportunities of girls and women. These improvements, in turn, can enable women to make broader contributions to economic and social development.

Acknowledgements

Lori Ashford is technical director of policy information at PRB. Thanks are due to several collaborators and reviewers who provided input and comments on this brief: Yvette Collymore, Mai Hijazi,

Deborah Mesce, Farzaneh Roudi, Diana Prieto, Barbara Seligman, Rhonda Smith, Ellen Starbird, and Nancy Yinger. Funding was provided by the U.S. Agency for International Development, under the BRIDGE Project (No. GPO-A-00-03-00004-00).

ENDNOTES

1. Lori Ashford and Donna Clifton, *Women of Our World* 2005 (Washington, DC: Population Reference Bureau, 2005).
2. United Nations, "Education and Training of Women: New Challenges," *Beijing at 10: Putting Policy into Practice* (New York: United Nations International Research and Training Institute for the Advancement of Women, 2005).
3. United Nations Statistics Division, "Progress toward the Millennium Development Goals, 1990-2003," available at http://millenniumindicatorsun.org.
4. International Labour Organization (ILO), *2001 Labour Overview, Latin America and the Caribbean* (Lima: ILO, 2001): 21-22.
5. United Nations, "Women in Power and Decision-making: New Challenges," *Beijing at 10: Putting Policy into Practice* (New York: United Nations International Research and Training Institute for the Advancement of Women, 2005).
6. International Parliamentary Union (IPU), "Women Elected in 2003: The Year in Perspective," accessed online at www.ipu.org, on March 16, 2005.
7. John Ross and William Winfrey, "Unmet Need for Contraception in the Developing World and the Former Soviet Union: An Updated Estimate," *International Family Planning Perspectives* 28, no. 3 (2002).
8. Lori Ashford and Haruna Kashiwase, *The Wealth Gap in Health: Data on Women and Children in 53 Countries* (Washington, DC: Population Reference Bureau, 2004).
9. WHO/UNICEF/UNFPA, *Maternal Mortality in 2000: Estimates Developed by WHO, UNICEF, and UNFPA* (Geneva: Department of Reproductive Health and Research, World Health Organization, 2004): 12.
10. UNAIDS, *2004 Report on the Global AIDS Epidemic* (Geneva: UNAIDS, July 2004): 3-10.

APPENDIX - II

GENDER PROFILE OF TAMIL NADU AND INDIA ON SELECT INDICATORS

Indicator	*Year*	*Gender*	*India (Million)*			*Tamil Nadu (Million)*			*Comments*
			Total	*Rural*	*Urban*	*Total*	*Rural*	*Urban*	
Population Totals	1981	P	685.20	525.50	159.70	48.41			Tamil Nadu holds 6.05% of the population of India according to the 2001 Census.
		M	354.40	269.40	850.00				
		F	330.80	256.10	747.00				
	1991	P	846.30	628.69	217.61	55.86			
		M	439.23	324.32	114.90				
		F	407.07	304.37	102.70				
	2001	P	1025.25	740.26	284.99	62.11	34.86	27.24	
		M	530.42	380.44	149.98	31.26	17.50	13.75	
		F	494.83	359.82	135.01	30.84	17.36	13.48	

Source : Census of India, 1991, Kerala State District Profile, 1991, Registrar General, India; and Census of India, 2001, Provisional Population Totals, Paper 2 of 2001, Rural-Urban Distribution; Tamil Nadu — An Economic Appraisal, 2001-2002, Department of Evaluation and Applied Research (DEAR), Government of Tamil Nadu, Chennai; Women in India, A Statistical Profile — 1997—Department of Women and Child Development, Ministry of Human Resource Development.

Indicator	*Year*	*Area*	*India*	*Tamil Nadu*	*Comments*
Distribution of Population (%)	1991	R	74.29	65.85	Tamil Naud has the highest proportion of urban population among the major States.
		U	25.71	34.15	
	2001	R	72.22	56.14	
		U	27.78	43.86	

Source : Census of India, 1991, Kerala State District Profile, 1991, Registrar General, India; and Census of India, 2001, Provisional Population Totals, Paper 2 of 2001, Rural-Urban Distribution.

Indicator	*Year*	*India*	*Tamil Nadu*	*Comments*
Decennian Growth rate	1971	24.80	22.30	The Growth rate has been declining significantly and more rapidly since 1981. The decline has been greater than for All India.
	1981	25.71	34.15	
	1991	72.22	56.14	
	2001	27.78	43.86	

Source : Registrar General, India; and Census of India, 2001; Tamil Nadu — An Economic Approach 2001–2002, Department of Evaluation and Applied Research (DEAR), Government of Tamil Nadu, Chennai.

Indicator	*Year*	*India*	*Tamil Nadu*	*Comments*
Density of Population (Per Sq.Km.)	1991	267	429	Density of population is higher than the national averages.
	2001	324	478	

Source: Registrar General, India; and Census of India, 2001; Tamil Nadu — An Economic Approach 2001–2002, Department of Evaluation and Applied Research (DEAR), Government of Tamil Nadu, Chennai.

Indicator	*Year*	*Area*	*India*	*Tamil Nadu*
Population of SC/ST Millions	1991	Total	838.58	55.86
		SC	138.22 (16.5%)	10.71 (19.2%)
		ST	67.75 (8.1%)	0.57 (1.0%)

Source : Registrar General, India; and Census of India, 1991; Women in India, A Statistical Profile — 1997.

Indicator	*Year*	*Gender*	*India*	*Tamil Nadu*	*Comments*
Life Expectancy at Birth	1970–75	Male	50.5	49.6	The state has picked up in life expectancy at birth above the national average since 1981.
		Female	49.0	49.5	
	1981–85	Male	55.4	56.5	
		Female	55.7	57.4	
	2001–06	Male	63.9	67.0	
		Female	66.9	69.7	

Source : Census of India, 2001 — Population Projections for India and States: 1996–2016, Registrar General of India (Gandhigram Rural Institute), New Delhi, 1996. SRS, RGI, New Delhi, 1999; Tamil Nadu—An Economic Appraisal, 2001–2002, Department of Evaluation and Applied Research (DEAR), Government of Tamil Nadu Chennai.

Indicator	*Year*	*Gender*	*India*	*Tamil Nadu*	*Comments*
Sex ratio	1971		930	978	Sex ratio is far above the All India level and has been improving in the aggregate though it is declining in the 0-6 age group.
	1981	All	927	977	
		Rural	939		
		Urban	894		
	2001	All	93	986	
		Rural		992	
		Urban		980	

Source: Census of India, 2001 —Provisional Population Totals, Tamil Nadu—An Economic Appraisal, 2001-2002, Department of Evaluation and Applied Research (DEAR), Government of Tamil Nadu, Chennai.

Indicators	*Year*	*India*	*Tamil Nadu*
Sex Ratio (0-6 years)	1971	964	974
	1981	962	967
	1991	945	948
	2001	927	939

Source : Registrar General, India; and Census of India, 2001; Women in India, A Statistical Profile—1997, Department of Women and Child Development, Ministry of Human Resource Development.

Indicators	*Year*	*Area*	*India*	*Tamil Nadu*	*Comments*
Birth Rate	1971	Total	36.9	31.4	Tamil Nadu has registered fast demographic transition (Please also see the following table on declining death rates).
		Rural	38.9	32.9	
		Urban	30.1	27.8	
	1981	Total	33.9	28.0	
		Rural	35.6	29.7	
		Urban	27.0	23.9	
	1991	Total	29.5	20.8	
		Rural	30.9	20.8	
		Urban	23.1	20.8	
	1997	Total	27.2	19.0	
		Rural	28.9	19.3	
		Urban	21.5	18.3	
	2000	Total	25.8	19.3	

Source : Compendium of India's Fertility and Mortality Indicators, 1971–1997 based on the Sample Registration System (SRS), RGI, 1991, Economic Survey, 2002.

Indicators	*Year*	*Area*	*India*	*Tamil Nadu*
Death Rate	1971	Total	14.9	14.4
		Rural	16.4	16.5
		Urban	9.7	9.3
	1981	Total	12.5	11.8
		Rural	13.7	13.5
		Urban	7.8	7.9
	1991	Total	9.8	8.8
		Rural	10.6	93.5
		Urban	7.1	7.6
	1997	Total	8.9	8.0
		Rural	9.6	8.7
		Urban	6.5	6.7
	2000	Total	8.5	7.9

Source : Compendium of India's Fertility and Mortality Indicators, 1971–1997 based on the Sample Registration System (SRS), RGI, 1991, Economic Survey, 2002.

Indicators	*Year*	*Area*	*India*	*Tamil Nadu*
Infant Mortality Rate	1971	Total	129	113
		Rural	138	127
		Urban	82	77
	1981	Total	110	91
		Rural	119	104
		Urban	62	55
	1991	Total	80	57
		Rural	87	65
		Urban	53	42
	1997	Total	71	53
		Rural	77	58
		Urban	45	40
	2000	Total	68	51
		Rural	67	49
		Urban	69	54

Source : Compendium of India's Fertility and Mortality Indicators, 1971–1997 based on the Sample Registration System (SRS), RGI, 1991, Economic Survey, 2002.

Indicators	*Year*	*Area*	*India*	*Tamil Nadu*
Neonatal Mortality	1992-93		48.6	46.2
	1998-99	Total	47.7	
		Rural	51.7	
		Urban	33.5	
Post-Neonatal Mortality	1992 – 93		29.9	21.5
	1998 – 99	Total	25.3	13.3
		Rural	28.0	
		Urban	15.8	
Child Mortality	1992 – 93		33.4	20.1
	1998 - 99	Total	30.6	15.9
		Rural	34.6	
		Urban	17.0	
Under Five Mortality	1992 – 93		109.3	86.5
	1998 - 99	Total	101.4	63.3
		Rural	111.5	
		Urban	65.4	

Source : National Family Health Survey (NFHS–1), 1992–93; National Family Health Survey (NFHS-2), 1998–99.

Indicators	*Year*	*India*	*Tamil Nadu*
Maternal Mortality	1997	408	76

Source : Compendium of Inida's Fertility and Mortality Indicators, 1971–1997 based on the Sample Registration System (SRS), RGI, 1999.

Indicators	*Year*	*Gender*	*India*	*Tamil Nadu*
Mean Age of Marriage	1971	Male	21.3	
		Female	17.2	
	1981	Male	23.3	
		Female	18.3	
	1991	Male	23.9	
		Female	19.5	20.3
	1997	Male	N.A	
		Female	19.5	20.6

Source : SRS–Fertility and Mortality Indicators for respective years, RGI, New Delhi.

Indicators	Year	Area	India	Tamil Nadu
Total Fertility Rate	1971	Total	5.2	3.9
		Rural	5.4	4.2
		Urban	4.1	3.3
	1981	Total	4.5	3.4
		Rural	4.8	3.7
		Urban	3.3	2.7
	1991	Total	3.6	2.2
		Rural	3.9	2.3
		Urban	2.7	2.0
	1997	Total	3.3	2.0
		Rural	3.6	2.1
		Urban	2.4	1.8

Source : Compendium of India's Fertility and Mortality Indicators, 1971–1997 based on the Sample Registration System (SRS), RGI, 1999.

Indicators	Year	Area	India	Tamil Nadu
Place of Delivery	1998 – 99	Ins.	33.6	79.3
		Home	65.4	20.7
		Other	1.0	

Source : National Family Heatlh Survey (NFHS) – 2, 1998–99.

Indicator	Year	Area	India	Tamil Nadu
Assistance During Delivery	1998 – 99	Professional	42.3	83.8
		TBA	35.0	
		Other	22.4	16.2

Source : National Family Health Survey (NFHS) – 2, 1998 – 99.

Indicators	***Year***	***Area***	***India***	***Tamil Nadu***
Literacy Rate	1971	Persons	34.45	39.39
		Male	45.96	51.78
		Female	21.97	26.86
	1981	Persons	43.57	45.70
		Male	56.38	57.19
		Female	29.76	34.12
	1991	Persons	52.21	63.74
		Male	64.13	74.88
		Female	39.29	52.29
	1997	Persons	65.38	73.47
		Male	75.85	82.33
		Female	54.16	64.55

Source : Registrar General, India; and Census of India, 2001; Tamil Nadu — An Economic Appriasal 2001–2002, Department of Evaluation and Applied Research (DEAR), Government of Tamil Nadu, Chennai, Literacy Tamil Nadu Experience: National Literacy Mission.

Indicators	***Year***	***Area***	***Gender***	***India***	***Tamil Nadu***
Work Population Rate	1981	Total	Persons	36.7	
			Male	52.6	
			Female	19.7	
		Rural	Persons	38.8	
			Male	53.8	
			Female	23.1	
		Urban	Persons	30.0	
			Male	49.1	
			Female	8.3	
	1991	Total	Persons	37.5	
			Male	51.6	
			Female	22.3	
		Rural	Persons	40.0	
			Male	52.5	
			Female	26.7	
		Urban	Persons	42.0	
			Male	52.4	
			Female	31.0	
	2001	Total	Persons	39.3	
			Male	51.9	
			Female	25.7	
		Rural	Persons	42.0	
			Male	52.4	
			Female	31.0	
		Urban	Persons	32.2	
			Male	50.9	
			Female	11.6	

Source : Census of India, 2001, Series — 33, Kerala, Provisional Population Totals, Paper-3, of 2001, Distribution of Workers and Non-Workers. Data Compiled from Statement 2.1.

Indicator	***Year***	***Gender***	***India***			***Tamil Nadu***		
			Total	***Rural***	***Urban***	***Total***	***Rural***	***Urban***
Work Participation Rate	1991	Persons	37.50	40.00	30.30	43.3	48.5	33.3
		Male	51.61	52.58	48.92	56.4	58.3	52.8
		Female	22.27	26.79	9.19	29.9	38.5	13.1
	2001	Persons	39.26	41.97	32.23	44.78	50.4	37.6
		Male	51.93	52.36	50.85	58.06	59.4	56.4
		Female	25.68	30.98	11.55	31.32	41.3	18.4
Main Workers	1991	Persons	34.10	35.70	29.50	40.8	45.1	32.6
		Male	51.00	51.88	48.57	56.1	57.9	52.6
		Female	16.03	18.75	8.15	25.1	32.0	11.8
	2001	Persons	30.5	31.0	29.3	38.13	41.0	34.5
		Male	45.3	44.5	47.5	52.28	51.8	52.9
		Female	14.7	16.8	9.1	23.79	30.1	15.7
Marginal Workers	1991	Persons	3.40	4.30	0.7	2.5	3.4	0.7
		Male	0.61	0.70	0.35	0.3	0.4	0.2
		Female	6.24	8.04	1.04	4.8	6.5	1.3
	2001	Persons	8.7	10.9	2.0	6.65	9.4	3.1
		Male	6.6	7.9	3.4	5.78	7.6	3.5
		Female	11.0	14.2	2.4	7.53	11.2	2.7
Non - Workers	2001	Persons	60.7	58.0	67.84	55.2	49.6	62.4
		Male	48.1	47.6	49.2	41.94	40.6	43.6
		Female	63.55	69.0	88.5	68.68	58.7	81.6

Source : Registrar General of India, Census 2001.

Indicator	***Year***		***India***	***Tamil Nadu***	***Comments***
Poverty Ratio (% of Population Below Poverty Line)	1973-74	Combined	54.88	54.94	The rate of reduction of the population below the poverty line has been much higher in Tamil Nadu compared to All India.
		Rural	56.44	57.44	
		Urban	49.01	49.40	
	1973-74	Combined	35.97	35.03	
		Rural	37.27	32.48	
		Urban	32.36	39.77	
	1999-2000	Combined	26.10	21.12	
		Rural	27.09	20.55	
		Urban	23.62	22.11	

Source : Government of India, Planning Commission.

Indicator	*Year*		*India*	*Tamil Nadu*
National / State Income at Constant Prices	2001-02	Net Domestic Product (Rs.Crores)	11,23,543	*93,066.16
		Per Capital Inocme (in Rs.)	10,754	13,108

Source : Government of Kerala, State Planning Board, Economic Review, 2002 for data on India; Commissioner of Economic Statistics, Chennai for Tamil Nadu.

* Gross State Domestic Product.

Indicator	*Year*	*India*	*Tamil Nadu*	*Comments*
Human Development Index	2001	0.472	0.657	Tamil Nadu hold the Third rank on the HDI in India following Kerala and Punjab.

Source : Government of India, Planning Commission, Tamil Nadu—An Economic Appraisal, 2001–2002, Department of Evaluation and Applied Research (DEAR), Government of Tamil Nadu, Chennai.

Fertility Indicators by Residence from 1971 to 1996 at Interval of 5 years

Indicators	*Age Group*	*1971*	*1976*	*1981*	*1986*	*1991*	*1996*
		Total					
Age Specific Fertility Rates	15-19	70.7	73.1	71.0	62.7	45.3	36.7
	20-24	217.5	224.6	207.7	208.2	186.7	187.1
	25-29	222.4	215.3	193.8	145.3	130.7	122.3
	30-34	160.0	135.7	124.6	73.7	54.6	49.1
	35-39	87.9	77.6	55.1	26.7	20.8	12.9
	40-44	25.0	25.2	19.5	10.3	4.2	3.1
	45-49	6.7	5.9	5.3	2.4	4.5	0.5
General Fertility Rate		127.0	119.5	107.0	90.1	77.1	70.4
Total Fertility Rate		3.9	3.8	3.4	2.7	2.2	2.1
Gross Reproduction Rate		3.9	3.8	3.4	2.7	2.2	2.1
Gross Reproduction Rate		1.9	1.8	1.6	1.3	1.1	1.0
		Rural					
Age Specific Fertility Rates	15-19	85.2	84.0	82.2	66.3	47.8	42.2
	20-24	237.5	245.0	228.8	215.5	184.2	198.8
	25-29	228.1	230.8	208.4	151.1	139.3	127.5
	30-34	168.2	146.7	136.0	82.4	62.2	53.3
	35-39	92.5	83.9	59.4	30.2	25.5	15.0
	40-44	26.3	28.4	20.8	12.6	5.8	3.6
	45-49	5.1	7.7	6.1	2.7	1.7	0.7
General Fertility Rate		135.0	127.3	115.0	92.5	78.4	73.8
		4.2	4.1	3.7	2.8	2.3	2.2
		2.0	2.0	1.8	1.4	1.1	1.1
		Urban					
Age Specific Fertility Rates	15-19	43.2	50.6	46.1	56.2	40.6	25.5
	20-24	175.3	188.6	164.6	196.5	191.3	166.5
	25-29	210.1	185.3	166.4	135.8	117.0	113.1
	30-34	138.0	111.4	100.6	57.4	41.2	41.2
	35-39	76.6	61.4	45.0	19.7	11.5	8.9
	40-44	21.3	17.3	16.0	5.4	1.0	2.1
	45-49	10.0	1.3	3.1	1.6	1.1	0.0
General Fertility Rate		108.8	102.8	89.4	85.8	74.6	63.8
Total Fertility Rate		3.3	3.1	2.7	2.4	2.0	1.8
Gross Reproductive Rate		1.7	1.5	1.3	1.2	0.9	0.9

Source : Compendium of India's Fertility and Mortality Indicators, 1971–1997 based on the Sample Registration System (SRS), Registrar General, India, 1999.

APPENDIX – III

National Policy for the Empowerment of Women 2001 — India

Source : Department of Women and Child Development

1. Introduction
   - Goal and Objectives
2. Policy Prescriptions
   - Judicial Legal Systems
3. Decision-making
4. Mainstreaming a Gender Perspective in the Development Process
5. Economic Empowerment of Women
   1. Poverty Eradication
   2. Micro Credit
   3. Women and Economy
   4. Globalization
   5. Women and Agriculture
   6. Women and Industry
   7. Support Services
6. Social Empowerment of Women
   1. Education
   2. Health
   3. Nutrition
   4. Drinking Water and Sanitation
   5. Housing and Shelter
   6. Environment
   7. Science and Technology
   8. Women in Difficult Circumstances
7. Violence against Women
8. Rights of the Girl Child
9. Mass Media
10. Operational Strategies
    - Action Plans
11. Institutional Mechanisms
12. Resource Management

13. Legislation
14. Gender Sensitization
15. Panchayati Raj Institutions
16. Partnership with the voluntary sector organizations
17. International Cooperation

1. Introduction

1. The principle of gender equality is enshrined in the Indian Constitution in its Preamble, Fundamental Rights, Fundamental Duties and Directive Principles. The Constitution not only grants equality to women, but also empowers the State to adopt measures of positive discrimination in favour of women.
2. Within the framework of a democratic polity, our laws, development policies, Plans and programmes have aimed at women's advancement in different spheres. From the Fifth Five Year Plan (1974-78) onwards has been a marked shift in the approach to women's issues from welfare to development. In recent years, the empowerment of women has been recognized as the central issue in determining the status of women. The National Commission for Women was set up by an Act of Parliament in 1990 to safeguard the rights and legal entitlements of women. The 73rd and 74th Amendments (1993) to the Constitution of India have provided for reservation of seats in the local bodies of Panchayats and Municipalities for women, laying a strong foundation for their participation in decision- making at the local levels.
3. India has also ratified various international conventions and human rights instruments committing to secure equal rights of women. Key among them is the ratification of the Convention on Elimination of All Forms of Discrimination Against Women (CEDAW) in 1993.
4. The Mexico Plan of Action (1975), the Nairobi Forward Looking Strategies (1985), the Beijing Declaration as well as the Platform for Action (1995) and the Outcome Document adopted by the UNGA Session on Gender Equality and Development & Peace

for the 21st century, titled “Further actions and initiatives to implement the Beijing Declaration and the Platform for Action” have been unreservedly endorsed by India for appropriate follow up.

5. The Policy also takes note of the commitments of the Ninth Five Year Plan and the other Sectoral Policies relating to empowerment of women.
6. The women’s movement and a wide-spread network of non-Government Organisations which have strong grassroots presence and deep insight into women’s concerns have contributed in inspiring initiatives for the empowerment of women.
7. However, there still exists a wide gap between the goals enunciated in the Constitution, legislation, policies, plans, programmes, and related mechanisms on the one hand and the situational reality of the status of women in India, on the other. This has been analyzed extensively in the Report of the Committee on the Status of Women in India, “Towards Equality, 1974 and highlighted in the National Perspective Plan for Women, 1988-2000, the Shramshakti Report, 1988 and the Platform for Action, Five Years After—An assessment”.
8. Gender disparity manifests itself in various forms, the most obvious being the trend of continuously declining female ratio in the population in the last few decades. Social stereotyping and violence at the domestic and societal levels are some of the other manifestations. Discrimination against girl children, adolescent girls and women persists in parts of the country.
9. The underlying causes of gender inequality are related to social and economic structure, which is based on informal and formal norms, and practices.
10. Consequently, the access of women particularly those belonging to weaker sections including Scheduled Castes/Scheduled Tribes/ Other Backward Classes and minorities, majority of whom are in the rural areas and in the informal, unorganized sector—to education, health and productive resources, among others, is inadequate. Therefore, they remain largely marginalized, poor and socially excluded.

Goal and Objectives

11. The goal of this Policy is to bring about the advancement, development and empowerment of women. The Policy will be widely disseminated so as to encourage active participation of all stakeholders for achieving its goals. Specifically, the objectives of this Policy include:
    - i. Creating an environment through positive economic and social policies for full development of women to enable them to realize their full potential.
    - ii. The de-jure and de-facto enjoyment of all human rights and fundamental freedom by women on equal basis with men in all spheres – political, economic, social, cultural and civil.
    - iii. Equal access to participation and decision-making of women in social, political and economic life of the nation.
    - iv. Equal access to women to health care, quality education at all levels, career and vocational guidance, employment, equal remuneration, occupational health and safety, social security and public office, etc.
    - v. Strengthening legal systems aimed at elimination of all forms of discrimination against women.
    - vi. Changing societal attitudes and community practices by active participation and involvement of both men and women.
    - vii. Mainstreaming a gender perspective in the development process.
    - viii. Elimination of discrimination and all forms of violence against women and the girl child; and
    - ix. Building and strengthening partnerships with civil society, particularly women's organizations.

2. Policy Prescriptions

Judicial Legal Systems

1. Legal-judicial system will be made more responsive and gender sensitive to women's needs, especially in cases of domestic violence and personal assault. New laws will be enacted and

existing laws reviewed to ensure that justice is quick and the punishment meted out to the culprits is commensurate with the severity of the offence.

2. At the initiative of and with the full participation of all stakeholders including community and religious leaders, the Policy would aim to encourage changes in personal laws such as those related to marriage, divorce, maintenance and guardianship so as to eliminate discrimination against women.
3. The evolution of property rights in a patriarchal system has contributed to the subordinate status of women. The Policy would aim to encourage changes in laws relating to ownership of property and inheritance by evolving consensus in order to make them gender just.

3. Decision-making

1. Women's equality in power sharing and active participation in decision-making, including decision-making in political process at all levels will be ensured for the achievement of the goals of empowerment. All measures will be taken to guarantee women equal access to and full participation in decision-making bodies at every level, including the legislative, executive, judicial, corporate, statutory bodies, as also the advisory Commissions, Committees, Boards, Trusts, etc. Affirmative action such as reservations/quotas, including in higher legislative bodies, will be considered whenever necessary on a time-bound basis. Women–friendly personnel policies will also be drawn up to encourage women to participate effectively in the developmental process.

4. Mainstreaming a Gender Perspective in the Development Process

1. Policies, programmes and systems will be established to ensure mainstreaming of women's perspectives in all developmental processes, as catalysts, participants and

recipients. Wherever there are gaps in policies and programmes, women specific interventions would be undertaken to bridge these. Coordinating and monitoring mechanisms will also be devised to assess from time to time the progress of such mainstreaming mechanisms. Women's issues and concerns as a result will specially be addressed and reflected in all concerned laws, sectoral policies, plans and programmes of action.

5. Economic Empowerment of Women

Poverty Eradication

1. Since women comprise the majority of the population below the poverty line and are very often in situations of extreme poverty, given the harsh realities of intra-household and social discrimination, macro-economic policies and poverty eradication programmes will specifically address the needs and problems of such women. There will be improved implementation of programmes which are already women oriented with special targets for women. Steps will be taken for mobilization of poor women and convergence of services, by offering them a range of economic and social options, along with necessary support measures to enhance their capabilities.

Micro Credit

2. In order to enhance women's access to credit for consumption and production, the establishment of new, and strengthening of existing micro-credit mechanisms and micro-finance institution will be undertaken so that the outreach of credit is enhanced. Other supportive measures would be taken to ensure adequate flow of credit through extant financial institutions and banks, so that all women below poverty line have easy access to credit.

Women and Economy

3. Women's perspectives will be included in designing and implementing macro-economic and social policies by institutionalizing their participation in such processes. Their contribution to socio-economic development as producers and workers will be recognized in the formal and informal sectors (including home based workers) and appropriate policies relating to employment and to her working conditions will be drawn up. Such measures could include:
   i. Reinterpretation and redefinition of conventional concepts of work wherever necessary e.g. in the Census records, to reflect women's contribution as producers and workers.
   ii. Preparation of satellite and national accounts.
   iii. Development of appropriate methodologies for undertaking (i) and (ii) above.

Globalization

4. Globalization has presented new challenges for the realization of the goal of women's equality, the gender impact of which has not been systematically evaluated fully. However, from the micro-level studies that were commissioned by the Department of Women & Child Development, it is evident that there is a need for re-framing policies for access to employment and quality of employment. Benefits of the growing global economy have been unevenly distributed leading to wider economic disparities, the feminization of poverty, increased gender inequality through often deteriorating working conditions and unsafe working environment especially in the informal economy and rural areas. Strategies will be designed to enhance the capacity of women and empower them to meet the negative social and economic impacts, which may flow from the globalization process.

Women and Agriculture

5. In view of the critical role of women in the agriculture and allied sectors, as producers, concentrated efforts will be made to ensure that benefits of training, extension and various programmes will reach them in proportion to their numbers. The programmes for training women in soil conservation, social forestry, dairy development and other occupations allied to agriculture like horticulture, livestock including small animal husbandry, poultry, fisheries, etc. will be expanded to benefit women workers in the agriculture sector.

Women and Industry

6. The important role played by women in electronics, information technology and food processing and agro industry and textiles has been crucial to the development of these sectors. They would be given comprehensive support in terms of labour legislation, social security and other support services to participate in various industrial sectors.
7. Women at present cannot work in night shift in factories even if they wish to. Suitable measures will be taken to enable women to work on the night shift in factories. This will be accompanied with support services for security, transportation etc.

Support Services

8. The provision of support services for women, like child care facilities, including crèches at work places and educational institutions, homes for the aged and the disabled will be expanded and improved to create an enabling environment and to ensure their full cooperation in social, political and economic life. Women-friendly personnel policies will also be drawn up to encourage women to participate effectively in the developmental process.

6. Social Empowerment of Women

Education

1. Equal access to education for women and girls will be ensured. Special measures will be taken to eliminate discrimination, universalize education, eradicate illiteracy, create a gender-sensitive educational system, increase enrolment and retention rates of girls and improve the quality of education to facilitate life-long learning as well as development of occupation/vocation/technical skills by women. Reducing the gender gap in secondary and higher education would be a focus area. Sectoral time targets in existing policies will be achieved, with a special focus on girls and women, particularly those belonging to weaker sections including the Scheduled Castes/Scheduled Tribes/ Other Backward Classes/Minorities. Gender sensitive curricula would be developed at all levels of educational system in order to address sex stereotyping as one of the causes of gender discrimination.

Health

2. A holistic approach to women's health which includes both nutrition and health services will be adopted and special attention will be given to the needs of women and the girl at all stages of the life cycle. The reduction of infant mortality and maternal mortality, which are sensitive indicators of human development, is a priority concern. This policy reiterates the national demographic goals for Infant Mortality Rate (IMR), Maternal Mortality Rate (MMR) set out in the National Population Policy 2000. Women should have access to comprehensive, affordable and quality health care. Measures will be adopted that take into account the reproductive rights of women to enable them to exercise informed choices, their vulnerability to sexual and health problems together with endemic, infectious and communi-

cable diseases such as malaria, TB, and water borne diseases as well as hypertension and cardio-pulmonary diseases. The social, developmental and health consequences of HIV/AIDS and other sexually transmitted diseases will be tackled from a gender perspective.

3. To effectively meet problems of infant and maternal mortality, and early marriage the availability of good and accurate data at micro-level on deaths, birth and marriages is required. Strict implementation of registration of births and deaths would be ensured and registration of marriages would be made compulsory.
4. In accordance with the commitment of the National Population Policy (2000) to population stabilization, this Policy recognizes the critical need of men and women to have access to safe, effective and affordable methods of family planning of their choice and the need to suitably address the issues of early marriages and spacing of children. Interventions such as spread of education, compulsory registration of marriage and special programmes like BSY should impact on delaying the age of marriage so that by 2010 child marriages are eliminated.
5. Women's traditional knowledge about health care and nutrition will be recognized through proper documentation and its use will be encouraged. The use of Indian and alternative systems of medicine will be enhanced within the framework of overall health infrastructure available for women.

Nutrition

6. In view of the high risk of malnutrition and disease that women face at all the three critical stages viz., infancy and childhood, adolescent and reproductive phase, focussed attention would be paid to meeting the nutritional needs of women at all stages of the life cycle. This is also important in view of the critical link between the health of adolescent girls, pregnant and lactating women with the health of infant

and young children. Special efforts will be made to tackle the problem of macro and micro nutrient deficiencies especially amongst pregnant and lactating women as it leads to various diseases and disabilities.

7. Intra-household discrimination in nutritional matters *vis-à-vis* girls and women will be sought to be ended through appropriate strategies. Widespread use of nutrition education would be made to address the issues of intra-household imbalances in nutrition and the special needs of pregnant and lactating women. Women's participation will also be ensured in the planning, superintendence and delivery of the system.

Drinking Water and Sanitation

8. Special attention will be given to the needs of women in the provision of safe drinking water, sewage disposal, toilet facilities and sanitation within accessible reach of households, especially in rural areas and urban slums. Women's participation will be ensured in the planning, delivery and maintenance of such services.

Housing and Shelter

9. Women's perspectives will be included in housing policies, planning of housing colonies and provision of shelter both in rural and urban areas. Special attention will be given for providing adequate and safe housing and accommodation for women including single women, heads of households, working women, students, apprentices and trainees.

Environment

10. Women will be involved and their perspectives reflected in the policies and programmes for environment, conservation and restoration. Considering the impact of environmental factors on their livelihoods, women's participation will be

ensured in the conservation of the environment and control of environmental degradation. The vast majority of rural women still depend on the locally available non-commercial sources of energy such as animal dung, crop waste and fuel wood. In order to ensure the efficient use of these energy resources in an environmental friendly manner, the Policy will aim at promoting the programmes of non-conventional energy resources. Women will be involved in spreading the use of solar energy, bio-gas, smokeless chulahs and other rural application so as to have a visible impact of these measures in influencing eco-system and in changing the life styles of rural women.

Science and Technology

11. Programmes will be strengthened to bring about a greater involvement of women in science and technology. These will include measures to motivate girls to take up science and technology for higher education and also ensure that development projects with scientific and technical inputs involve women fully. Efforts to develop a scientific temper and awareness will also be stepped up. Special measures would be taken for their training in areas where they have special skills like communication and information technology. Efforts to develop appropriate technologies suited to women's needs as well as to reduce their drudgery will be given a special focus too.

Women in Difficult Circumstances

12. In recognition of the diversity of women's situations and in acknowledgement of the needs of specially disadvantaged groups, measures and programmes will be undertaken to provide them with special assistance. These groups include women in extreme poverty, destitute women, women in conflict situations, women affected by natural calamities, women in less developed regions, the disabled widows,

elderly women, single women in difficult circumstances, women heading households, those displaced from employment, migrants, women who are victims of marital violence, deserted women and prostitutes, etc.

7. Violence against Women

1. All forms of violence against women, physical and mental, whether at domestic or societal levels, including those arising from customs, traditions or accepted practices shall be dealt with effectively with a view to eliminate its incidence. Institutions and mechanisms/schemes for assistance will be created and strengthened for prevention of such violence, including sexual harassment at work place and customs like dowry; for the rehabilitation of the victims of violence and for taking effective action against the perpetrators of such violence. A special emphasis will also be laid on programmes and measures to deal with trafficking in women and girls.

8. Rights of the Girl Child

1. All forms of discrimination against the girl child and violation of her rights shall be eliminated by undertaking strong measures both preventive and punitive within and outside the family. These would relate specifically to strict enforcement of laws against pre-natal sex selection and the practices of female foeticide, female infanticide, child marriage, child abuse and child prostitution, etc. Removal of discrimination in the treatment of the girl child within the family and outside and projection of a positive image of the girl child will be actively fostered. There will be special emphasis on the needs of the girl child and earmarking of substantial investments in the areas relating to food and nutrition, health and education, and in vocational education. In implementing programmes for eliminating child labour, there will be a special focus on girl children.

9. Mass Media

1. Media will be used to portray images consistent with human dignity of girls and women. The Policy will specifically strive to remove demeaning, degrading and negative conventional stereotypical images of women and violence against women. Private sector partners and media networks will be involved at all levels to ensure equal access for women particularly in the area of information and communication technologies. The media would be encouraged to develop codes of conduct, professional guidelines and other self-regulatory mechanisms to remove gender stereotypes and promote balanced portrayals of women and men.

10. Operational Strategies

Action Plans

1. All Central and State Ministries will draw up time-bound Action Plans for translating the Policy into a set of concrete actions, through a participatory process of consultation with Centre/State Departments of Women and Child Development and National /State Commissions for Women. The Plans will specifically including the following: —
   - i. Measurable goals to be achieved by 2010.
   - ii. Identification and commitment of resources.
   - iii. Responsibilities for implementation of action points.
   - iv. Structures and mechanisms to ensure efficient monitoring, review and gender impact assessment of action points and policies.
   - v. Introduction of a gender perspective in the budgeting process.
2. In order to support better planning and programme formulation and adequate allocation of resources, Gender Development Indices (GDI) will be developed by networking with specialized agencies. These could be analyzed and

studied in depth. Gender auditing and development of evaluation mechanisms will also be undertaken along side.

3. Collection of gender disaggregated data by all primary data collecting agencies of the Central and State Governments as well as Research and Academic Institutions in the Public and Private Sectors will be undertaken. Data and information gaps in vital areas reflecting the status of women will be sought to be filled in by these immediately. All Ministries/Corporations/Banks and financial institutions, etc. will be advised to collect, collate, disseminate and maintain/publish data related to programmes and benefits on a gender disaggregated basis. This will help in meaningful planning and evaluation of policies.

11. Institutional Mechanisms

1. Institutional mechanisms, to promote the advancement of women, which exist at the Central and State levels, will be strengthened. These will be through interventions as may be appropriate and will relate to, among others, provision of adequate resources, training and advocacy skills to effectively influence macro-policies, legislation, programmes, etc. to achieve the empowerment of women.
2. National and State Councils will be formed to oversee the operationalisation of the Policy on a regular basis. The National Council will be headed by the Prime Minister and the State Councils by the Chief Ministers and be broad in composition having representatives from the concerned Departments/Ministries, National and State Commissions for Women, Social Welfare Boards, representatives of Non-Government Organizations, Women's Organisations, Corporate Sector, Trade Unions, financing institutions, academics, experts and social activists, etc. These bodies will review the progress made in implementing the Policy twice a year. The National Development Council will also be informed of the progress of the programme undertaken under the policy from time to time for advice and comments.

3. National and State Resource Centres on women will be established with mandates for collection and dissemination of information, undertaking research work, conducting surveys, implementing training and awareness generation programmes, etc. These Centers will link up with Women's Studies Centres and other research and academic institutions through suitable information networking systems.
4. While institutions at the district level will be strengthened, at the grassroots, women will be helped by Government through its programmes to organize and strengthen into Self-Help Groups (SHGs) at the Anganwadi/Village/Town level. The women's groups will be helped to institutionalize themselves into registered societies and to federate at the Panchyat/Municipal level. These societies will bring about synergistic implementation of all the social and economic development programmes by drawing resources made available through Government and Non-Government channels, including banks and financial institutions and by establishing a close Interface with the Panchayats/ Municipalities.

12. Resource Management

1. Availability of adequate financial, human and market resources to implement the Policy will be managed by concerned Departments, financial credit institutions and banks, private sector, civil society and other connected institutions. This process will include:
   a. Assessment of benefits flowing to women and resource allocation to the programmes relating to them through an exercise of gender budgeting. Appropriate changes in policies will be made to optimize benefits to women under these schemes.
   b. Adequate resource allocation to develop and promote the policy outlined earlier based on (a) above by concerned Departments.

c. Developing synergy between personnel of Health, Rural Development, Education and Women & Child Development Department at field level and other village level functionaries.
d. Meeting credit needs by banks and financial credit institutions through suitable policy initiatives and development of new institutions in coordination with the Department of Women & Child Development.

2. The strategy of Women's Component Plan adopted in the Ninth Plan of ensuring that not less than 30 per cent of benefits/funds flow to women from all Ministries and Departments will be implemented effectively so that the needs and interests of women and girls are addressed by all concerned sectors. The Department of Women and Child Development being the nodal Ministry will monitor and review the progress of the implementation of the Component Plan from time to time, in terms of both quality and quantity in collaboration with the Planning Commission.
3. Efforts will be made to channelize private sector investments too, to support programmes and projects for advancement of women.

13. Legislation

1. The existing legislative structure will be reviewed and additional legislative measures taken by identified departments to implement the Policy. This will also involve a review of all existing laws including personal, customary and tribal laws, subordinate legislation, related rules as well as executive and administrative regulations to eliminate all gender discriminatory references. The process will be planned over a time period 2000-2003. The specific measures required would be evolved through a consultation process involving civil society, National Commission for Women and Department of Women and Child Development. In appropriate cases the consultation process would be widened to include other stakeholders too.

2. Effective implementation of legislation would be promoted by involving civil society and community. Appropriate changes in legislation will be undertaken, if necessary.
3. In addition, following other specific measures will be taken to implement the legislation effectively:
   a. Strict enforcement of all relevant legal provisions and speedy redressal of grievances will be ensured, with a special focus on violence and gender related atrocities.
   b. Measures to prevent and punish sexual harassment at the place of work, protection for women workers in the organized/ unorganized sector and strict enforcement of relevant laws such as Equal Remune-ration Act and Minimum Wages Act will be undertaken.
   c. Crimes against women, their incidence, prevention, investigation, detection and prosecution will be regularly reviewed at all Crime Review fora and Conferences at the Central, State and District levels. Recognised, local, voluntary organizations will be authorized to lodge complaints and facilitate registration, investigations and legal proceedings related to violence and atrocities against girls and women.
   d. Women's Cells in Police Stations, Encourage Women Police Stations Family Courts, Mahila Courts, Counselling Centers, Legal Aid Centers and Nyaya Panchayats will be strengthened and expanded to eliminate violence and atrocities against women.
   e. Widespread dissemination of information on all aspects of legal rights, human rights and other entitlements of women, through specially designed legal literacy programmes and rights information programmes will be done.

14. Gender Sensitization

1. Training of personnel of executive, legislative and judicial wings of the State, with a special focus on policy and

programme framers, implementation and development agencies, law enforcement machinery and the judiciary, as well as non-governmental organizations will be undertaken. Other measures will include:

a. Promoting societal awareness to gender issues and women's human rights.
b. Review of curriculum and educational materials to include gender education and human rights issues.
c. Removal of all references derogatory to the dignity of women from all public documents and legal instruments.
d. Use of different forms of mass media to communicate social messages relating to women's equality and empowerment.

15. Panchayati Raj Institutions

1. The 73rd and 74th Amendments (1993) to the Indian Constitution have served as a breakthrough towards ensuring equal access and increased participation in political power structure for women. The PRIs will play a central role in the process of enhancing women's participation in public life. The PRIs and the local self-Governments will be actively involved in the implementation and execution of the National Policy for Women at the grassroots level.

16. Partnership with the voluntary sector organizations

1. The involvement of voluntary organizations, associations, federations, trade unions, non-governmental organizations, women's organizations, as well as institutions dealing with education, training and research will be ensured in the formulation, implementation, monitoring and review of all policies and programmes affecting women. Towards this end, they will be provided with appropriate support related to resources and capacity building and facilitated to participate actively in the process of the empowerment of women.

17. International Cooperation

1. The Policy will aim at implementation of international obligations/commitments in all sectors on empowerment of women such as the Convention on All Forms of Discrimination Against Women (CFDAW), Convention on the Rights of the Child (CRC), International Conference on Population and Development (ICPD+5) and other such instruments. International, regional and sub-regional cooperation towards the empowerment of women will continue to be encouraged through sharing of experiences, exchange of ideas and technology, networking with institutions and organizations and through bilateral and multi-lateral partnerships.

APPENDIX - IV

Social Welfare and Nutritious Meal Programme Department
Policy Note — 2005-2006
Demand No. 43

CHAPTER 4 : DEVELOPMENT OF WOMEN

4.1 Introduction

Tamil Nadu Corporation for Development of Women Limited was established for the empowerment of women in December 1983 by the Government of Tamil Nadu.

The Corporation implements the following schemes for the socio-economic development of women throughout Tamil Nadu:

- Tamil Nadu Women's Development Project (Mahalir Thittam)
- Setting up of Recreation Centres for Women
- Entrepreneurship Development Programme for Women (EDP)
- District Level Training-cum-Marketing Centres
- Provision of Free Gas connections to newly married couples under poverty line
- Assistance to Vocational and Skill Training Programme (VTP)
- Assistance for formation of 25000 Self-Help Groups
- Total Economic Development Project for Theni
- World Bank assisted Tamil Nadu Empowerment and Poverty Reduction Project

4.2 Tamil Nadu Women Development Project (Mahalir Thittam)

Tamil Nadu Women's Development Project, funded by International Fund for Agricultural Development (IFAD), was started on an experimental basis during 1991-92 in Dharmapuri District. It received its first growth thrust and was extended to Salem, South Arcot, Madurai and Ramanathapuram Districts during the period from 1992 to1994. By 1995-96, the project was well established and was taken up as a model for future growth and extended to all other districts in a phased manner under the State Budget. This Project, more popularly known as "Mahalir Thittam", is implemented with the support of Non-Governmental Organisations (NGOs) and Banks and is functioning through a network of Women's Self-Help Groups (SHGs), established and monitored with the assistance of NGOs. The project also plans for the growth of SHG movement with a view to promote sustainability combined with deepening of coverage at habitations and ward/slums in urban areas.

The project has a consistently growing membership and as on 31.01.2005, the membership has crossed 32.44 lakhs women in 1,92,893 SHGs with 1,67,090 Rural Self-Help Groups (28,17,817 members) and 25,803 Urban Self-Help Groups (4,23,190 members). The Self-Help Groups have mobilized a saving of Rs. 621.92 crores. Apart from commercial banks, the Self-Help Groups open bank accounts in Primary Agricultural Cooperative Banks and avail loans as per the norms laid down by the Project.

Tamil Nadu Women Development Project and Swarna Jayanthi Gram Swarozgar Yojana (SGSY) Scheme implemented by the Rural Development Department have been converged for Rural Self-Help Groups and common guidelines and norms have been adopted. Similarly, in respect of Self-Help Groups in Urban areas, Swarna Jayanthi Shehari Rozgar Yojana (SJSRY) and Tamil Nadu Women Development Project are being operated in a converged manner.

Mahalir Thittam has created awareness among women of their own strengths, resources and ability to face risks. As the bank loan liability is entirely on the women and the group, the women themselves act as best judges in respect of economic activities and levels of credit required. The project implementation units and the NGOs serve as mere facilitators and advisors in this process, with decision-making left entirely to the participating women.

Under the project, members of matured Self-Help Groups ready to absorb loans are linked with banks and other financial institutions to avail credit. As on 31.1.2005, 1,78,251 SHGs have been linked with bank credit at a total financial outlay of Rs.1054.10 crores for various economic activities such as Agriculture, Horticulture,

Sericulture, Animal Husbandry, Cottage and Village Industries and other small businesses/micro enterprises in Urban areas.

The Government is supporting and motivating women from families below poverty line to join SHGs and shall achieve the plan of covering another 15 lakhs women over the next 3 years. Entrepreneurship Development Training followed by Vocational and Skill Training is being given as a special thrust for the benefit of SHG members to start their own Micro Enterprises. A sum of Rs. 20 crores has been provided under Mahalir Thittam for the year 2005-2006 to improve the quality of life of women.

The focus areas of this project for 2005-2006 will be:

- Socio-economic empowerment of Minority Community, Scheduled Caste and Scheduled Tribe women and protecting them against exploitation, by making them join the SHG movement.
- Facilitating markets for SHG products through arrangement of marketing facilities such as shops at public places like bus stands, Government Commercial complexes, etc., and helping SHGs to participate in the National, State, District level Sales Melas/ Exhibitions organized by Government departments. Besides this, District level and Block level marketing workshops will also be conducted to familiarize the SHG women with marketing techniques and to the concepts of quality, pricing, packaging and promotion.
- For further economic development, all assistance under Mahalir Thittam will be extended to the women groups formed under various Government programs by absorbing them under Mahalir Thittam.
- The role of Panchayat Level Federations and Block Level Federations will be strengthened by imparting capacity building training and involving them in imparting capacity building, EDP training to the SHG members and monitoring the SHGs in their villages.
- A special skill training on 'Preserving and Processing of Fish products' will be imparted to the SHG fisher women in the coastal Districts.

4.3 Women Recreation Centres

Apart from the needs of nutrition, health, education, etc., the need for recreation for working poor women is very important. Women Recreation Centres have therefore been created at Village Panchayat Level for the benefit of SHGs. The members of the SHGs use these centres to meet, interact and discuss matters of interest, play games, etc. with the other SHG women. Newspapers and weekly/monthly magazines including Mutram are also made available for reading to the SHG members and their children by these centers. There are 300 WRCs functioning in Tamil Nadu including 25 WRCs established during 2004-05. About 60,000 SHG members including 20,000 SC/ST women are benefited by this Scheme.

4.4 District Level Training-cum-Marketing Centres

With a view to demonstrate and promote micro enterprises in the IT sector for SHG women and training the poor, downtrodden and SC/ST girls in computer appliances, it is planned to establish 30 Information centres with Internet access, one each in all the districts. Under this program, so far 12 Internet browsing centers with computer training facilities have been established at a cost of Rs. 2.50 lakhs per center. The Government has provided a sum of Rs. 7.50 lakhs for establishing 3 more centers during 2005-06.

4.5 Free Gas Connection to the Newly Married Couples under Poverty Line

This scheme, started during the year 2001-2002, has so far benefited 7343 newly married couples of BPL families. A sum of Rs. 56.48 lakhs has been deposited with the respective Gas Agencies in the districts for the first gas cylinder connection to the beneficiaries. To reduce indoor pollution and to relieve the drudgery of poor women, this scheme would be given thrust in the coming years. Though the scheme was originally planned for family members of the SHG women, the scheme has now been extended to all the newly married women who have been benefited under Government assisted marriage schemes. For the year 2005-2006, Rs. 40 lakhs has been provided for the scheme to benefit 5,000 newly married couples.

4.6 Assistance for Formation of 25,000 Self-Help Groups

To give momentum to the SHG movement and to cover another 15 lakhs women over a period of 3 years from 2003-04 to 2005-06, the Government have provided a sum of Rs. 262.50 lakhs for forming 75,000 new SHGs and released a sum of Rs. 87.50 lakhs each for the years 2003-04 and 2004-05. So far, about 50,000 new groups have been formed and 8.52 lakhs women have been enrolled by utilizing the released amount of Rs. 175 lakhs. For the year 2005-06, the Government have provided Rs. 87.50 lakhs to form 25,000 new women groups in the remote rural and tribal areas, fishermen villages, weavers' habitations and urban slums.

4.7 Entrepreneurship Development Training Programme for Women (EDP)

This scheme was announced by the Hon'ble Chief Minister during 2001-02 to cover 5 lakhs women over a period of 5 years at the rate of 1 lakh women per year. In the past three years, Tamil Nadu Corporation for Development of Women Ltd., being the nodal agency for implementation of the programmes, has trained a total of 4,74,254 women (of which the share of TNCDW is 83,881 women), in coordination with other Government departments such as Rural Development, Agriculture, Industries & Commerce, Backward Classes, Most Backward Classes and Minorities Welfare, Sericulture, THADCO, Slum Clearance Board, etc. For the year 2005-06, an amount of Rs.166.95 lakhs has been provided to this Corporation for imparting this training programme to 22,000 SHG women, skill training to 3,000 SHG women and skill up-gradation training to 650 SHG women.

4.8 Vocational and Skill Training Programme (VTP)

The Government have launched the Vocational and Skill training programme during the year 2003-04 to give Skill training to 50,000 EDP trained SHG women so as to enable them to start their own income generating economic activities. The estimated cost of the programme which has been planned to be implemented over a period of 5 years from the year 2003-04 to 2007-08 is Rs. 500 lakhs at the rate of Rs.100 lakhs per year for training 12,500 women annually. The sanctioned amount of Rs.100 lakhs per year was released for the years 2003-04 and 2004-05 to train 12,500 women per year. As on 31.01.2005, about 19,282 SHG women have been trained under this programme at a cost of Rs. 173 lakhs. For the year 2005-06, Rs. 100 lakhs has been provided by the Govern-ment for imparting training to 12,500 SHG women. Apart from the funds provided by the State Government, funds available under programs of Government of India such as NORAD and STEP will also be utilised for imparting skill/vocational training to the SHG women.

4.9 Total Economic Development Project for Theni

In pursuance of the Hon'ble Chief Minister's announcement, the schemes of various Government organisations are being integrated for the total economic development of Theni District. As self-help as a strategy for Poverty alleviation has made impressive strides in the State, the Government has sanctioned a sum of Rs. 220.57 lakhs to this Corporation to implement the Total Economic Development Project for Theni District over a period of four years from 2003-04 to 2006-07.

- The main focus of this project is to cover all habitations and to provide credit linkage to all eligible credit rated SHGs,
- Entrepreneurship Development training,
- Skill and skill up-gradation training on specific Land based activities,
- Health and nutrition coverage to make the District malnutrition free and to make all SHGs members literate.

As part of the scheme, new SHGs are formed among affected weavers, Minority families, Scheduled Caste and in Tribal Areas and the SHG members will be imparted with Entrepreneurship Development Training (EDP) and Vocational and Skill Training (VTP).

With the sum of Rs. 55.30 lakhs provided by the Government for the year 2004-05, a special district specific action plan for Theni has been prepared, which is being implemented under the direct supervision of the District Collector. A sum of Rs. 55.30 lakhs has been provided for the year 2005-06 for this project.

4.10 State Policy for Women

This Government has been effectively implementing a *State Policy for Women* that guides the developmental policies of all departments and sectors which help to eliminate gender gaps and enable women to gain equitable access to resources, decision-making and improved quality of life.

In order to mainstream gender in all Government policies and departments, a *Women's Development Report,* including women's development Index and women's empowerment indicators, is being commissioned to measure and evaluate the impact of the Government's pro-women policies and programs annually. Mother Theresa University has taken up this project and is in the process of preparing the report.

4.11 Tamil Nadu on Governmental Organizations and Volunteers Resource Centre (TNVRC)

TNVRC is a resource center promoted by TNCDW in the year 2001, for the purpose of Capacity Building of Development Agencies (Government based, Non-Government based and Community based), Research, Documentation and Promotion of Volunteerism. This centre, funded and monitored by TNCDW, is conducting various trainings and workshops to improve the capacity of the staff of NGOs.

During the year 2004-05, TNVRC has conducted the following programs for the officials of NGOs involved in women Development activities, mainly from Mahalir Thittam NGOs:

- One batch of Report Writing and Documentation Training,
- Three batches of Book keeping and Accounting Training,
- Two batches of Information Technology Awareness Training,
- 6 batches of Computer Training,
- One batch of PRA Training, and
- Two Workshops on Organizational Ethics etc.

These trainings develop the efficiency of the Mahalir Thittam NGOs and help them monitor the SHGs more effectively.

Besides the training activities, the TNVRC has conducted a study on need assessment of the Neighbourhood groups formed under SJSRY Scheme in urban areas. One state level, six regional level and twenty-two district level convergence workshops have also been conducted by TNVRC.

The TNVRC is presently involved in preparing strategy papers for Tamil Nadu Empowerment and Poverty Reduction Project (TNEPRP) on Gender Strategy. It is planned to focus more attention towards Quality Assessment and Quality Enhancement in the areas of Development. Management Trainings and Accounting Software Trainings to NGOs, Communication and Team Work Training to Government Officials, Evaluation of EDP Training Program, Study on Micro Finance in Tamil Nadu are some of the activities proposed by the TNVRC for the year 2005-06.

4.12 Waste Land Rejuvenation and Micro-watershed Development

This Government has accorded high priority to wasteland development as well as management and conservation of soil and water resources so as to ensure self-sufficiency in food production, adequate returns to the farming community and increased agricultural productivity. Under this scheme, wasteland is being allocated to the federations/SHGs with the co-ordination of other Government Organisations. The Project Officers of Mahalir Thittam and District

Rural Development Agency are working with NABARD and Non-Governmental Voluntary Organisations at district levels to develop land rejuvenation strategies for the land-holding SHG members. Training to the SHGs in land based agriculture and allied activities and micro enterprises is being organized in co-ordination with the Agriculture Department at district level.

4.13 World Bank Aided Tamil Nadu Empowerment and Poverty Reduction Project (TNEPRP)

Tamil Nadu Empowerment and Poverty Reduction Project is the Government of Tamil Nadu's initiative to reduce poverty and empower the women and disadvantaged in the State, with the assistance of the World Bank.

The overall goal of the project is to support Government of Tamil Nadu's strategy of reducing rural poverty through support for productive activities and investments, using the Community Driven Development (CDD) approach.

The objectives of the proposed project would be to empower the poor and improve livelihoods through:

a. Developing and strengthening pro-poor local institutions / groups;
b. Building skills and capacities of the poor; and
c. Financing productive demand–driven sub-project investments.

It is proposed to form a State level society to implement this innovative project. It is also proposed to constitute autonomous registered district level societies in each of the fifteen project districts, to implement the project.

This project is to be implemented in 2300 Panchayats in 70 Blocks covering 15 Districts in Tamil Nadu and will benefit 3.5 lakh poor families.

This project aims at organizing the poor women and disadvantaged sections like the disabled into self-help groups and federations. The project has a specific livelihood focus and will build the capacity of self-help groups and activity based groups to undertake viable livelihood activities. Substantial technical support is proposed to be provided to the self-help groups in selecting income generating activities, getting credit linkage from the banks and for sustaining their activities through market linkages and marketing support. The project has a special component to address the rehabilitation and livelihood needs of the disabled and other vulnerable sections of the society like destitutes, widows, deserted women, etc. The project will also be promoting and supporting federations of women self-help groups and activity based federations which will help the self-help groups in achieving economies of scale and sustainability in their income generating activities.

At the Panchayat level a Village Poverty Reduction Committee will be constituted which will play a pivotal role in implementation of the project with the facilitation of the project staff.

The total cost of the project is around Rs.715 crores. Project preparation has reached the final stages. After approval by the World Bank, this scheme will be implemented during 2005-06.

APPENDIX – V

WOMEN OF OUR WORLD 2005 — POPULATION REFERENCE BUREAU

	DEMOGRAPHY						REPRODUCTIVE HEALTH							
							MDG		MDG	MDG			MDG	
	Total Females (in millions) 2005	Per cent of Women in Ages: 2005 <15	15-49	>50	Lifetime Births per Woman (TFR)	Per cent of women aged 15-19 giving birth in one year	Per cent of Married Women using contraception any method Contra-ceptive	modern Modern	Per cent of Births attended by Skilled Personnel	Maternal Deaths per 100,000 Live Births 2000	Life time chances of dying from maternal causes 1 in:	Abortion Policy 2004	Per cent of Adults Ages 15-49 With HIV/AIDS 2003/04	Per cent of HIV-Infected Adults Who Are Women
(1)	(2)	(3)	(4)	(5)	(6)	(7)	(8)	(9)	(10)	(11)	(12)	(13)	(14)	(15)
Haiti	4.3	36	51	13	4.7	6	28	22	24	680	29	●	5.6	58
Jamaica	1.4	29	54	18	2.4	8	66	63	95	87	380	O	1.2	48
Trinidad and Tobago	0.7	21	58	21	1.6	3	—	—	92	160	330	O	3.2	50
SOUTH AMERICA	188	28	54	18	2.5	7	74	65	85	210	157	-	0.6	34
Argentina	20	26	49	25	2.4	6	—	—	97	82	410	O	0.7	20
Bolivia	4.6	37	49	14	3.8	8	58	35	65	420	47	O	0.1	27
Brazil	92.9	26	56	18	2.2	7	76	70	88	260	140	O	0.7	37
Chile	8.2	26	52	22	2.4	4	—	—	100	31	1,100	●	0.3	33
Colombia	23.1	30	54	16	2.6	8	76	64	86	130	240	●	0.7	34
Ecuador	6.7	31	53	16	3	6	66	50	69	130	210	O	0.3	34
Guyana	0.4	28	56	16	2.4	6	37	36	86	170	200		2.5	55
Paraguay	3.1	37	50	12	3.8	7	57	48	58	170	120	●	0.5	26
Peru	13.9	32	53	15	2.8	5	68	50	59	410	73	O	0.5	34
Suriname	0.2	29	56	15	2.5	4	42	41	85	110	340	●	1.7	34
Uruguay	1.8	23	47	30	2.2	7	—	—	99	27	1,300	O	0.3	33

(1)	(2)	(3)	(4)	(5)	(6)	(7)	(8)	(9)	(10)	(11)	(12)	(13)	(14)	(15)
Venezuela	13.2	31	53	16	2.8	9	—	—	95	96	300	●	0.7	32
ASIA	1,920	28	53	19	2.6	5	62	57	59	330	94	-	0.4	34
Asia (Excl. China)	1,287	31	52	17	3	7	51	43	49	53	—	-	0.6	35
WESTERN ASIA	104	34	52	14	3.7	4	49	30	75	190	120	-	—	—
Armenia	1.6	17	58	25	1.2	3	59	22	97	55	1,200	o	0.1	36
Azerbaijan	4.4	26	58	16	1.8	3	55	12	88	94	520	o	z	—
Bahrain	0.3	32	57	11	2.7	2	65	—	98	28	1,200	o	0.2	—
Cyprus	0.4	20	49	31	1.6	1	—	—	100	47	890	o	—	—
Georgia	2.6	16	51	33	1.4	3	41	20	96	32	1,700	o	0.1	33
Iraq	13.1	40	49	11	5	4	—	—	72	250	65	●	z	—
Israel	3.4	26	48	25	2.9	2	—	—	99	17	1,800	o	0.1	—
Jordan	2.8	37	52	10	3.7	3	56	41	100	41	450	o	z	—
Kuwait	1.1	31	60	9	4	3	52	39	98	5	6,000	o	—	—
Lebanon	1.9	27	56	17	3.2	2	63	40	88	150	240	●	0.1	—
Oman	1.3	42	49	8	4.1	6	24	18	91	87	170	●	0.1	—
Palestinian Territory	1.9	45	45	10	5.7	9	51	37	—	100	140	●	—	—
Qatar	0.2	34	55	11	4	2	43	32	98	7	3,400	o	—	—
Saudi Arabia	11.9	40	51	9	4.8	4	32	29	91	23	610	● o	—	—
Syria	9.2	36	54	10	3.8	3	49	32	98	160	130	●	z	—
Turkey	36.4	29	54	17	2.5	4	64	38	81	70	480	o	—	—
United Arab Emirates	1.1	34	58	9	2.5	5	28	24	99	54	500	●	—	—
Yemen	10.6	48	44	8	7	11	21	10	22	570	19	●	0.1	—
SOUTH CENTRAL ASIA	786	33	52	15	3.3	9	48	41	39	520	46	-	0.7	37
Afghanistan	12.6	43	46	10	6.8	11	5	4	14	1,900	6	●	—	—
Bangladesh	74.4	37	52	11	3	11	54	43	13	380	59	●	—	15

	EDUCATION							WORK & PUBLIC LIFE					
	MDG									MDG		MDG	
	Per cent Literate (ages 15-24) 2000-2004		Literate Women as per cent of Literate Men (ages 15-24)	Per cent Enrolled in Secondary School 2000-2003		Female Secondary School Enrollment as per cent of Male Enrollment		Per cent Economically Active Ages 15+ 1995-2002		Women as per cent of Non-farm Wage Earners		Women as per cent of Parliament	
	Female	Male	2000-04	Female	Male	1995	2000-03	Female	Male	1990	2001-02	1995	2004
(1)	(2)	(3)	(4)	(5)	(6)	(7)	(8)	(9)	(10)	(11)	(12)	(13)	(14)
WORLD	82	89	92	62	67	90	93	54	80	35	38	12	16
More Developed	—	—	—	103	101	103	101	52	69	45	47	14	20
Less Developed	81	88	92	55	61	84	91	55	83	32	34	11	14
Less Developed (Excl. China)	76	85	89	53	59	82	91	47	82	28	—	9	13
AFRICA	69	81	86	36	41	84	88	53	80	30	—	9	13
Sub-Saharan Africa	69	80	85	—	—	83	—	62	84	31	—	10	14
NORTHERN AFRICA	72	84	86	66	69	86	95	21	68	21	20	4	9
Algeria	86	94	91	74	69	90	107	7	47	8	14	7	6
Egypt	67	79	85	85	91	85	93	20	69	21	20	2	2
Libya	94	100	94	108	102	94	106	23	78	19	—	—	—
Morocco	61	77	79	36	45	75	80	27	77	26	26	1	11
Sudan	69	82	85	30	34	87	88	29	75	22	15	8	10
Tunisia	91	98	93	81	78	94	104	24	73	20	—	7	23
WESTERN AFRICA	66	77	87	—	—	73	—	56	86	35	—	6	10
Benin	39	73	53	16	35	42	46	69	67	52	—	8	7

(1)	(2)	(3)	(4)	(5)	(6)	(7)	(8)	(9)	(10)	(11)	(12)	(13)	(14)
Burkina Faso	14	26	55	8	12	55	65	77	90	13	14	4	12
Cape Verde	86	92	94	67	64	—	105	44	89	50	—	8	11
Côte d'Ivoire	52	70	74	16	30	51	54	44	88	23	20	5	9
Gambia	49	65	76	28	40	57	70	70	90	24	—	—	13
Ghana	89	94	95	34	41	64	83	73	77	57	—	8	10
Guinea	—	—	—	7	20	35	35	78	87	30	—	7	19
Guinea-Bissau	44	73	60	13	23	47	57	57	92	11	—	10	8c
Liberia	55	86	64	28	40	—	70	54	84	28	—	6	5
Mali	17	32	52	9	18	50	50	72	90	36	—	2	10
Mauritania	42	57	73	19	25	56	76	64	86	43	—	0	4
Niger	16	37	42	5	8	48	63	70	93	9	—	4	1
Nigeria	87	91	95	—	—	84	—	48	87	36	—	—	6
Senegal	42	62	68	15	22	61	68	61	86	28	—	12	19
Sierra Leone	30	47	64	22	31	57	71	44	84	32	—	—	15
Togo	63	83	76	22	51	35	43	53	87	47	—	1	7
EASTERN AFRICA	67	81	82	18	23	78	78	76	88	30	—	12	16
Burundi	70	76	92	9	61	75	83	93	10	—	12	18	
Comoros	52	66	80	25	81	83	63	86	16	—	0	3	
Djibouti	79	89	90	15	72	63	—	—	—	—	0	11	
Eritrea	60	80	75	22	73	67	75	87	—	—	21	22	
Ethiopia	52	63	82	15	83	65	72	90	40	—	5	8	
Kenya	95	96	99	30	85	88	74	89	21	38	3	7	
Madagascar	68	72	94	14	100	93	79	86	26	—	4	4	
Malawi	71	82	86	29	62	74	76	79	11	12	6	15	
Mauritius	95	94	102	78	106	96	41	80	37	38	3	6	
Mozambique	49	77	64	10	16	64	63	83	91	15	—	25	30

(1)	(2)	(3)	(4)	(5)	(6)	(7)	(8)	(9)	(10)	(11)	(12)	(13)	(14)
Reunion	100	96	104	—	—	—	—	47	67	31	—	—	—
Rwanda	76	77	98	14	15	77	93	85	87	17	—	4	49
Somalia	—	—	—	—	—	—	—	64	87	28	—	—	—
Tanzania	89	94	95	5	6	82	81	87	90	33	—	11	21
Uganda	74	86	86	15	19	59	79	81	91	43	—	17	25
Zambia	86	91	94	21	27	63	78	66	86	36	—	7	12
Zimbabwe	96	99	97	38	43	79	88	65	79	15	21	15	10
MIDDLE AFRICA	64	79	81	—	—	61	—	62	86	29	—	7	11
Angola	63	83	76	17	21	66	81	73	90	35	—	10	16
Cameroon	88	92	96	29	36	68	81	48	86	24	—	12	9
Central African Republic	47	70	67	—	—	41	—	69	87	36	—	4	7c
Chad	23	55	42	5	18	24	28	67	88	4	—	16	6
Congo	97	98	99	27	37	72	73	58	83	33	—	2	9
Congo, Dem. Rep. of	61	77	80	—	—	61	—	62	85	32	—	5	12
Equatorial Guinea	95	99	97	22	38	—	58	45	91	13	—	8	18
Gabon	—	—	—	42	49	—	86	63	84	43	—	6	9
SOUTHERN AFRICA	94	93	102	85	78	119	109	48	62	—	—	19	25
Botswana	93	86	109	75	70	106	107	46	65	48	45	10	7
Lesotho	99	83	119	38	30	147	127	56	69	40	—	5	12
Namibia	94	91	104	65	57	118	114	54	81	39	50	18	26
South Africa	94	94	101	90	83	120	108	48	61	—	—	25	33
Swaziland	89	87	103	45	45	98	100	36	58	37	29	3	11
NORTH AMERICA	—	—	—	93	95	101	98	60	75	47	49	14	17
Canada	—	—	—	105	106	99	99	61	73	47	49	18	21
United States	—	—	—	92	94	101	98	60	75	47	49	11	14

(1)	(2)	(3)	(4)	(5)	(6)	(7)	(8)	(9)	(10)	(11)	(12)	(13)	(14)
LATIN AMERICA/CARIBBEAN	96	95	101	90	83	114	108	49	79	38	43	13	19
CENTRAL AMERICA	94	95	99	72	68	102	106	38	81	37	38	12	17
Belize	85	84	101	74	68	—	109	34	79	38	41	3	3
Costa Rica	99	98	101	68	66	109	103	42	80	37	40	14	35
El Salvador	88	90	98	56	56	114	100	46	79	32	31	11	11
Guatemala	74	86	86	38	41	91	93	23	74	37	39	8	8
Honduras	91	87	105	—	—	123	—	43	85	48	50	7	6
Mexico	97	97	100	78	73	101	107	38	81	35	37	14	23
Nicaragua	89	84	106	61	52	118	117	36	91	49	—	16	21
Panama	96	97	99	72	67	107	107	46	79	44	44	8	17
CARIBBEAN	89	88	101	—	—	112	—	47	77	40	—	18	26
Bahamas	98	96	102	93	90	—	103	66	74	49	49	8	20
Cuba	100	100	100	89	90	105	99	47	77	37	38	23	36
Dominican Republic	95	93	102	75	60	140	125	38	86	35	35	12	17
Bhutan	—	—	—	—	—	—	—	58	90	12	—	0	10
India	65	80	81	42	57	65	74	41	86	13	18	8	8
Iran	91	96	95	75	79	84	95	11	75	18	—	4	3
Kazakhstan	100	100	100	88	90	101	98	65	76	60	48	—	10
Kyrgyzstan	—	—	—	87	86	111	101	55	74	46	45	5	10
Maldives	99	99	100	68	64	—	106	37	72	21	40	6	6
Nepal	60	81	75	37	50	51	74	57	86	12	—	—	6
Pakistan	42	66	64	19	29	55	65	16	83	7	8	2	22
Sri Lanka	97	97	100	89	84	109	106	36	77	39	45	5	5
Tajikistan	100	100	100	74	90	94	82	55	74	40	50	3	13
Turkmenistan	100	100	100	—	—	99	—	61	78	—	—	18	26

(1)	(2)	(3)	(4)	(5)	(6)	(7)	(8)	(9)	(10)	(11)	(12)	(13)	(14)
Uzbekistan	100	100	100	97	100	89	97	61	74	46	42	6	7
SOUTH-EAST ASIA	96	97	99	63	64	93	99	59	84	39	—	11	15
Brunei	99	99	100	91	85	—	107	47	83	40	—	—	—
Cambodia	76	85	90	16	27	59	59	74	81	41	53	6	10
Indonesia	98	99	99	58	58	85	100	52	85	29	30	12	11
Laos	75	83	90	34	47	63	72	75	89	42	—	9	23
Malaysia	97	97	100	73	66	109	111	44	79	38	35	8	9
Myanmar	93	96	97	38	41	103	93	66	88	35	—	—	—
Philippines	96	95	101	86	78	103	110	53	82	40	41	9	15
Singapore	100	99	100	—	—	103	—	56	81	43	47	4	16
Thailand	98	98	100	81	85	98	95	65	81	45	46	6	9
Viet Nam	95	95	100	67	72	—	93	75	84	53	—	19	27
EAST ASIA	99	99	99	65	71	91	93	70	84	38	39	17	18
China	99	99	99	62	68	88	91	74	86	38	39	21	20
China, Hong Kong SAR	—	—	—	78	78	—	100	52	72	41	46	—	—
Japan	—	—	—	103	102	102	101	48	74	38	41	3	7
Korea, North	—	—	—	—	—	—	—	62	82	50	—	20	20
Korea, South	100	100	100	90	90	101	100	49	75	38	40	2	13
Mongolia	98	97	101	83	69	135	120	56	61	49	47	4	5
EUROPE	—	—	—	105	103	104	102	49	66	45	48	15	20
NORTHERN EUROPE	—	—	—	152	133	110	115	58	72	49	50	22	28
Denmark	—	—	—	132	126	104	105	73	82	47	49	33	38
Estonia	100	100	100	97	95	111	102	52	66	52	52	13	19
Finland	—	—	—	133	120	114	111	56	66	51	51	34	38
Iceland	—	—	—	115	108	—	106	79	87	53	53	25	30
Ireland	—	—	—	110	100	106	110	48	71	42	48	13	13

(1)	(2)	(3)	(4)	(5)	(6)	(7)	(8)	(9)	(10)	(11)	(12)	(13)	(14)
Latvia	100	100	100	95	94	104	101	50	65	52	53	15	21
Lithuania	100	100	100	100	101	104	99	53	64	58	50	7	21
Norway	—	—	—	115	112	95	103	69	77	47	49	39	36
Sweden	—	—	—	160	132	105	121	76	80	51	51	40	45
United Kingdom	—	—	—	169	145	112	117	55	71	48	50	10	18
WESTERN EUROPE	—	—	—	107	107	98	100	50	65	41	46	19	26
Austria	—	—	—	97	101	96	96	51	68	40	44	24	34
Belgium	—	—	—	166	148	106	112	40	56	40	45	12	35
France	—	—	—	108	107	99	101	49	63	44	47	6	12
Germany	—	—	—	99	100	98	99	49	65	41	46	26	32
Luxembourg	—	—	—	100	93	—	108	43	64	35	38	20	20
Netherlands	—	—	—	120	124	95	97	56	73	38	45	31	37
Switzerland	—	—	—	95	101	—	94	59	77	43	47	18	25
EASTERN EUROPE	100	100	100	93	93	106	100	—	65	49	50	10	14
Belarus	100	100	100	88	84	105	105	53	66	56	56	—	29
Bulgaria	100	100	100	93	95	99	98	44	55	54	51	13	26
Czech Republic	—	—	—	97	95	103	102	51	69	46	47	10	17
Hungary	100	99	100	104	103	105	101	47	61	46	47	11	10
Moldova	99	98	101	73	71	104	103	54	59	53	54	5	13
Poland	100	100	100	100	103	101	97	48	62	47	48	13	20
Romania	98	98	100	85	84	101	101	48	63	43	45	4	11
Russia	100	100	100	92	92	108	100	53	67	50	50	13	10
Slovakia	100	100	100	90	89	104	101	53	68	48	52	15	19
Ukraine	100	100	100	97	97	107	100	58	67	51	53	4	5
SOUTHERN EUROPE	100	100	100	103	101	105	101	—	65	37	41	10	17
Albania	100	99	100	80	77	102	103	49	71	40	40	6	6

(1)	(2)	(3)	(4)	(5)	(6)	(7)	(8)	(9)	(10)	(11)	(12)	(13)	(14)
Bosnia-Herzegovina	100	100	100	—	—	—	—	44	75	43	—	5	17
Croatia	100	100	100	89	88	103	101	45	62	44	46	6	18
Greece	100	100	100	97	95	93	102	38	61	35	41	6	14
Italy	100	100	100	96	100	102	96	37	62	34	41	15	12
Macedoniab	—	—	—	83	85	101	97	43	66	38	42	3	18
Malta	100	98	102	91	92	—	99	31	70	26	34	2	9
Portugal	100	100	100	117	111	110	106	55	70	44	47	9	19
Serbia and Montenegro	—	—	—	89	88	—	101	50	71	46	—	—	8
Slovenia	100	100	100	108	107	103	100	50	63	49	48	14	12
Spain	100	100	100	119	112	110	106	43	67	33	40	16	36
OCEANIA	—	—	—	112	112	98	100	—	72	42	49	—	13
Australia	—	—	—	153	155	99	99	56	71	45	49	10	25
Fiji	99	99	100	83	78	101	106	39	79	30	35	4	6
New Zealand	—	—	—	116	109	98	106	57	72	48	51	21	28
Papua-New Guinea	71	80	—	21	27	68	78	71	74	24	—	0	1

BIBLIOGRAPHY

Agarwal, Bina, (1994) "Gender and Command Over Property: A Critical Gap in Economic Analysis and Policy in South Asia", *World Development,* Vol. 22, No.10.

Ahmed, Ariz (April 1992), "Women Empowerment and Self-Help Groups", *Kurukshetra.*

Akroyd S, Duncan A. (1998), "The Sector Approach and Sustainable Rural Livelihoods" in *Sustainable Rural Livelihoods* by Carney, London: DFID.

Alkire, Sabina (2002), *Valuing Freedoms: Sen's Capability Approach and Poverty Reduction,* New Delhi: Oxford University Press.

Armendáriz de Aghion, Beatriz, and Jonathan Morduch (2000). "Microfinance Beyond Group Lending." *Economics of Transition,* 8 (2).

Asian Development Bank, (2000), *Finance for the Poor: Micro Finance Development Strategy,* Manila: Asian Development Bank.

Bhuimali, A. & Biswas, A.K. (June 2004) "Development and Empowerment of Disadvantaged People of India", *Indian Journal of Economics & Business,* Vol. 3 (1).

Brocklesby, M.A. and J. Holland, (1998), *Participatory Poverty assessments and public services key messages from the poor,* London: Social Development Division, DFID.

Chambers, Robert (1995), *"Poverty and Livelihood: Whose Reality Counts*?", IDS Discussion Paper 347.

Dadhich, C.L, (July- Sept., 2001) "Micro Finance – A Panacea for Poverty Alleviation: A Case Study of Oriental Grameen Project In India", *Indian Journal of Agricultural Economics,* Vol. 56 (3).

Gayatri, A. Menon and Suranjana Gupta (October 1999), "*From Margin to Mainstream – Building Stakes in the SHG –Bank Linkage Programme*", Swayam Shikshan Prayog.

Girija, S., (1996) "*Group approach to empowerment of women – IFAD experience in Tamil Nadu*", Working Paper No. 5, Lucknow: Bankers Institute of Rural Development.

Government of Tamil Nadu, (2000), *Evaluation Report on Self Help Groups (SHGs) in Tamil Nadu.* Chennai: Government of Tamil Nadu, Department of Evaluation & Applied Research.

Hall, C.M. (1992) *Women and Empowerment: Strategies for Increasing Autonomy,* Washington: Hemisphere Publishing Corporation.

Jones S. (1999), *Increasing aid effectives in Africa? The World Bank and Sector Investment Programmes,* Oxford: OPM.

Kanitkar, Ajit (2002) "Exploring Empowerment and Leadership at The Grassroots: Local Entrepreneurship on the SHG Movement in India" in *Beyond Micro Credit* by Fisher and Sriram (Eds.) New Delhi: Vistar Publications.

Marilyn, Carr, Marcha Chen, Ramana Jhabrala (Eds.) (1996) *Speaking Out: Women's Economy in South Asia,* New Delhi: Vistaar Publications.

Meenai, Zubair (2003) *Empowering Rural Women: An Approach to Empowering Women Through Credit Based Self-Help Groups,* New Delhi: Aakar Books.

Moser Caroline (1989) "Gender Planning in Third World: Meeting Practical and Strategic Gender Needs", *World Development,* Vol.17: No.11.

Murthy K. Ranjani (Ed.) (2001), *Building Women's Capacities,* New Delhi: Sage Publications.

Narasimhan, Sakuntala (1999), *Empowering Women: An Alternative Strategy from Rural India,* New Delhi: Sage Publications.

Narayan, Deepa et.al. (2000), *Voices of the Poor: Can anyone hear us*? New York: Oxford University Press for World Bank.

Nussbaum, M. and J. Glover (Eds.) (1995), *Women, Culture and Development: A Study of Human Capabilities,* Oxford: Clarendon Press.

Nocleen, Heizer and Gita Sen (Eds.) (1994), *Gender, Economic Growth and Poverty,* New Delhi: Kali for Women.

Nussbaum, M (2000), *Women and Human Development: The Capabilities Approach,* Cambridge: Cambridge University Press.

Olson, M. (1965) *The Logic Of Collective Action,* Harvard: Harvard University Press.

Qizilbash, Muzaffar (1996), "Capabilities, Well-being and Human Development: A Survey", *Journal of Development Studies,* 33/2.

Rainuka, Dagar (Ed.) (1998), *Manual on Women's Development and Gender Justice*, Chandigarh: Institute of Development and Communication.

Raju, S., P. J. Aakkins, N.Kumar and J.S.Jownsend (1999), *Atlas of Women and Mass in India,* New Delhi: Kali for Women.

Sahay, Sushma (1998), *Women Empowerment: Approaches and Strategies,* New Delhi: Discovery Publishing House.

Sen Amartya (2005b), *The Argumentative Indian: Writings on Indian History, Culture and Identity,* New Delhi: Allenlane an imprint of Penguin Books.

Sen Amartya (2002), *Inequality Re-examined,* New Delhi, Oxford University Press.

Sen Amartya (2005a), *Development as Freedom,* New Delhi: Oxford University Press.

Seth, Mira (2000) *Women and Development: The Indian Experience*, New Delhi: Sage Publication.

Sharma, Kumud (1992), *"Grassroots Organization and Women's Empowerment: Some Issues in the Contemporary Debate",* Samyashakti, Vol. 6.

UN (2005), *The Millennium Development Goals Report,* New York: United Nations.

World Bank, (1999), *Building Poverty Reduction Strategies in Developing Countries,* Washington: World Bank.

INDEX